THE EAST RIVER TIDAL BARRAGE
A SYMPOSIUM ON A MULTIPURPOSE ADDITION TO NEW YORK CITY'S INFRASTRUCTURE

EAST RIVER TIDAL BARRAGE

TAMS Consultants, Inc.

ANNALS OF THE NEW YORK ACADEMY OF SCIENCES

Volume 742

THE EAST RIVER TIDAL BARRAGE
A SYMPOSIUM ON A MULTIPURPOSE ADDITION TO NEW YORK CITY'S INFRASTRUCTURE

Edited by Douglas Hill

The New York Academy of Sciences
New York, New York
1994

Copyright © 1994 by the New York Academy of Sciences. All rights reserved. Under the provisions of the United States Copyright Act of 1976, individual readers of the Annals are permitted to make fair use of the material in them for teaching and research. Permission is granted to quote from the Annals provided that the customary acknowledgment is made of the source. Material in the Annals may be republished only by permission of the Academy. Address inquiries to the Executive Editor at the New York Academy of Sciences.

Copying fees: For each copy of an article made beyond the free copying permitted under Section 107 or 108 of the 1976 Copyright Act, a fee should be paid through the Copyright Clearance Center, Inc., 222 Rosewood Drive, Danvers, MA 01923. For articles of more than 3 pages, the copying fee is $1.75.

∞ The paper used in this publication meets the minimum requirements of American National Standard for Information Sciences—Permanence of Paper for Printed Library Materials, ANSI Z39.48-1984.

COVER ART: Map of New York Harbor showing tidal currents. The map is taken from *Tidal Current Charts, New York Harbor,* seventh edition (1956) published by the U.S. Department of Commerce, Coast and Geodetic Survey.

FRONTISPIECE: Design concept for the East River Tidal Barrage at a midtown location. (TAMS Consultants, Inc.)

Library of Congress Cataloging-in-Publication Data

Symposium on a Multipurpose Addition to New York City's Infrastructure (1993 : New York, N.Y.)
 The East River tidal barrage : a Symposium on a Multipurpose Addition to New York City's Infrastructure / edited by Douglas Hill.
  p. cm. — (Annals of the New York Academy of Sciences; v. 742)
  Includes bibliographical references and index.
  ISBN 0-89766-868-5. — ISBN 0-89766-869-3 (pbk.)
  1. City planning—New York (N.Y.) 2. Barrages—New York (State)—East River. 3. East River (N.Y.) I. Hill, Douglas, 1925– . II. Series.
 Q11.N5 vol. 742
 [Ht168.N5]
 500 s—dc20
 [307.1'2164'097471]   94-31202
                                                                                         CIP

&/PCP
Printed in the United States of America
ISBN 0-89766-868-5 (cloth)
ISBN 0-89766-869-3 (paper)
ISSN 0077-8923

ANNALS OF THE NEW YORK ACADEMY OF SCIENCES

Volume 742
December 16, 1994

THE EAST RIVER TIDAL BARRAGE
A SYMPOSIUM ON A MULTIPURPOSE ADDITION TO NEW YORK CITY'S INFRASTRUCTURE[a]

Editor
DOUGLAS HILL

Sponsors
AMERICAN SOCIETY OF CIVIL ENGINEERS, METROPOLITAN SECTION, INFRASTRUCTURE GROUP

COLUMBIA UNIVERSITY, DEPARTMENT OF CIVIL ENGINEERING AND ENGINEERING MECHANICS, CENTER FOR INFRASTRUCTURE STUDIES

THE NEW YORK ACADEMY OF SCIENCES, ENGINEERING SECTION

NEW YORK SEA GRANT INSTITUTE

THE STATE UNIVERSITY OF NEW YORK AT STONY BROOK, MARINE SCIENCES RESEARCH CENTER

CONTENTS

Preface. By D. HILL	ix
Welcome. By V. WOUK	xi
Why an East River Tidal Barrage? By D. HILL	1
Part I. Tide Gates and the Estuarine Environment R. L. SWANSON, *Chairman*	
Tide Gates and Their Effect on Water Quality. By M. J. BOWMAN	7
Hydrodynamic and Water Quality Impacts of the Proposed East River Tidal Barrage. By J. P. ST. JOHN	23
Sedimentation Associated with an East River Tidal Barrage. By H. BOKUNIEWICZ	51
Effects of Tide Gates on the Fish Community of the East River. By P. M. J. WOODHEAD	57

[a]Held at Columbia University, New York, New York 29 April 1993.

Rapporteurs:

M. L. Thatcher 69

R. Will 73

L. M. Bocamazo... 77

Tide Gates and the Estuarine Environment: A New York City Perspective. *By* E. O. Wagner.................................. 81

General Discussion.. 87

Part II. The Tidal Barrage as a Bridge

Another East River Crossing? *By* L. J. Riccio 93

Part III. Conceptual Designs of the East River Tidal Barrage
F. H. ("Bud") Griffis, *Chairman*

East River Tidal Barrage. *By* M. J. Abrahams and A. Matlin 101

General Concepts for and Design Issues Related to an East River Tidal Barrage. *By* J. J. Szeligowski, H. Ekezian, and L. H. Hixenbaugh.. 115

Part IV. Commentary
C. Meyer, *Chairman*

Infrastructure as Public Place. *By* A. C. Webster 129

Prospects of Tidal Electricity Generation. *By* G. Birman 147

Permitting the East River Tidal Barrage. *By* J. W. Haggerty........ 151

Some Initial Thoughts from a Member of the Environmental Community. *By* T. D. Searchinger............................. 155

Part V. Conclusion

A Summary of the Symposium *By* D. F. Squires 171

Curricula Vitae 179

Subject Index.. 189

Index of Contributors 193

The New York Academy of Sciences believes it has a responsibility to provide an open forum for discussion of scientific questions. The positions taken by the participants in the reported conferences are their own and not necessarily those of the Academy. The Academy has no intent to influence legislation by providing such forums.

To
William McIlroy
Engineer, modeler, colleague, friend
1924–1992

Preface

The East River Tidal Barrage is a concept for a multipurpose addition to New York City's infrastructure. It would consist essentially of tide gates in the East River that would be used to improve water quality by altering the circulation patterns in the waterways around New York City. If such a structure were built, it might also serve other purposes: as a bridge, to mount water turbines to generate electricity, as a place for the public to enjoy the waterfront. The purpose of this symposium is to give shape to this concept and examine its merits.

The modern idea for East River tide gates to improve water quality originated with Malcolm J. Bowman, who first published his proposal in 1976; the literature reveals that Sidney A. Reeve made a similar proposal in 1922. Interest in the idea was renewed at a workshop on alternatives for alleviating hypoxia in western Long Island Sound held under the recent Long Island Sound Study. The symposium is intended to provide a hearing for the tide gate proposal, taking advantage of the knowledge that has been gained in marine science since 1976 and making use of the advanced models of hydrodynamics and water quality developed for the New York City area.

The symposium is entirely the product of voluntary effort. I should like to thank the heads of the sponsoring organizations: Christian Meyer, Chairman, Infrastructure Group, Metropolitan Section, American Society of Civil Engineers; F. H. ("Bud") Griffis, Director, Center for Infrastructure Studies, Department of Civil Engineering and Engineering Mechanics, Columbia University; Richard H. Tourin, Chair, Engineering Section, The New York Academy of Sciences; Anne McElroy, Director, New York Sea Grant Institute; and J. R. Schubel, Dean and Director, Marine Sciences Research Center, The State University of New York at Stony Brook. The New York Academy of Sciences, New York Sea Grant Institute, the Marine Sciences Research Center, and the Metropolitan Section, American Society of Civil Engineers, contributed to meeting the costs of the symposium and these proceedings.

For the major new work that provided so much of the substance of the symposium, I wish to thank in particular HydroQual, Inc., Parsons Brinckerhoff Quade & Douglas, and TAMS Consultants, Inc. I thank Col. Thomas York, District Engineer, for the support of the New York District, U.S. Army Corps' of Engineers, and Bruce Bergmann for arranging the Corps contributions. It should be noted, however, that the the participation by any organization in this technical meeting does not constitute support for the idea of tide gates in preference to other forms of water quality control.

Donald F. Squires of the University of Connecticut was instrumental in planning the marine science portion of the program. The members of the ASCE Met Section Intrastructure Group served as an advisory committee, especially Peter Gyulavary, Theresa Z. Johnson, Therios Lefcochilos, Mohammad Longi, Albert Machlin, Robert A. Olmstead, Bolivar Sarmiento-Zamora, and Robert Schumacher. Lori Palmer of the Marine Sciences Research Center assisted with graphic design.

Finally, thanks to The New York Academy of Sciences for making these proceedings part of the scientific record.

DOUGLAS HILL

Welcome

VICTOR WOUK
Victor Wouk Associates
1225 Park Avenue, 5B
New York New York 10128-1758

It is a pleasure to welcome you here, on behalf of sponsors of the symposium: American Society of Civil Engineers, Metropolitan Section, Infrastructure Group; Columbia University, Department of Civil Engineering and Engineering Mechanics, Center for Infrastructure Studies; The New York Academy of Sciences, Engineering Section; New York State Sea Grant Institute; and The State University of New York at Stony Brook, Marine Sciences Research Center.

I see names and faces that I recognize from meetings at The New York Academy of Sciences; since I am of the Columbia Class of '39, I cannot expect to see many, if any, names and faces from then.

I'm also *glad* to welcome you; I have had more than a passing interest in events around and about the East River, since my childhood. Most recently, I designed the Electric Bus system that operated on Roosevelt Island so successfully for about a decade, beginning in the early 1970s. This E-bus system kept the air-pollution and noise-pollution levels low in the canyons that are unavoidable with high-rise apartments on the narrow island.

As a child, I enjoyed walking around the shores of the East River, where the Bronx River empties into it. The sea breezes were fresh and invigorating. The water was clean and blue. The Hell Gate railroad bridge, with its powerful structure, stood dramatically alone. There was no clutter of other roads or bridges, nor high-rise buildings on Wards or Randalls Islands. The Woolworth Building was too far downtown to affect the view in the background.

The area I roamed is known as Hunts Point. Not only has the natural environment changed, but so has the physical. I and my cousin, both aged 10, would walk the length of Hunts Point Avenue, about 1 ½ miles, from the Hunts Point subway station, past Con Ed's Hell Gate generating plant, to where the trolley cars turned around. The only fear we had was that a billy goat might come at us from one of the farms along the way.

Boys would swim in the waters at the junction of the East and Bronx Rivers. They were the *tough* boys. *We* would never do that. Today, only *crazy* boys would swim in these waters.

I would like to see both developments since my childhood reversed. It may be a Sisyphean task to undo the social problems wrought in the South Bronx in the past 60 years. However, it would be only a Herculean task to clean the waters in the East River.

The proposed East River Tidal Barrage would indeed be a Herculean task. Various engineering and scientific disciplines would be involved. Economic and political considerations are critical. The New York Academy of Sciences has always been a "neutral territory" for a forum on subjects as potentially controversial as this one. It is therefore with anticipation of being present at the formal "Birth of a Notion", that I again welcome you all, and say "Let us listen to the speakers with open minds and hopeful spirits."

Why an East River Tidal Barrage?

DOUGLAS HILL

Douglas Hill, P. E., P. C.
15 Anthony Court
Huntington, New York 11743-1327

The title of this introduction might suggest that I am going to justify the East River Tidal Barrage in the next few pages. What I actually hope to do in the next few pages is to justify a symposium on the subject.

The East River Tidal Barrage is an idea for a structure in the East River that could serve several purposes. Basically, it would consist of a set of tide gates that would greatly improve water quality from Long Island Sound through the East River and New York Harbor into the New York Bight. One way to design the tide gates would be to mount them on a series of piers spanning the river. The piers could also serve as the foundation for another bridge across the East River for road, rail, or pedestrian traffic. The structure could be designed to provide opportunities for the public to enjoy the waterfront: an esplanade for walking and fishing, restaurants and shops in the superstructure, as suggested in the artist's conception (FIG. 1). It could be used also to house underwater turbines that would generate electricity when the tide is flowing, probably at least enough to meet its own needs. To allow for all of these possibilities in our hypothetical structure, we have given it the general name of the East River Tidal Barrage, as opposed to just the tide gates.

Where it would best be located—between the Battery and the Throgs Neck Bridge—will depend upon a number of factors: its cost and effectiveness in improving water quality, its effect on river traffic, and its possible use as a bridge, for example.

Building a tidal barrage in the East River would clearly have serious consequences, however. It would obviously impede river navigation, at least the half of the time when the tide gates were closed. It would basically alter the water circulation in this region and affect the aquatic ecosystems that depend upon it.

Moreover, over a period of decades, there has been steady improvement in the quality of the waters surrounding New York City in most respects and in most places, due to the construction of sewage plants and other improvements in wastewater disposal.[1]

What then would justify even considering such a departure from conventional wastewater treatment for improving water quality? The main reason is that water quality in the East River remains seriously degraded, and western Long Island Sound may be becoming worse.

The East River from the Battery to the Whitestone Bridge, a narrow stretch of water that receives 60 percent of New York City's treated wastewater, is classified "B-1", meaning that its best use is for fishing

FIGURE 1. Artist's conception of the East River Tidal Barrage.

and secondary contact recreation.[2] I have to admit that I have always had difficulty visualizing what "secondary contact recreation" is like. It sounds like safe sex. The water is OK, as long as there is a boat between you and it.

Even by this diminished standard, however, the water quality in the East River falls short, with dissolved oxygen readings in summer months often below the specified 4 milligrams per liter.

The waters east of the Whitestone Bridge extending into western Long Island Sound, are classified to be suitable for swimming and shellfishing. As a boy living in the Bronx, I swam in Eastchester Bay and and fished for flounder off Hart Island, New York City waters in Long Island Sound.

Close study of these waters in the past several years suggests worsening conditions of hypoxia: oxygen deficiency due to overfertilization by nitrogen that adversely affects fish and invertebrates, at times leading even to fish kills. The recent Long Island Sound Study found that the effluent from sewage treatment plants and polluted runoff from streets and storm sewers entering the Sound "threaten its very existence as a functioning ecosystem," and states that "it is clear from the years of research that the Sound will not recover by itself."[3]

To remedy the overconcentration of nitrogen that causes hypoxia, the draft management plan of the Long Island Sound Study primarily recommends additional treatment to reduce the nitrogen in the effluent from scores of sewage treatment plants that affect the sound, including New York City plants on the East River. Half of the nitrogen comes from sewage treatment plants.

Ironically, the problem of overfertilization due to nitrogen is exacerbated by the steps being taken to dispose of sewage sludge that was formerly dumped far at sea. To comply with the Ocean Dumping Ban Act of 1988, the city has been installing sludge dewatering facilities at several of the sewage treatment plants located on the East River, one of which also takes sludge from the North River plant. The effluent ("centrate") from these dewatering plants further increases the nitrogen concentration of the treated wastewater entering the East River.

The Long Island Sound Study management plan recommends, in addition to upgrading sewage treatment plants, a wide variety of measures to try to control nonpoint sources of nitrogen. Altogether, however, these steps are not expected in the short term to meet the goal of increasing dissolved oxygen levels. In the long term, nitrogen removal from sewage treatment plants—estimated to cost $8 billion—and other measures to reduce the nitrogen load may well be offset by growth in population.

Let us then look at something entirely different.

By changing a waterway—the East River—that is never completely flushed to one that is flushed daily, tide gates may improve water quality not only in the river but in western Long Island Sound and New York Harbor. Moreover, the tidal barrage, imaginatively designed to serve also as a bridge and public place, could become part of the life of the city.

As part of the Long Island Sound Study, a workshop of oceanographic experts selected tide gates as the most promising alternative to biological removal of nitrogen at sewage treatment plants to alleviate hypoxia and recommended further examination.[4] It must be said, however, that the draft management plan would only begin to explore such alternatives upon the completion of a eutrophication model of the entire complex of waterways in the New York City region in 1996.

We hope that this symposium will make an earlier start toward that evaluation by assembling what is known or can be judged with the tools at hand now. Our purpose is to introduce the concept of the East River Tidal Barrage and examine its ramifications—good and bad.

The first part will be devoted to an explanation of the tide gates and several evaluations of their effects on the estuarine environment. Next will be a presentation on where such a tidal barrage might best be located as a river crossing and what kind of traffic it should carry. In the third section two prominent engineering firms will discuss the technical feasibility and cost of their conceptual designs of an East River Tidal Barrage. Then we will have several commentaries on the idea:

- How the barrage might be designed to provide public amenities
- The state of the art in electric generation from underwater turbines
- What would be necessary to provide permits to build the barrage
- Some initial thoughts on the barrage from a member of the environmental community

Everybody will undoubtedly have his or her own assessment of the prospects of an East River Tidal Barrage, but a prominent marine scientist and historian of the port of New York will conclude the book by putting it in his perspective for us.

I wish to emphasize that this symposium is not intended to seek nor to provide an endorsement of the concept of the East River Tidal Barrage. In particular, the participation of any individual or organization in this symposium is not to be construed as their endorsement of the idea of tide gates in preference to other alternatives for improving New York's water quality. On its merits, however, the idea of an East River Tidal Barrage at least deserves a day of examination now.

Time and tide...

REFERENCES

1. APPLETON, A. F. & E. O. WAGNER. 1991. New York Harbor Water Quality Survey, 1988-1990. Bureau of Clean Water, Department of Environmental Protection, City of New York. New York, NY.
2. INTERSTATE SANITATION COMMISSION. 1992. 1992 Annual Report. New York, NY.
3. UNITED STATES ENVIRONMENTAL PROTECTION AGENCY, LONG ISLAND SOUND STUDY. 1993. Draft January 1993, Comprehensive conservation and management plan. New York, NY.
4. SCHUBEL, J. R. 1991. The second phase of an assessment of alternatives to biological nutrient removal at sewage treatment plants for alleviating hypoxia in western Long Island Sound. Report of a workshop, 21-22 November 1991. COAST Institution of the Marine Sciences Research Center, State University of New York, Stony Brook, NY.

Part I

TIDE GATES AND THE ESTUARINE ENVIRONMENT

R. LAWRENCE SWANSON, *Chairman*

Tide Gates and Their Effect on Water Quality

MALCOLM J. BOWMAN

Marine Sciences Research Center
State University of New York
Stony Brook, New York 11794

HYDROGRAPHIC AND TIDAL REGIMES OF NEW YORK HARBOR AND ENVIRONS

New York Harbor (FIG. 1) is located at the mouth of the Hudson River, one of the two largest sources of fresh water in the northeastern United States (the Connecticut River is the other). The Hudson River drains a watershed of about 35,000 km^2 with about 50% of the annual discharge occurring between February and May.[1] The long-term annual mean discharge is about 560 m^3 s^{-1} (20,000 cfs), peaking in April with a monthly mean flow of 1,200 m^3 s^{-1}, and is at a minimum in August with a monthly mean flow of 190 m^3 s^{-1}. Mean monthly discharge for a given month can vary by a factor of 4 to 10 from year to year.

The tides in the Hudson River are semidiurnal, progressive in nature, and propagate upstream until blocked by the federal dam at Troy, NY. The root mean square (RMS) tidal transport at the Narrows is about 41,000 m^3 s^{-1} (1.5 million cfs), about 75 times larger than the mean river discharge. The mean tidal range at the Battery is 1.4 m.

Long Island Sound (FIG. 2) is a shallow estuary, some 165 km in length and with a mean depth of 20 m. Its main opening to the Atlantic Ocean is at its eastern mouth where RMS tidal transport is about 4×10^5 m^3 s^{-1}. Tidal transport drops monotonically westward to ~8,000 m^3 s^{-1} near the confluence of the Sound with the upper East River. The tidal wave in the Sound is standing in nature, with only a short time interval existing between high tide along its entire length. Tidal currents are weak in the western Sound, and the associated lack of tidal stirring allows an appreciable water column stratification to develop in the summer. Insolation provides about half of the summer buoyancy input to the surface layers of the western Sound with the balance derived from Hudson River water, transported through the East River (J. St John, personal communication). Strong summer stratification results, which coupled with high sewage (nitrogen) inputs (FIG. 3), leads to a serious hypoxia problem.[3]

The East River, connecting New York Harbor and western Long Island Sound, is not a river *per se*, but is more correctly characterized as a tidal strait. The river, of length ~25 km, is divided into lower and upper sections by the Hell Gate Sill, which represents a severe restriction to

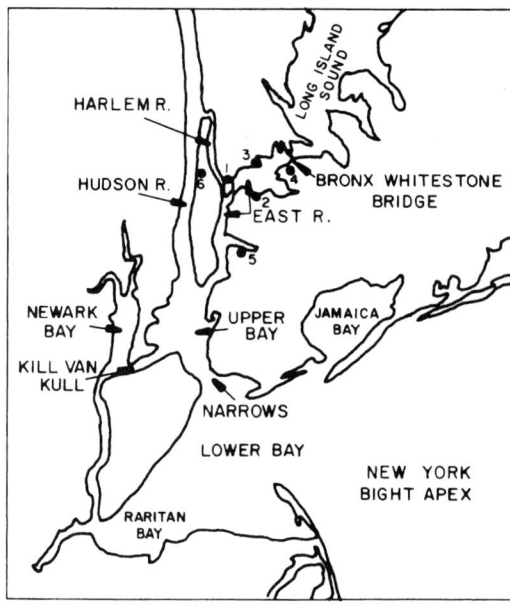

FIGURE 1. Locator map of greater New York Harbor. There are 76 sewage treatment plants situated within the area shown. The six plants referred to in the text are: 1—Wards Island; 2—Bowery Bay; 3—Hunts Point; 4—Tallman Island; 5—Newtown Creek; and 6—North River (from ref. 7).

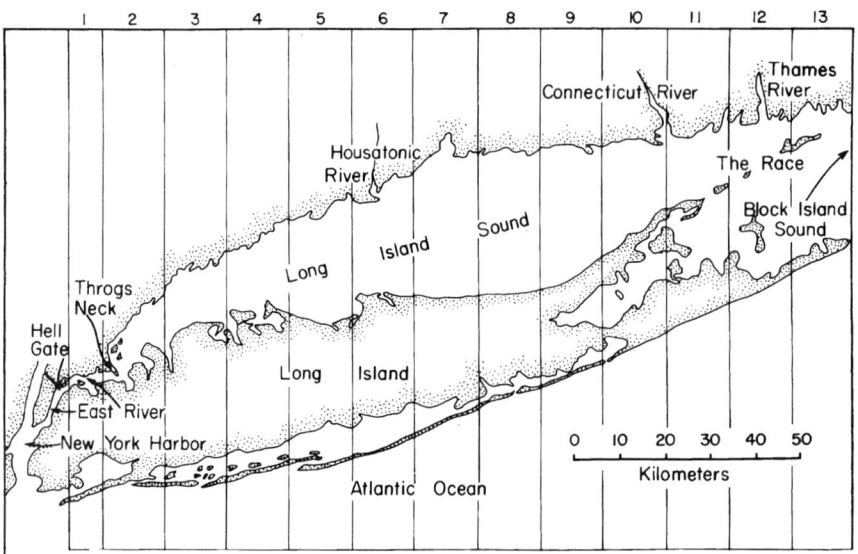

FIGURE 2. Locator map of Long Island Sound illustrating the 13 model sections. Section 1 covers the upper East River. The main connection to the ocean is at The Race (section 12) where about 98% of the tidal exchange with the coastal ocean takes place, with only 2% exchanging via the East River (from ref. 7).

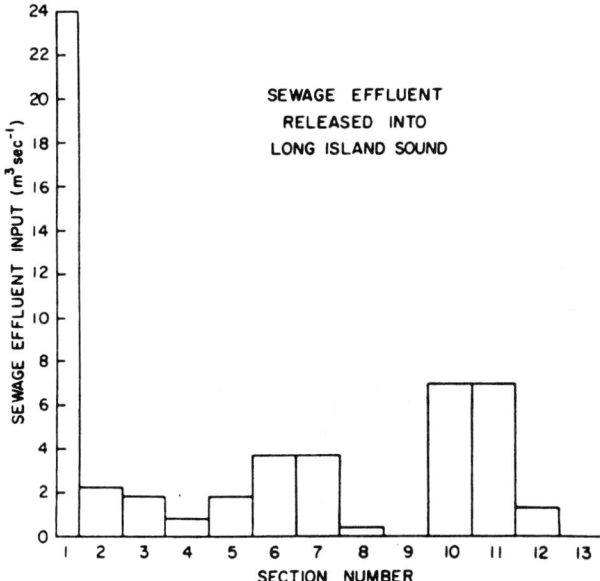

FIGURE 3. Longitudinal distribution (both shores combined) of sewage effluents released into Long Island Sound including the upper East River. By far the largest contribution is into the upper East River (section 1) where five major New York City sewage plants are located; see FIGURE 1 (from ref. 7).

tidal flow and a hazard to shipping. The lower East River, ~12 km in length, has the narrower and deeper channel and extends from the Battery to Hell Gate. The upper East River, ~13.5 km in length, is shallower and wider than the lower East River, and its irregular shoreline encompasses several bays and islands. The depth of the shipping channel throughout the length of the River is at least 11 m below mean low water (MLW).

The predominant flow is a co-oscillating tidal current (FIGS. 4 and 5) at the semidiurnal frequency (period = 12 h 25 min.). There is also a weak diurnal component, a number of internally generated overtides, and a variable subtidal residual flow.[4] Root mean square semi-diurnal tidal transport through the East River is ~6,700 $m^3 s^{-1}$ (peak transport ~ 9,500 $m^3 s^{-1}$); the former is 12 times the mean Hudson River discharge. Because the tides in Long Island Sound (a standing wave) and New York Harbor (a progressive wave) are 90° out of phase, there is a 3 hour time difference in high tides across the ends of the River, leading to large hydraulic gradients and swift currents within the river. Peak tidal currents exceeding 3 $m s^{-1}$ are common. Slack water is almost synchronous along the river, except in the eastern half of the upper East River where a 1.5 hour phase shift occurs. The tidal excursion (the maximum distance a

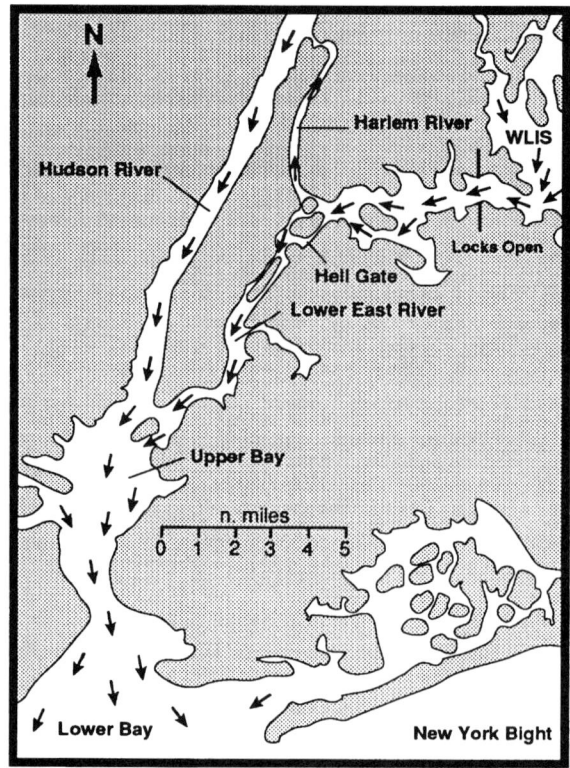

FIGURE 4. Schematic diagram of present ebbing tidal currents through New York Harbor, at low water at The Battery. The tidal gates are located at the eastern end of the East River, one of the preferred sites (see the discussion of other sites elsewhere in this volume).

particle would travel during either flooding or ebbing tides) is about 70% of the length of the River itself, which explains why the river is never completely flushed of contaminants by the tides.

The Harlem River is also a tidal strait, ~11 km in length and connects the East River at Hell Gate to the Hudson River at Spuyten Duyvil. The RMS tidal transport through the Harlem River (~330 m^3s^{-1}) is approximately in phase with that through the lower East River (*i.e.*, both flow toward the Hudson River together), but is only ~5% of the East river tidal transport, and its influence on the dynamics of the East River is small.[5]

In addition to tidal oscillations, subtidal flows through the East River influence water, salt, sediment and contaminant transport. The subtidal flow may be broken down into two parts: i) that tidally averaged component also averaged over the water column, known as the tidal residual

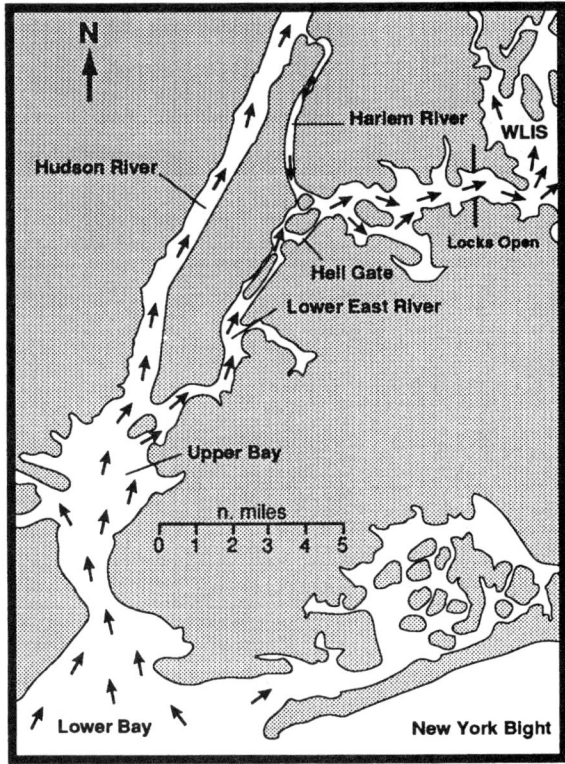

FIGURE 5. Schematic diagram of present flooding tidal currents through New York Harbor, at high water at The Battery.

flow; and ii) that tidally averaged component not averaged over the water column, known as the estuarine circulation.

The tidal residual flow is quite variable in speed, direction and duration. It is caused by nonlinearities in the tidal dynamics, changing water depths during the tidal cycle (the river is deeper while flowing towards New York Harbor), and meteorological effects. Numerous measurements and analyses over the last 120 years have shown that the residual transport, averaged over the cross-section and over one or more tidal cycles lies in the range +9% to −16% of the RMS tidal transport (a positive flow is taken towards the Harbor[5]).

The residual flow is quite sensitive to meteorological influences, with northeasterly winds capable of driving storm surges into western Long Island Sound. These surges may partially discharge through the East River and New York Harbor and into the New York Bight. The situation is quite complicated as coastal storm surges also occur along the Atlantic Coast in response to atmospheric low pressure centers and onshore

Ekman transport. Such surges enter New York Harbor through the Narrows and may to some extent reduce the nontidal hydraulic head across the East River. Over the long term, however, the residual flow through the East River lies in the range of 125-350 $m^3\ s^{-1}$, directed towards the Harbor.[5,6]

The last component of transport that is important to the hydrology of the East River, especially the upper river, is the two-layered estuarine circulation, with a surface flow directed towards Long Island Sound and an equal and opposite bottom flow directed towards the Harbor. This estuarine or gravitational circulation is driven by the input of fresh water of Hudson River origin into the system via the lower East River. This estuarine circulation steadily strengthens eastwards throughout Long Island Sound as further buoyancy is added from other rivers emptying into the Sound (primarily the Housatonic and Connecticut Rivers). The estuarine component of the circulation contributes to the transport into western Long Island Sound of (buoyant) sewage effluent released into the surface waters of the East River.

In summary, New York Harbor is surrounded by a complex network of tidally dominant but poorly flushed waterways, which has led to numerous water quality problems for at least the last 150 years. The juxtaposition of Long Island Sound and New York Harbor, each with its own connection to the sea, each with a fundamentally different tidal regime, and connected by a narrow tidal strait (the East River) provides an unique opportunity, not found in any other major city, to harness the energy of the tides by constructing tide gates to modify the circulation in order to greatly increase the dilution and flushing of contaminants out to sea. Tide gates, similar in principle to those described here, have been in continuous operation for almost 100 years in Shinnecock Canal, eastern Long Island. Clean Peconic Bay water is allowed to flow into Shinnecock Bay, but not vice versa. Small locks allow ~32,000 small pleasure boats annually to traverse the locks in order to bypass the gates.

WHY IS THERE A SERIOUS HYPOXIA PROBLEM IN WESTERN LONG ISLAND SOUND?

There are many factors contributing to the water quality problems experienced in New York Harbor, the Hudson River, and western Long Island Sound. The sewage from an estimated population of 16 million, representing about 7% of the population of the United States, is released into New York Harbor and environs: Upper Bay, Lower Bay, Jamaica Bay, lower Hudson River, and East River.[7] The sewage from an estimated 7.4 million people residing in the watershed of Long Island Sound, including the four eastern plants in the East River and both shorelines of the Sound: New York and Connecticut, but not Massachusetts, Vermont and Quebec (D. Squires, personal communication) enter the Sound.

Most of these people live crowded around the narrow, poorly flushed waterways, rivers and estuaries of New York City, northern New Jersey, and western Long Island Sound (FIG. 1). Over 68 m^3 s^{-1} (1.6 billion gallons per day) of effluent are released from New York City water pollution control plants (WPCPs). Another 22 m$^{3-1}$ (500 million gallons per day [MGD]) of sewage effluent are released from treatment facilities in New Jersey into the waters surrounding the City.[8] Approximately, 24 m^3 s^{-1} (560 MGD) are released directly into the East River (region 1 in FIG. 2) from six of the largest sewage works in the city (Wards Island, Bowery Bay, Hunts Point, Tallman Island, Newtown Creek, and Red Hook; FIG. 1), representing about 60% of all New York City discharge. The North River plant is located on the Hudson River and is rated at 7 m^3 s^{-1} (163 MGD).

The problem of combined storm and municipal waste sewer systems in New York City remains a serious problem, with over 700 combined sewer overflows (CSO) located around the perimeter of the Harbor.[9]

A number of factors combine to contribute to hypoxia in western Long Island Sound.

i) The population density along both the north and south shores increases exponentially towards New York City, resulting in ~6m^3 s^{-1} (140 MGD) of sewage discharge released from local communities directly into western Long Island Sound (regions 2–4 in FIG. 2). In addition, Bowman[7] estimated that ~15 m^3 s^{-1} (400 MGD) of sewage is transported eastwards through the upper East River boundary at Throgs Neck.

ii) Tidal circulation in Long Island Sound approximates a standing wave, where tidal currents become progressively weaker westward (although tidal ranges become progressively larger). Hence eastward flushing by tidal dispersion and aeration of the water column by vertical stirring generated by tidal turbulence are both very weak in the western Sound.

iii) Bottom water replacement with higher oxygenated water from central Long Island Sound is limited by the presence of the Hempstead and Mattituck Sills. In some ways western Long Island acts like a shallow fjord. Anoxia is common in the bottom waters of many fjords, owing to the restriction or absence of exchange of bottom waters with the ocean because of a shallow sill located at their entrance.

iv) The surface area of western Long Island Sound decreases westward, diminishing wind stirring and thus atmospheric exchange of dissolved oxygen with its surface waters.

v) High summer sea surface temperatures in western Long Island Sound and weak winds promote strong stratification and diminish vertical exchange.

Thus the exponential increase westward in nutrient loadings, sluggish tidal currents and hence poor flushing and water column aeration, strong summer stratification, and the presence of major sills lying across the Sound, all contribute to the inability of the western Sound to dissipate effluents, leading to hypoxia.

Dissolved oxygen levels in the bottom water of New York Harbor are considerably higher than in western Long Island Sound, and have been steadily increasing since about 1950[9] as additional water pollution control plants have been brought into operation. Also, tidal stirring in New York Harbor is more vigorous than in western Long Island, and so vertical water column stratification is correspondingly weaker and aeration of bottom waters more efficient.

BASIC CONCEPTS OF TIDAL RECTIFICATION

If the oscillating tidal flow in the East River were half-wave rectified by constructing tide gates and locks for shipping across the river to allow ebbing flow into New York Harbor from Long Island Sound, but not the reverse, the presently small residual flow in the river would be increased from a few hundred m^3s^{-1} to about 6,500 m^3s^{-1} (FIG. 6). During flooding tides (second half of the tidal cycle), the gates would be closed and only weak flow would exist in the East River, sufficient to lift the water level west of the gates to that at the Battery (FIGS. 7 and 8). Thus over the tidal cycle, the flow would average about 3,250 m^3s^{-1} directed towards the Harbor. It is important to note that this flow is not generated by piling up water behind the barrier and releasing it suddenly. Tide levels would not be significantly different than at present, except for a 20 cm rise in high tide level at The Battery (J. St.John, this volume; his FIG. 7).

The major connections of the Sound and the Harbor to the Atlantic Ocean are at The Race (FIG. 2.), and the Sandy Hook-Rockaway transect

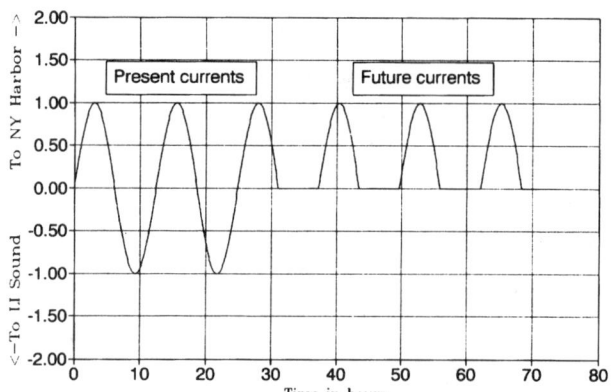

FIGURE 6. Schematic diagram of present and future tidal currents after tide gate and lock emplacement in the East River. The vertical scale is normalized to a peak value of unity; the diagram is intended to display the nature of half-wave rectified currents produced by the gates.

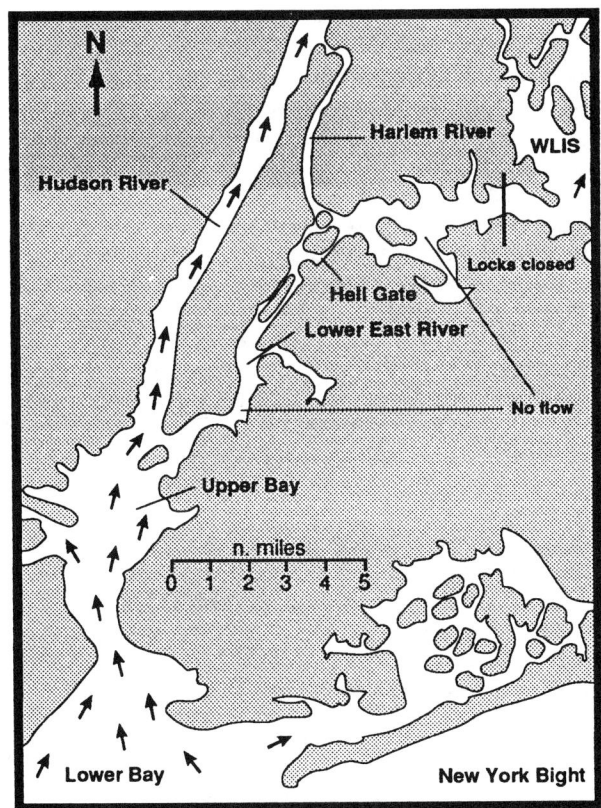

FIGURE 7. Schematic diagram of future flooding tidal currents through New York Harbor after tide gate and lock emplacement, at high water at The Battery.

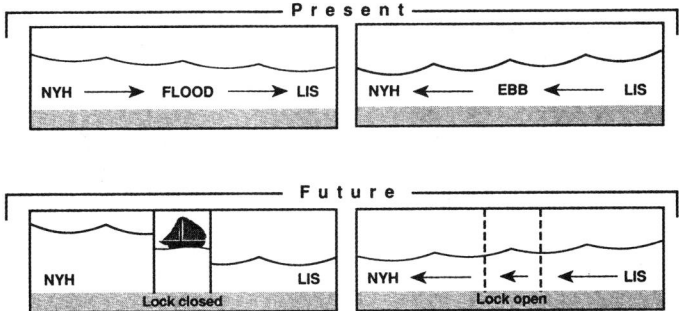

FIGURE 8. Side view sketch of sea surface along the East River during flooding and ebbing tides, at present (*upper two panels*) and in the future after lock emplacement (*lower two panels*).

south of the Verrazano Narrows (FIG. 1), respectively. Long Island Sound and New York Harbor would continue to fill and empty much as they do now whether the East River existed or not. Only 2% of the filling of Long Island Sound takes place through the East River and 98% takes place through The Race. For New York Harbor, the East River contributes only 16% to the tidal exchange, while 84% is contributed through the Verrazano Narrows.

Tidal rectification is based on the supposition that modifying the tidal currents in the East River would not significantly alter tidal elevations in Long Island Sound or New York Harbor, both of which drive the currents through the river in the first place. During ebbing tides, Long Island Sound water would flow into New York Harbor (as it does now, except that with gates the water would now be much cleaner) and out into the New York Bight. During rising tide in New York Harbor, flow through the East River would be blocked. This immediately raises the question as to where the flooding tidal waters entering New York Harbor through the Verrazano Narrows would go if the East River were blocked. Less water (~41,000-6,500 = 34,500 $m^3 s^{-1}$) would enter New York Harbor than at present, in response to a nonexistent hydraulic head in the East River west of the gates. The tidal wave would continue to propagate up the Hudson River. During ebb tides, the same flow as at present would ebb out to sea through the Narrows (~41,000 $m^3 s^{-1}$), with contributions from both the Hudson and East Rivers.

While it is clear that tide gates would benefit western Long Island Sound, it might appear that regions downstream of the gates would suffer. New York Harbor would face an increased sewage loading (that fraction of sewage released into the upper East River that presently disperses into western Long Island Sound).

Fortunately, however, this is only half the story. After the gates were in operation for a few months, significantly cleaner western Long Island Sound water would be drawn through the East River, into New York Harbor, and out into the Bight. Each day, ~200 billion cubic meters of new water would flow into the Harbor, equal to 60% of the volume of the Upper Bay. For comparison, the mean flow of the Hudson River replaces ~7%, and the tidal prism of the Upper Bay (the difference in volume between low and high water) represents 20% of the volume. Significant flushing of New York Harbor would result.

Tide gates would harness the natural energy of the tides for its basis of operation, so the system would not require any significant external source of power.

EXPECTED IMPROVEMENTS IN WATER QUALITY

Long Island Sound

First-order estimates were made by Bowman,[7] using a mass balance (non-hydrodynamical) model, of the expected changes in nitrogen concentrations in New York Harbor and western Long Island Sound after gate emplacement. The model was constructed around one-dimensional steady state, water, salt, and nutrient (NH_3, NO_2, NO_3) balance equations for each of 13 regions of Long Island Sound, as well as New York Harbor (FIGS. 1 and 2).

Computed values of present nutrient concentrations (FIGS. 9 and 10) reflect the combined efforts of tidal dispersion, nontidal residual flow, local sewage inputs around Long Island Sound (including contributions from sources up the Housatonic and Connecticut Rivers), agricultural runoff, and first-order nutrient uptake kinetics. Boundary conditions at the western end of the model are estimates of the net fluxes of water, salt and nutrient through the East River. A sufficient condition at the eastern end of the model is an oceanic source (or sink) of constant concentration.

The model was run under both present conditions and with a modified East River flow. Future/present mean concentrations of various nutrients in far western Long Island Sound ranged from a low of 3.2% for NH_3 in summer, to 36% for NO_3 in winter (TABLE 1). Concentrations east of region 4 (FIG. 2) remain essentially unaltered during summer, as most of the nutrients there are utilized by high rates of local phytoplankton production. The essential result of deploying tide gates is to reduce nutrient concentrations in the western Sound down to levels found in the central basin, which are only slightly higher than adjacent

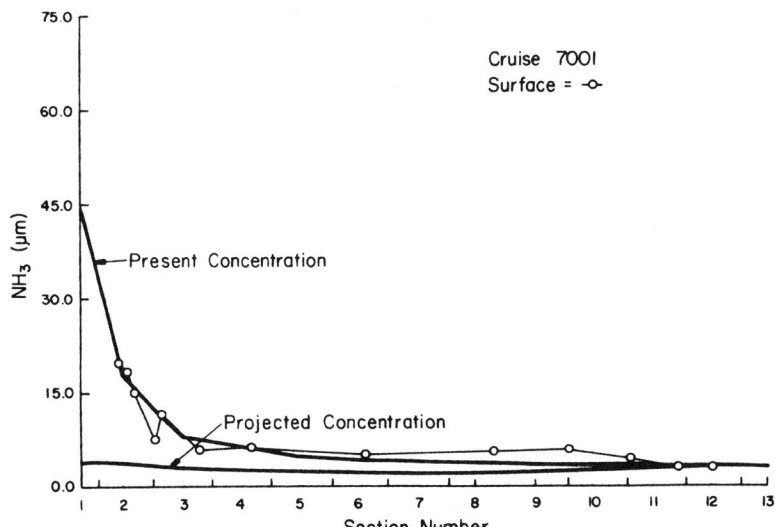

FIGURE 9. Present and projected depth-mean ammonia concentrations along the axis of Long Island Sound in winter. The thicker lines represent the predictions of the model; the thinner line joins concentration measurements (from ref. 7).

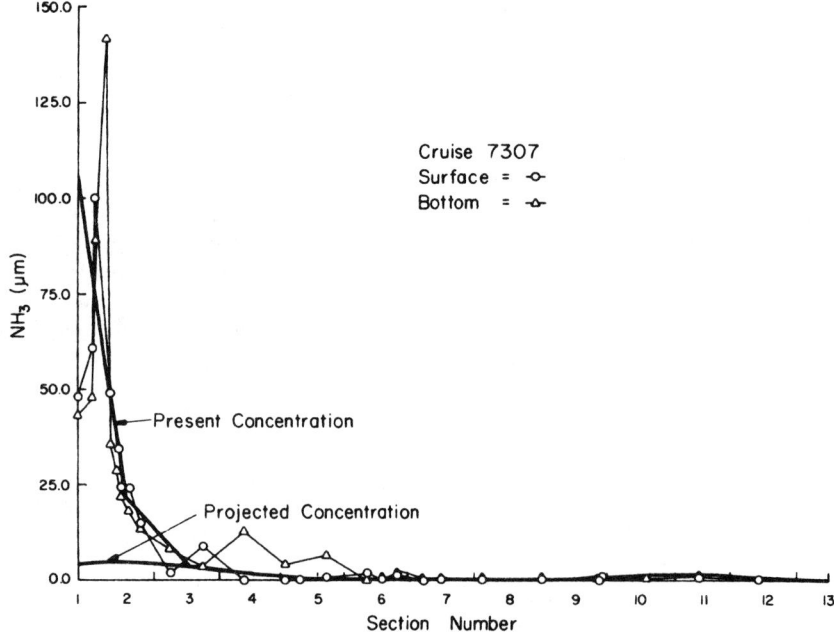

FIGURE 10. Present and projected depth-mean ammonia concentrations along the axis of Long Island Sound in summer. The thicker lines represent the predictions of the model; the thinner lines join surface and bottom concentration measurements (from ref. 7).

TABLE 1. Ratio of Future/Present Nitrogenous Nutrient Concentrations in Far Western Long Island Sound (Region 1 of FIG. 2)

Nutrient	Future/Present Concentration in Western Long Island Sound in %	
	Summer	Winter
NH_3	3.2% +/− 0.4%	7.9% +/− 1.1%
NO_2	2.0% +/− 0.5%	12% +/− 1.6%
NO_3	5.6% +/− 0.6%	36% +/− 2.6%
Conservative tracer	20% +/− 5%	20% +/− 5%

The uncertainties arise from variations in sewage effluent source concentrations, biochemical decay rates, and the fraction of East River nutrients that disperse into western Long Island Sound (from Bowman[7]).

coastal waters. A similar prediction has been obtained by J. St John (this volume; his FIG. 13) using the HydroQual LIS 2.0 model.[6]

New York Harbor

Predicted changes in salinity and nutrient concentrations in New York Harbor (Upper Bay) were estimated to first order with a similar one-dimensional mass balance model.[7] The Harbor was assumed to be well mixed with a mean salinity of 21 parts per thousand (o/oo). The model predicted that total nitrogen concentrations (considered as a conservative substance) in the Upper Bay would drop to 55% of present levels with an uncertainty of +/−10%. A similar result has been predicted by J. St John (this volume; his FIG. 17) using the HydroQual NYH 208 model.[10]

Two opposing factors control the change in nitrogen concentrations in the Harbor. First is the dilution attributable to the influx of cleaner Long Island Sound water, and second is the increase in nitrogen loading through the addition of sewage-derived effluents which were previously transported, or released directly, into western Long Island Sound. The calculations indicate, fortunately, that the former effect predominates, and effluent concentrations drop significantly in the Upper Bay. Nitrogen concentrations in Raritan Bay, Lower Bay, and the New York Bight Apex will also decrease as a consequence of increased dilution. Thus the effect of the tide gates is not to transport the problem downstream, but to significantly reduce the concentration of nitrogen throughout the system by greatly increasing the net circulation of the sea.

RATE OF IMPROVEMENT IN WATER QUALITY

An estimate of the rate at which water quality in the western Sound would improve was estimated by calculating the residence time of water in the western Sound after tide gate emplacement (regions 1–4 in FIG. 2). The residence times would be 11 hours, 5 days, 10 days, and 16 days for regions 1–4 (FIG. 2), respectively, or ~32 days for the entire region. Thus, in about 1 month a volume of water equal to that in the western Sound would be drawn through the East River, New York Harbor, and out to sea.

In seven months, a volume equal to that of the entire Long Island Sound (sections 1–13 in FIG. 2) would be transmitted through the East River. (This is not the same as saying that all of the Sound's water *per se* would be drawn through the East River, since there is a vigorous and continuous exchange of Sound and ocean water through The Race.) Sound water would drift westward slowly at an average speed of ~1 cm s^{-1}; this drift would be essentially undetectable, masked by the tidal and

SALINITY CHANGES IN LONG ISLAND SOUND AND NEW YORK HARBOR

Westward motion induced in western Long Island Sound by tide gates in the East River would increase the salinity in the Sound and New York Harbor by a few parts per thousand. In western Long Island Sound this would be due both to the elimination of water of Hudson River origin entering the Sound, and also to the indraw of saltier water from central and eastern Long Island Sound. The increase in depth-mean salinity predicted by the model[7] is shown in FIGURE 11, assuming that Block Island Sound salinity remains constant at 31 o/oo. The salinity increases ~4.5 o/oo just east of the gates.

The resulting reduction in horizontal salinity gradient would reduce the intensity of estuarine circulation, especially in the western Sound. Conditions would approximate more closely those of a coastal embayment with a reduced horizontal density gradient in the central and eastern basins maintained principally by the outflows of the Housatonic and Connecticut Rivers.

Mean salinity in the Harbor would increase by ~5 o/oo to 26 o/oo as a consequence of the injection of western Long Island water of salinity 28 o/oo. J. St.John (this volume; his FIG. 20) predicts a smaller increase in salinity of 1-2 o/oo using the HydroQual NYH 208 model.[10]

Although the improvement in water quality in western Long Island

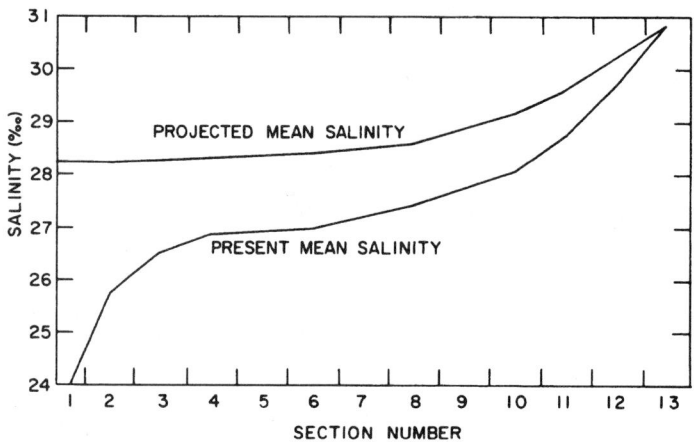

FIGURE 11. Present and projected depth-mean salinities along the axis of Long Island Sound. It is assumed that the oceanic salinity in Block Island sound (section 13) remains unaltered at ~31 o/oo (from ref. 7).

Sound may enable the reopening of significant numbers of shellfishing beds, the small increase in salinity might also increase the predation of oysters which depend on low salinity water for their survival.

CONCLUSION

The concept of East River tide gates offers a number of interesting possibilities for water pollution control in western Long Island Sound and New York Harbor which deserve careful investigation. Potential drawbacks and unforeseen deleterious water quality and ecological effects need to be identified and thoroughly investigated. Included in future studies should be an analysis of the potential benefits and problems arising from a combined approach of tide gate emplacement to effect an improvement in the main bodies of water, and improved sewage treatment in critical locations to reduce or eliminate local contamination.

REFERENCES

1. GIESE, G. L. & J. W. BARR. 1967. The Hudson River estuary: A preliminary investigation of flow and water-quality characteristics. New York State Department of Conservation. Water Resources Comm. Bull. 61. Albany, NY.
2. BOWMAN, M. J. & L. D. WUNDERLICH. 1977. Hydrographic Properties. MESA New York Monograph #1. Albany, NY.
3. UNITED STATES ENVIRONMENTAL PROTECTION AGENCY. 1993. Long Island Sound Study. Draft, January 1993, Comprehensive conservation and management plan. New York, NY.
4. BOWMAN, M. J. 1976a. The tides of the East River, New York. J. Geophys. Res. **81**:1069-1616.
5. JAY, D. A. & M. J. BOWMAN. 1975. The physical oceanography and water quality of New York Harbor and western Long Island Sound. Marine Sciences Research Center. Technical Report #23. State University of New York, Stony Brook, New York.
6. HYDROQUAL. 1978. Water quality modeling analysis of hypoxia in Long Island Sound. Job No. NENG0012 for the Management Committee, Long Island Sound Estuary Study, and New England Water Pollution Control Commission.
7. BOWMAN, M. J. 1976b. Tidal locks across the East River: An engineering solution to the rehabilitation of western Long Island Sound. In Estuarine Processes. M. Wiley, Ed. Academic Press. New York. Vol I: pp 541.
8. INTERSTATE SANITATION COMMISSION. 1991. 1991 Annual Report. New York, NY.
9. NEW YORK CITY DEPARTMENT OF ENVIRONMENTAL PROTECTION. 1991. New York Harbor Water Quality Survey, 1988-1990. New York, NY.
10. HYDROQUAL. 1978. New York City 208 Study: Task report-seasonal steady-state modeling (PCP 314). Hazen and Sawyer, P.C., for the New York City Department of Environmental Protection.

DISCUSSION OF THE PAPER

JEFF KANE: You have talked about Long Island Sound and New York Harbor. I am concerned about the Hudson River. It seems that after constructing the tide gates you will have a saltier New York Harbor, and then you may have more tidal currents going up the Hudson River. You are going to have an extended salinity problem in the Hudson River either in terms of higher salinity or salt penetration further up the Hudson. The fresh water intakes at Poughkeepsie are pretty close to the salt water now. Did you look at that at all?

MALCOLM J. BOWMAN: Your first point was that you are worried about an increase in the salinity of New York Harbor. My early calculations indicated that there would be a 5 part per thousand increase in salinity. John St. John will show you that his calculations suggest a one to two parts per thousand salinity increase. The natural fluctuations from season to season in the salinity of New York Harbor are much greater than that. Right now, the month of April, is the time of maximum discharge from the Hudson, and August is the low point; there are natural changes in salinity of six, eight, or ten parts per thousand over the year. There will be changes in the circulation and mixing of New York Harbor—you are entirely correct—and that needs to be investigated.

KANE: And did you look at all at what the effects would be further up the Hudson?

BOWMAN: We have to look at that.

R. LAWRENCE SWANSON: Do you propose that the tide gates would be used continuously?

BOWMAN: I think I will defer the answer to your question to some of the engineers who will be speaking this afternoon on some of the possible ways to operate them, but I will just say that a number of strategies could be developed. For example, the gates might not necessarily have to be used year-round. As I mentioned earlier, late winter and spring is critical for preconditioning summer hypoxia. The weather we have right now is critical, and if we experienced a very early warm spring this year— and we haven't—but if we had, then we might expect Long Island Sound hypoxia to be serious next summer. Perhaps the gates could be used on a seasonal basis, for example, to control the flow of water during the spring and early summer, and it may be unnecessary to use them during the wintertime.

Hydrodynamic and Water Quality Impacts of the Proposed East River Tidal Barrage

JOHN P. St. JOHN
HydroQual, Inc.
1 Lethbridge Plaza
Mahwah, New Jersey 07430

INTRODUCTION

The concept of a tidal barrage, a collection of tide gates, across the East River was originally conceived in the mid-1970s and presented in a series of papers by Bowman.[1,2] The stimulus for the concept was the objective to improve water quality conditions in western Long Island Sound and in New York Harbor by rectifying tidal currents in the East River to produce a one-way current from Long Island Sound toward New York Harbor. This procedure would thereby induce an enlarged flushing and dilution flow as compared to what presently exists, thus reducing the impact of point and nonpoint waste inputs. In addition, depending upon the exact location of the structure, the effects of large treated wastewater discharges in the East River would be physically prevented from reaching sensitive (in terms of water quality) areas such as western Long Island Sound, and instead be diluted and flushed in an accelerated manner through New York Harbor toward the Atlantic Ocean.

Recently, the Long Island Sound Study[3] has indicated the severity of the hypoxia problem in the western sound and that substantial reductions in nitrogen discharges may be required to restore dissolved oxygen values to acceptable levels. As such reductions are likely to be very expensive, there is renewed interest in more cost-effective alternatives to nitrogen removal at the sources to improve dissolved oxygen in western Long Island Sound and elsewhere. The concept of tide gates in the East River is therefore potentially relevant and worthy of consideration.

OBJECTIVES OF THE ANALYSIS

The purpose of this paper is neither to endorse nor to oppose the concept of a tidal barrage in the East River. Rather, it is to summarize the results of preliminary analyses which were performed by mathematical modeling to evaluate the hydrodynamic and water quality impacts which may result from operations of such a structure. The preliminary analyses were performed as a professional contribution to address the following questions:

- How would tide gates affect water elevations in the East River and adjacent waterways and what is the area of influence of such effects?
- How much volume flux or uni-directional tidally averaged flow would be induced by rectification of tidal currents in the East River by tide gate operations?
- What changes would occur in water quality conditions in western Long Island Sound by tide gate operations, specifically with regard to total nitrogen, total phosphorus, algal biomass (chlorophyll-a), and dissolved oxygen?
- What changes would occur in water quality conditions in the East River and in New York-New Jersey Harbor by tide gate operations, specifically with regard to total nitrogen, dissolved oxygen and total coliform bacteria?
- How would tide gate operations alter salinity distributions in western Long Island Sound and New York-New Jersey Harbor?

METHODS OF ANALYSIS

The methodology used to address the foregoing objectives is application of mathematical modeling technology. At present, no perfect mathematical model exists to answer all of the questions which may be posed regarding the impacts of tide gates in the East River. However, models do exist which can be used to place some perspective on tide gate impacts, at least in a preliminary manner. The objective at this point is to assess approximately the order of some of the beneficial and potentially adverse impacts of a tidal barrage. These initial assessments, together with construction feasibility and estimated costs developed by others, can then be used to establish the cost effectiveness of the concept for its intended purpose, and whether it is worth while to further develop this approach, at least on the basis of its technical merit. Navigational alterations, ecological and environmental impacts and public acceptability must also be considered.

Three mathematical models were used for this preliminary analysis to address impacts in the following order: hydrodynamic effects, water quality impacts in Long Island Sound and water quality impacts in New York-New Jersey Harbor.

For hydrodynamic effects, a comprehensive System-Wide Hydrodynamic Model of New York-New Jersey harbor, Long Island Sound and New York Bight was constructed specifically for purposes of this investigation. The model is based on models developed in previous studies.[4] The New York-New Jersey Harbor component was developed during work performed for the New York City Department of Environmental Protection for combined sewer overflow facilities planning projects.[5] The New York Bight component is based on a model developed for the U.S. Environmental Protection Agency as part of the New York Bight Restoration Plan.[6] The Long Island Sound component is based on work currently in progress for the Long Island Sound Study.

Water quality impacts in Long Island Sound were addressed by application of the second generation water quality model, LIS2.0, prepared as part of the Long Island Sound Study.[7,8] Water quality impacts in New York-New Jersey Harbor were estimated using the New York Harbor 208 Water Quality Model developed for the New York City Department of Environmental Protection as part of comprehensive wastewater management studies conducted under Section 208 of the Water Act.[9]

The LIS2.0 Model and the New York Harbor 208 Model have both been extensively calibrated against observed field data collected specifically for that purpose during the original studies. The limitations of this paper prevent a discussion or demonstration of the models' calibration. However, for purposes herein, model projections for baseline (without barrage) conditions are offered as reasonable representations of water quality conditions as may be expected for the input conditions subsequently discussed. The models are then re-executed to simulate the presence of the tidal barrage and the resulting water quality conditions are compared to the baseline cases.

For purposes of this analyses, it was assumed that the East River tidal barrage would be located at a position between the Whitestone and Throgs Neck Bridges as shown on FIGURE 1. The diagram also shows the locations of wastewater treatment plants discharging directly to New York-New Jersey Harbor. As shown, the position of the barrage is to the east of those treatment plants discharging directly to the East River, and tide gate operations would prevent any treated effluent from these plants from reaching western Long Island Sound.

HYDRODYNAMIC IMPACTS

FIGURE 2 shows the spatial domain and grid system used for the System-Wide Hydrodynamic Model. Not shown on the diagram is that portion of the model grid which extends up the Hudson River to the dam at Troy, New York. The spatial domain is necessarily extensive as boundary forcings of the model must be beyond the area affected by the subject structure, a zone not known with certainty before computations. In addition to the horizontal grid, the model is segmented into 10 vertical layers and is structured to include density effects on system hydrodynamics. For purposes of this analysis, the model was executed in a barotropic mode, that is, ignoring density effects for these preliminary computations, which substantially reduces computational requirements and execution times.

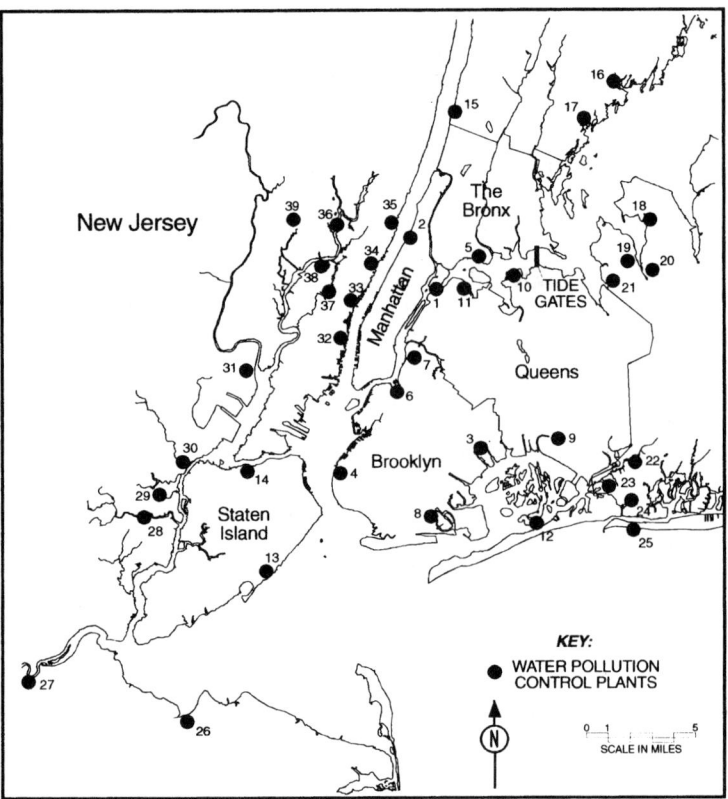

FIGURE 1. Locations of water pollution control plants and East River tide gates.

As the System-Wide Hydrodynamic Model has been only recently constructed for purposes of this analysis, the model has not yet been subjected to rigorous skill assessment. However, preliminary comparisons have been made of model predictions and the hydrodynamic properties of the study area. For this purpose, the System-Wide Hydrodynamic Model was executed to represent conditions for a 60 day period beginning June 10, 1990, using boundary forcing information on hand from another study.[10] Constants for tidal harmonics were abstracted for nine locations along the open boundaries of the model from published literature[11] and were used to generate time-varying water surface elevations.[12] Wind stresses were not included in the preliminary analysis.

Model results for water surface elevation variations were compared to predicted variations at 19 locations within the model domain. A

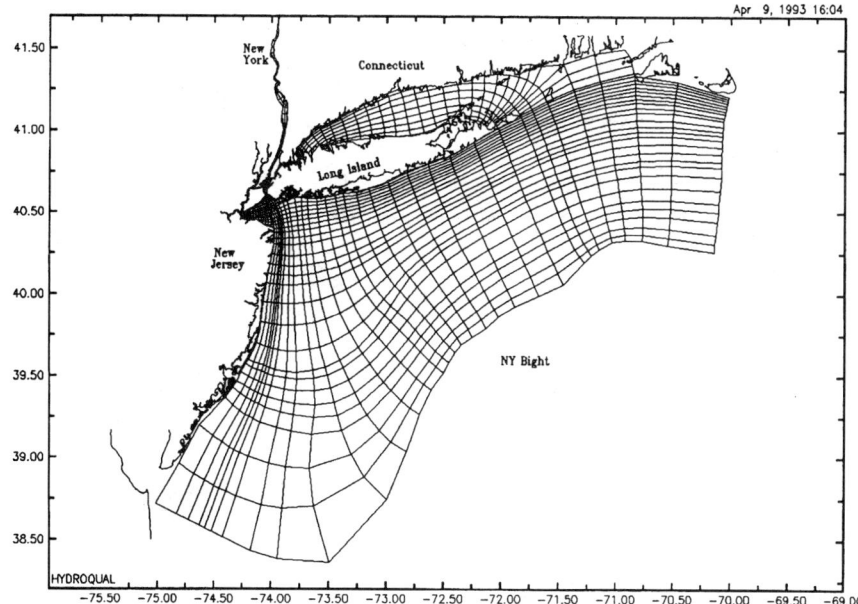

FIGURE 2. System-wide hydrodynamic model grid.

representative sampling of model generated and predicted results for a 20-day period incorporating a spring tide is presented. FIGURE 3 shows results for stations along New Jersey (Cape May, Atlantic City) and Long Island coastlines (Shinnecock Inlet, Montauk Point) and FIGURE 4 presents comparisons for the New York-New Jersey Harbor area (Sandy Hook, the Battery, Willets Point) and Long Island Sound (Bridgeport). The comparisons among model generated and predicted results are favorable.

After the preliminary skill assessment, the System-Wide Hydrodynamic Model was used for a preliminary analysis of tide gate operations. The model was re-executed for the 60-day period beginning June 10, 1990 to simulate tide gate operations as follows.

Tide gates were assumed to be open when current velocities in the East River were directed toward New York Harbor. At slack water, prior to current reversal, the gates were assumed to close. Water surface elevations would then rise on the western side of the gates and fall on the eastern side with tidal forcing. After water surface elevations began to fall on the western side and rise on the eastern side, the gates were assumed to open at that point when water elevations were equal on both sides of the gate.

FIGURE 5 shows the calculated current velocities from model grid cells immediately to the west and east of the tidal barrage. For each side, two

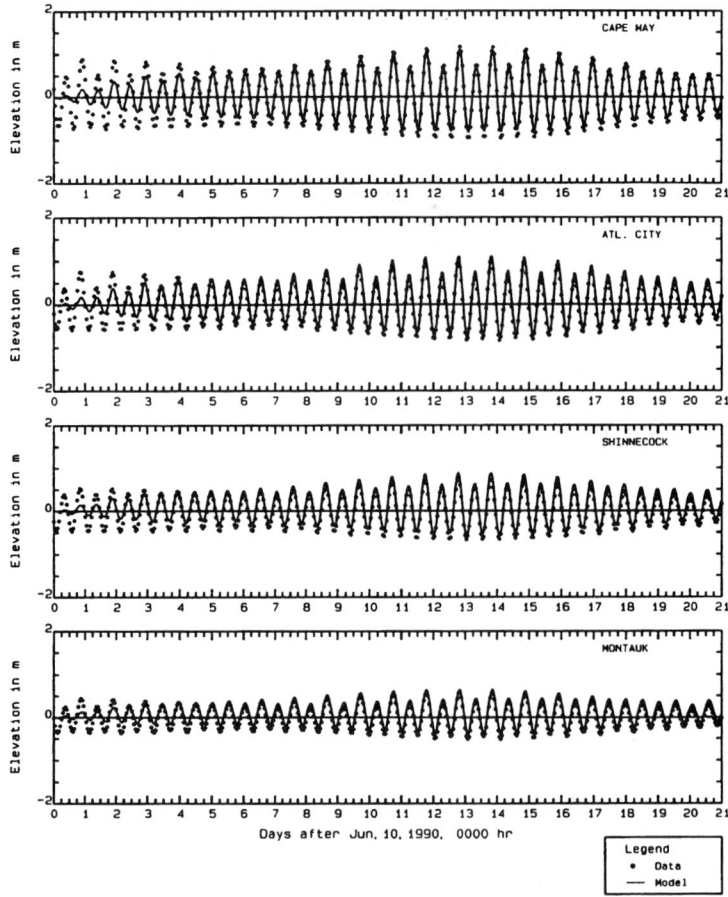

FIGURE 3. Comparison of water elevations, June 10-30, 1990.

conditions are shown; existing conditions without tide gates and then with gates in operation. The rectification in tidal currents produced by tide gate operations is evident from the successful simulation with currents being directed toward the harbor (negative velocity convention) at all times.

FIGURES 6 to 8 show projected results of tide gate operations on water surface elevations in affected areas. Review of model results indicated that the area of influence of the tidal barrage on water elevation is confined primarily to the East River/New York Harbor area and western Long Island Sound. FIGURE 6 shows water surface elevation variations with and without tide gate operations at locations from the Battery to Willets Point, including locations immediately adjacent to the structure.

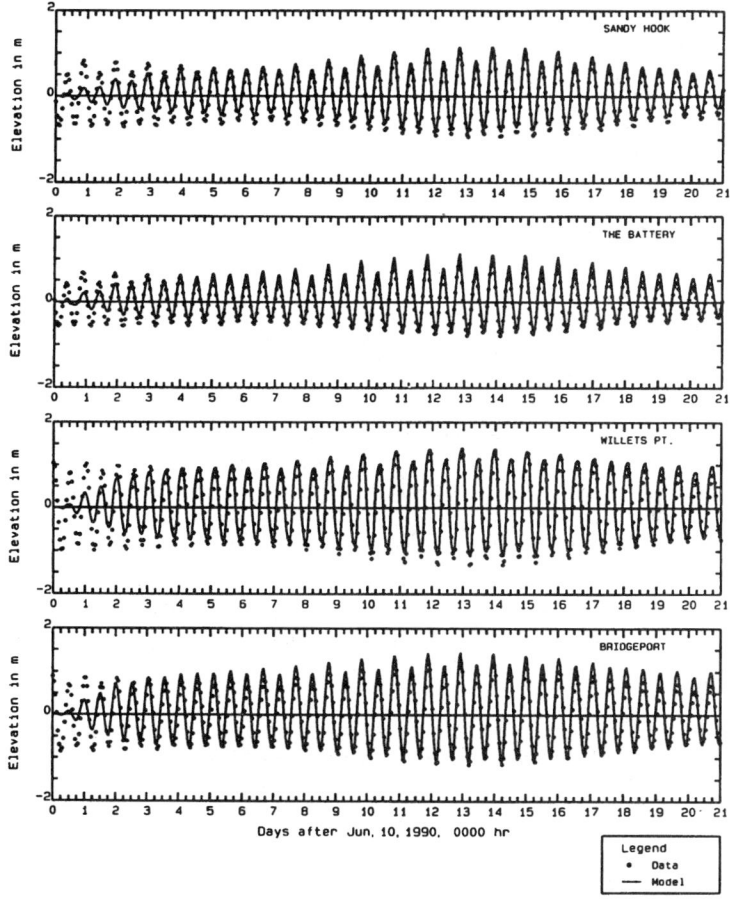

FIGURE 4. Comparison of water elevations, June 10-30, 1990.

By taking the differences of the results shown on FIGURE 6, alterations to water elevations produced by the gates are more clearly shown on FIGURES 7 and 8. These diagrams show changes produced in high water (above mean water level) and low water (below mean water level) surface elevations by tide gate operations. It is observed from FIGURE 7 that increases to approximately 20 centimeters (cm) are predicted for high water elevations at the Battery with minimal changes (2 cm) expected to low water elevations. Immediately to the west of the gates in the East River, relatively minor increases (3 cm) in high water elevations are forecast, but low water elevations may increase approximately 20 cm. FIGURE 8 shows that, on the east side of the tide gates and at Willets Point, low water elevations may be decreased by approximately 25 to 30

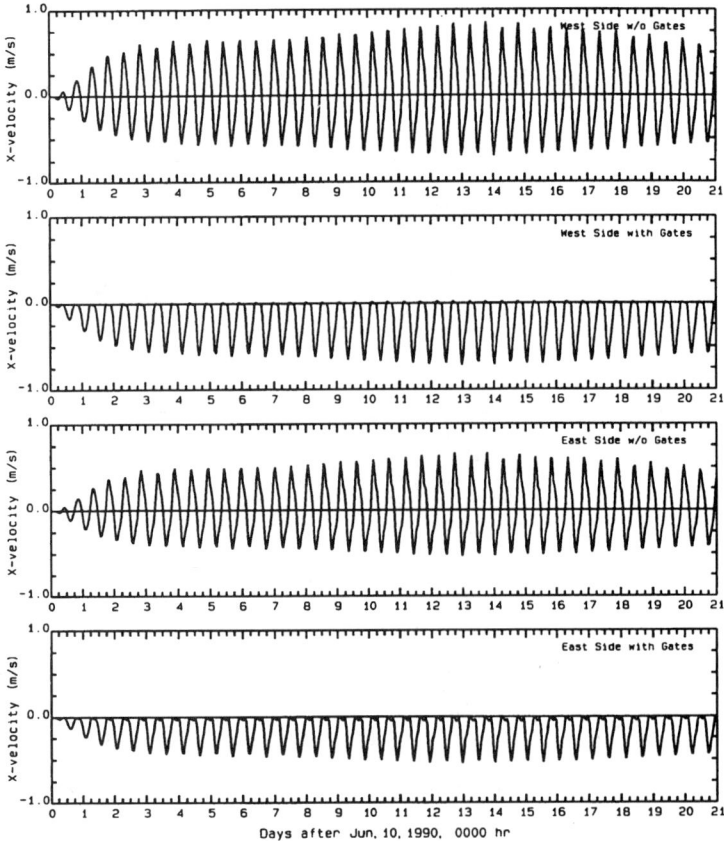

FIGURE 5. Comparison of current velocity, June 10-30, 1990.

cm. Thus, "high tide" at the Battery may be expected to be 20 cm higher than at present at certain times; "low tide" immediately to the west of the structure in the East River would not be as low as at present; while "low tide" to the east of the gates in westernmost Long Island Sound could be 25 to 30 cm lower than at present at certain times.

Low water elevations are decreased to the east of the barrage as much water volume is temporarily stored by closed tide gates in the East River and New York-New Jersey Harbor. The storage of water in the Hudson River could conceivably affect current velocities as a result. FIGURE 9 shows calculated current velocities at 4 representative locations in the Hudson River with and without tide gate operations. Maximum flood currents at the Battery could be decreased on the order of 10 cm/sec as a result of tide gate operations.

A final aspect of the tidal barrage which was evaluated with the

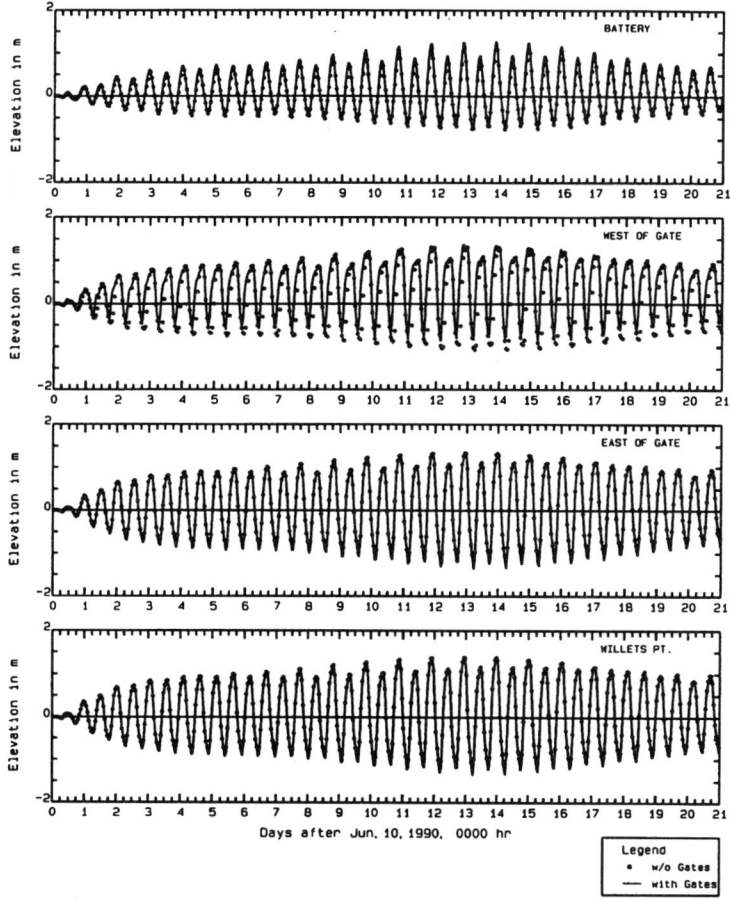

FIGURE 6. Comparison of calculated water elevations, June 10-30, 1990.

System-Wide Hydrodynamic Model was change in volume flux (tidally averaged net flow) through Long Island Sound and the East River induced by tide gate operations. FIGURE 10 shows calculated fluxes for the entire 60-day simulation period at four locations in the system: the eastern end of Long Island Sound, mid-Sound, Throgs Neck, and the Narrows. It is observed that average flow toward New York Harbor is increased substantially throughout the system. At Throgs Neck, the entrance to the East River, the calculated time averaged flow for the 60-day period increases from 128 cubic meters per second (m^3/sec) without tide gates to 3544 m^3/sec with tide gate operations. This projected substantial additional flow is available for dilution and transport of waste inputs in the East River and New York-New Jersey Harbor.

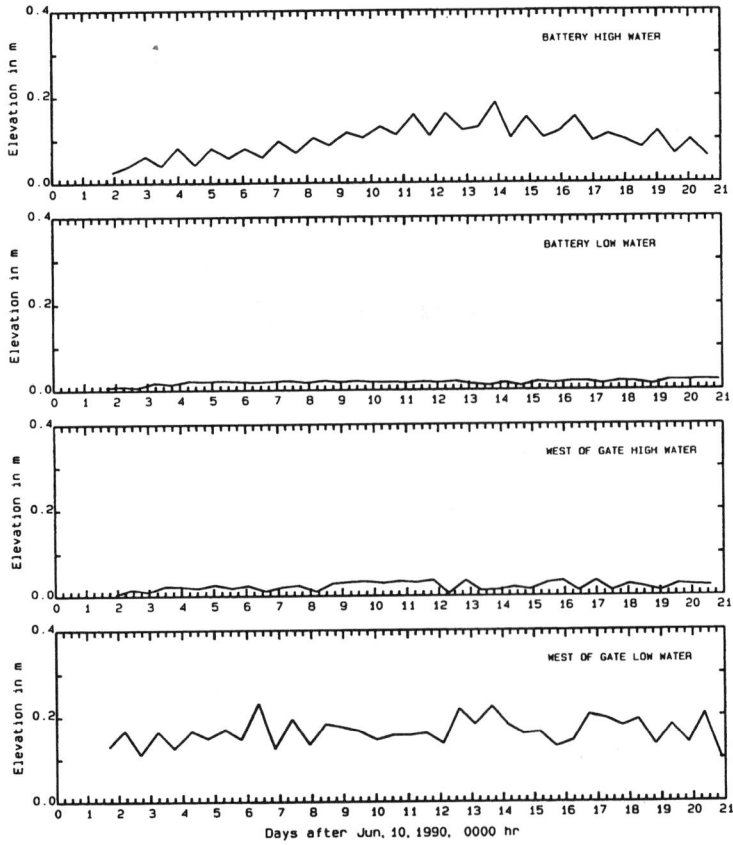

FIGURE 7. Calculated changes in water elevations, June 10-30, 1990.

WATER QUALITY IMPACTS IN LONG ISLAND SOUND

The effects of an East River tidal barrage on water quality conditions in Long Island Sound were calculated using the second generation Long Island Sound Water Quality Model, LIS2.0. The locations of point source wastewater discharges into Long Island Sound and the East River are shown on FIGURE 11; the sound also receives pollutant inputs from seven tributary rivers and from its boundaries, *i.e.*, New York-New Jersey Harbor to the west and the coastal Atlantic Ocean to the east. The spatial domain and segmentation of the LIS2.0 Model are shown on FIGURE 12; the segments shown are in two vertical layers to account for both horizontal and vertical water quality variations. The LIS2.0 Model also contains a bed sediment layer which interacts with the water column for nutrient and oxygen fluxes.

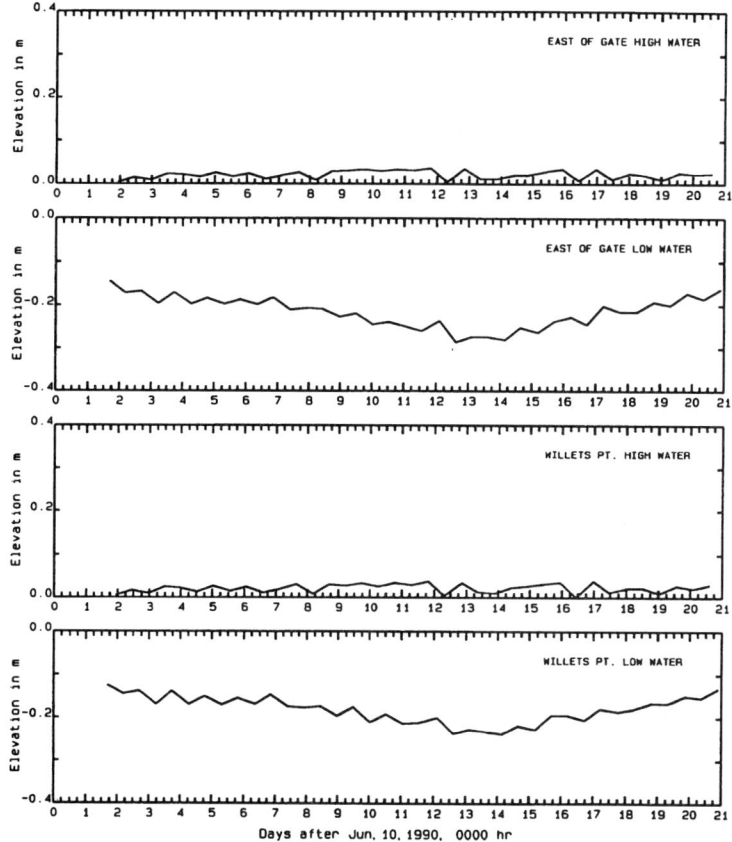

FIGURE 8. Calculated changes in water elevations, June 10-30, 1990.

The LIS2.0 Model has been extensively calibrated during the Long Island Sound Study with field data collected from April 1988 through September 1989. The characteristic 2-layer estuarine circulation pattern of Long Island Sound is computed for each of the 18 months of the calibration period from observed salinity data collected throughout the sound and the East River using an analytical procedure.[13] Net vertically integrated tidally averaged flow through the sound and East River was estimated from acoustic Doppler current profilers on the order of 200 m^3/sec. The water quality component of the LIS2.0 Model includes modern eutrophication kinetics for 25 state variables for the interactions of carbon, nitrogen, phosphorus and silica on the growth of algal biomass, and permits an analyses of all oxygen sources and sinks on the Long Island Sound dissolved oxygen balance. The model computes changes in dissolved oxygen and the other state variables in a time-

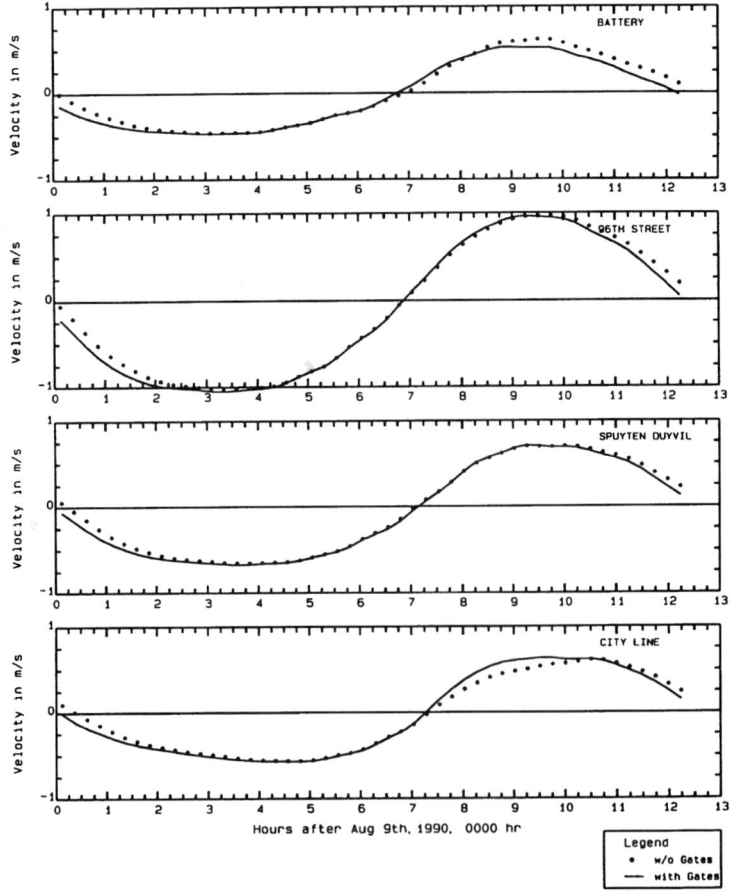

FIGURE 9. Comparison of calculated current velocities, August 9, 1990.

varying manner (daily) over an 18-month period using monthly average circulation patterns.

It was beyond the scope of this effort to reanalyze the changes in estuarine circulation of Long Island Sound caused by tide gate operations. Rather, the LIS2.0 Model was used solely to assess the impact of physically preventing waste loadings discharged to the west of the tidal barrage from reaching Long Island Sound proper. Thus, the increase in vertically integrated tidally averaged flow which brings additional ocean water into the sound from its eastern end and any changes to vertical density stratification caused by increased ocean water (from the east) and reduced fresh water (from the west) are not explicitly included in the computation.

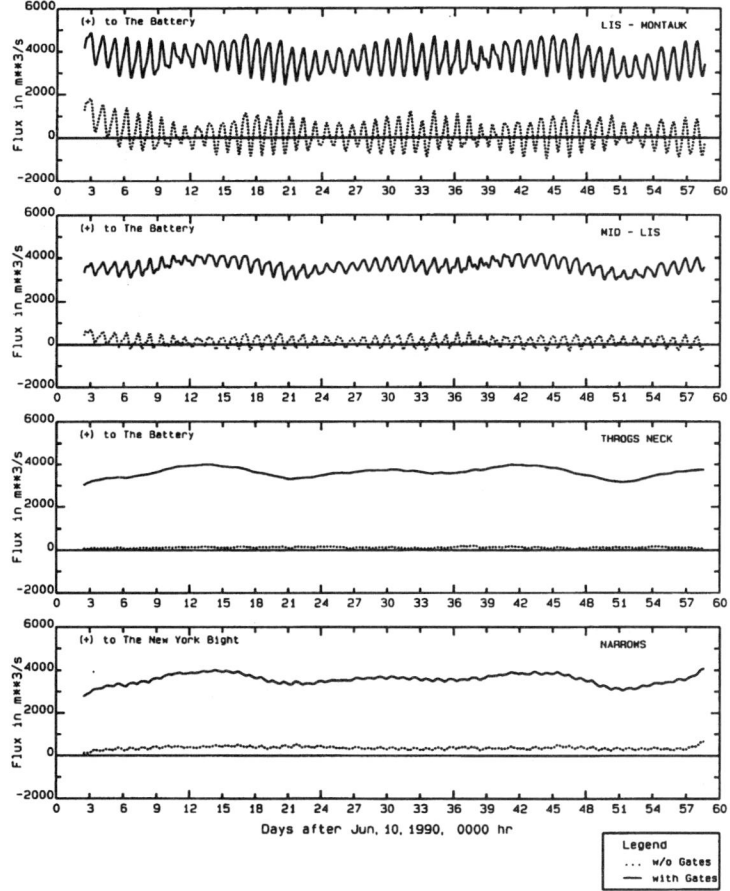

FIGURE 10. Calculated changes in volume flux, June 10-August 10, 1990.

Model calculations were performed for two conditions: a baseline case which basically represents existing waste loading conditions used for management planning in the Long Island Sound Study, and the same condition repeated with a tidal barrage acting as a barrier thus preventing waste loadings on the west side from reaching Long Island Sound.

FIGURES 13 and 14 show the results of the two calculations. The diagrams show calculated spatial profiles of water quality variables for August conditions with and without a tidal barrier on a distance scale from the Battery in New York City. FIGURE 13 shows that, with a tidal barrier in place, total nitrogen and total phosphorus concentrations are substantially reduced by a factor of 3 to 4 in the western sound from baseline conditions to values that are relatively constant and approxi-

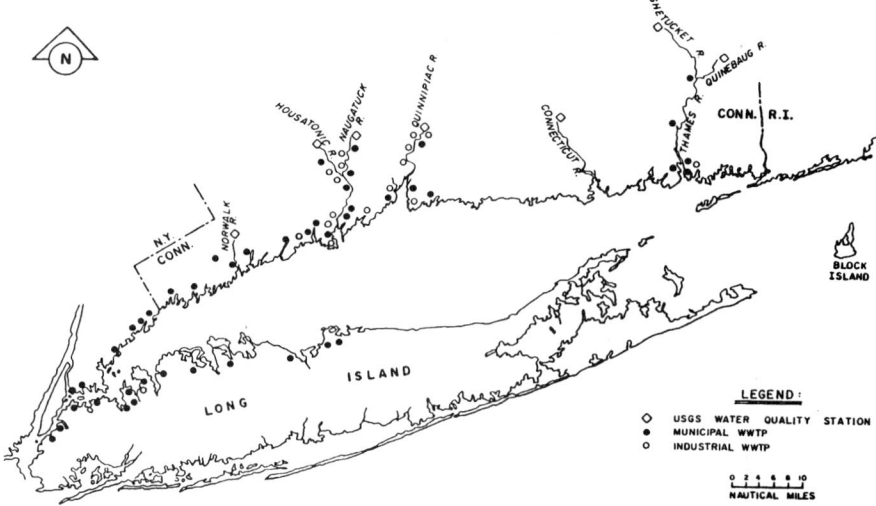

FIGURE 11. Location map of point source discharges to Long Island Sound.

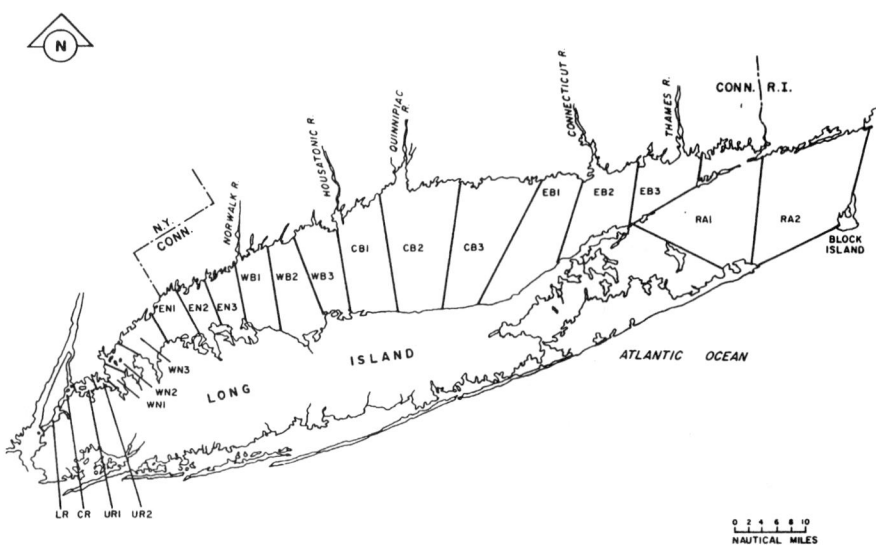

FIGURE 12. Segmentation map for Long Island Sound Water Quality Model.

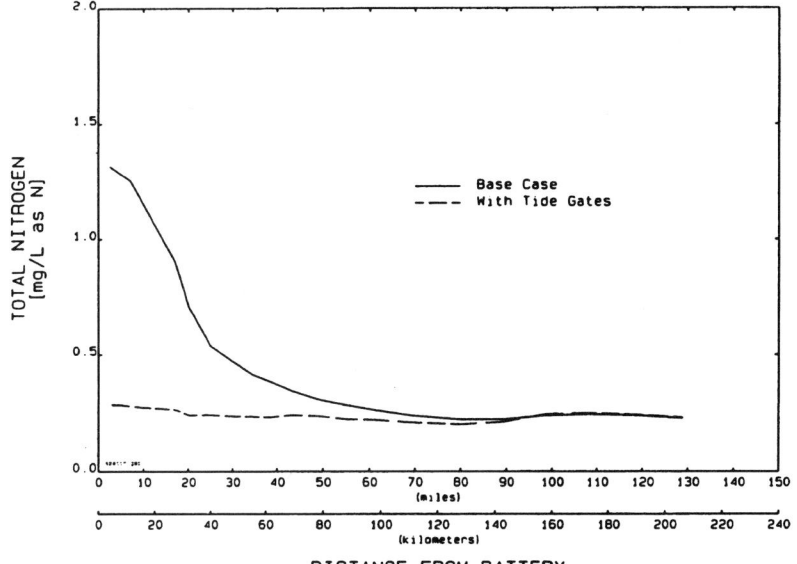
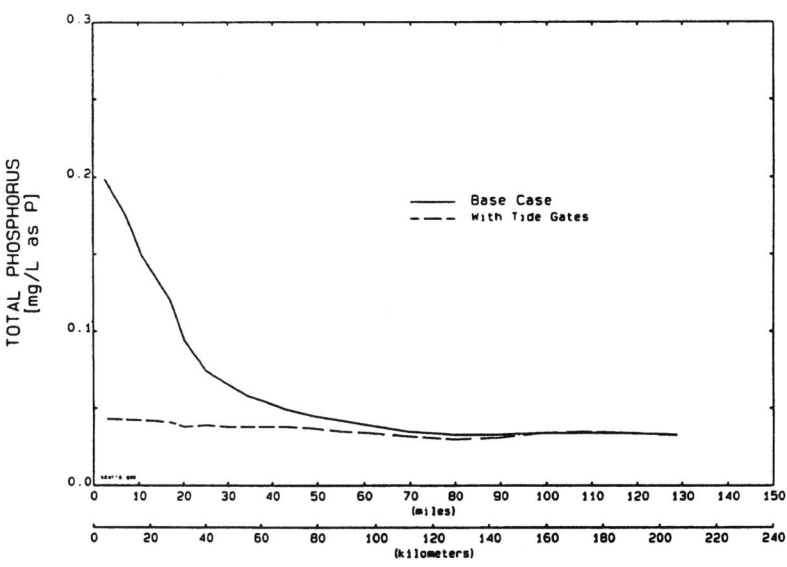

FIGURE 13. Calculated nitrogen and phosphorus profiles.

mate those entering the sound at the eastern boundary. FIGURE 14 illustrates that the reduced nutrients suppress the development of algal biomass (chlorophyll-a) at the critical location in the western sound by a similar factor. The effect on bottom water dissolved oxygen is also shown with minimum monthly average dissolved oxygen in the western sound calculated to increase from approximately 1.8 mg/l to 3.8 mg/l.

FIGURE 15 compares the baseline and tidal barrier case with other results developed for the Long Island Sound Study, which investigated the effect of three levels of total nitrogen reductions at the sources. It is observed that the increase in dissolved oxygen above baseline conditions projected to result from a tidal barrier exceeds that forecasted for high level nutrient reductions.

WATER QUALITY IMPACTS IN NEW YORK-NEW JERSEY HARBOR

A preliminary analysis of the effects an East River tidal barrage on water quality conditions in New York Harbor was performed using the New York Harbor 208 Water Quality Model. The spatial domain and model segmentation are shown on FIGURE 16. The 208 Model is three-dimensional and has two vertical layers in the East River, Long Island Sound, Upper New York Bay and the Hudson River to the Bear Mountain Bridge. The model is steady-state and computes average water quality conditions in all model segments on a seasonal (*e.g.*, summer) or monthly basis. The 208 Model has been extensively calibrated for salinity, dissolved oxygen, total and fecal coliform bacteria, and has received preliminary calibration for nitrogen, phosphorus, and toxic metals. Water circulation patterns in the 208 Model are deduced from salinity distributions and information available from other studies.[14] The dissolved oxygen kinetics in the 208 Model do not explicitly account for eutrophication effects, but rather the oxidation of carbonaceous and nitrogenous (where active) biochemical oxygen demand (BOD) and specified algal photosynthesis and respiration.

For the present analysis, the model was executed using representative summer freshwater flow in tributary rivers and an average summer rainfall. Waste inputs from point source municipal and industrial wastewater treatment plants, tributary rivers, area-wide combined sewer overflows and storm water runoff and other discharges were assigned for 1990 secondary treatment conditions, a planning scenario routinely used for model application. The model was then executed for conditions with and without an East River tidal barrage. For present conditions, the tidally averaged flow in the East River was assigned as 280 m^3/sec (10,000 cfs) as determined from other studies. For the tide gate condition, the tidally averaged flow in the East River was increased to 3,544 m^3/sec (125,000 cfs) as determined from the System-Wide Hydrodynamic Model. As the 208 Model is steady-state, the closing and opening of the tide

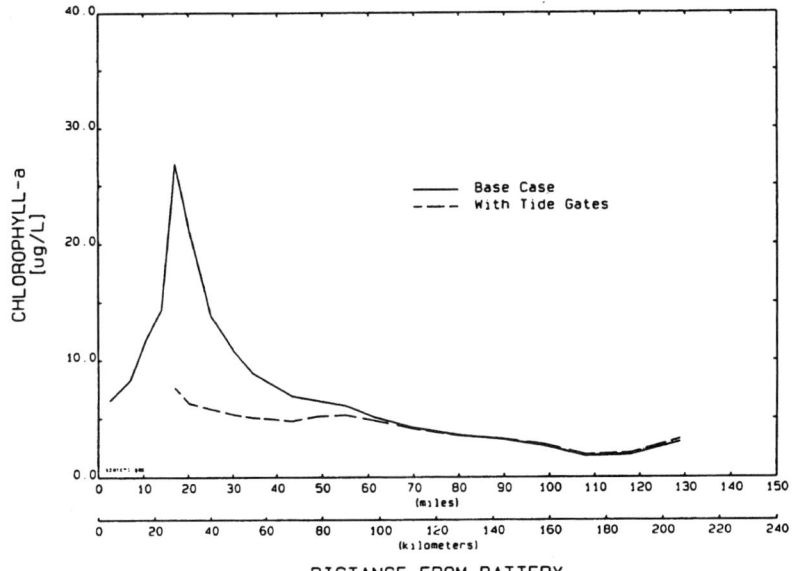
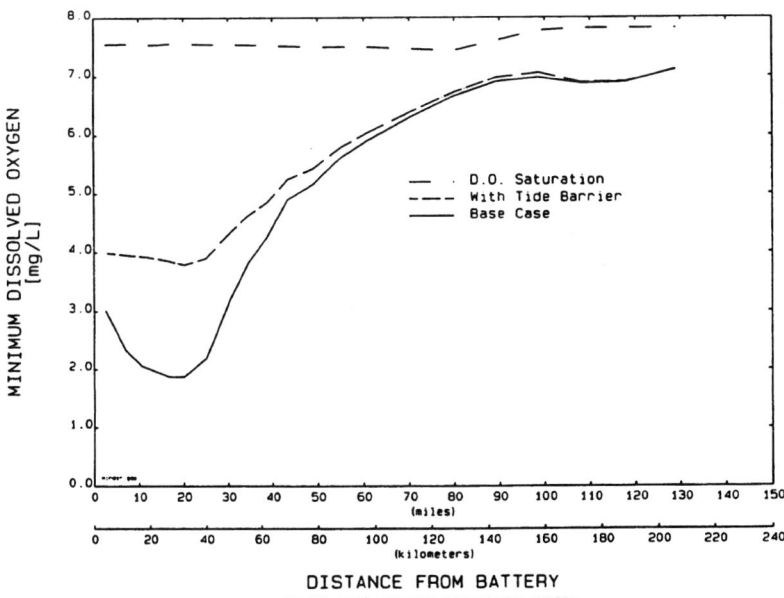

FIGURE 14. Calculated chlorophyll-a and dissolved oxygen profiles.

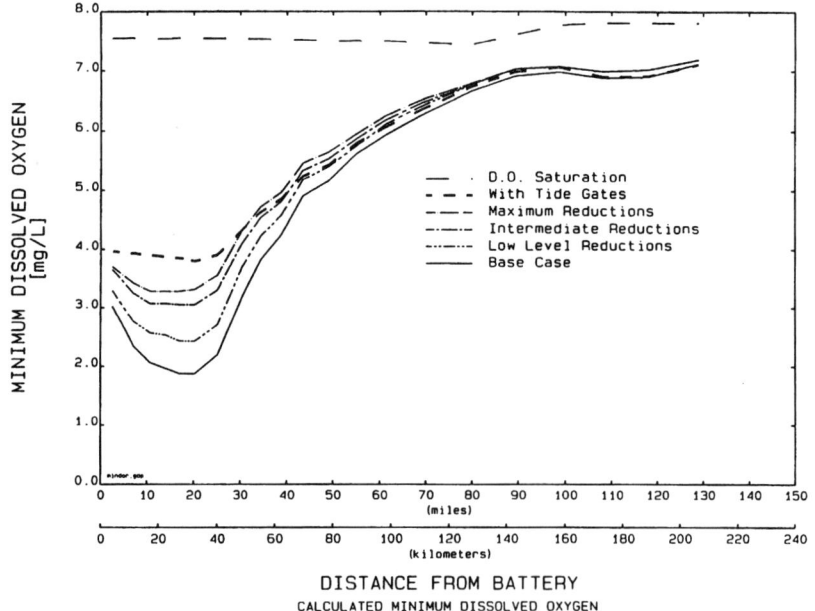

FIGURE 15. Calculated minimum dissolved oxygen.

gates could not be simulated directly, and the tidally averaged flow was assumed to be constant rather than pulsed. To account for the reducing effects of the physical structure of the barrage on tidal dispersion in the steady-state model, horizontal dispersion coefficients at the location of the barrage in the East River were assigned as zero. Water quality conditions for total nitrogen and dissolved oxygen at the open boundary of the 208 Model in Long Island Sound were assigned from the simulations of the LIS2.0 Model.

FIGURES 17 through 20 show the results of the 208 Model application. Spatial water quality profiles are presented for various waterways in New York-New Jersey Harbor for conditions with and without tide gates. The model calculates profiles in two layers in certain waterways as previously noted. However, for clarity of presentation, the results from only one (more critical) layer is presented (upper layer for total nitrogen, total coliforms; lower layer for dissolved oxygen, salinity).

FIGURE 17 shows calculated results for total nitrogen as a conservative substance. The increased tidally averaged flow in the East River and lower concentrations in western Long Island Sound affected by the tide gates combine to produce concentration reductions in the East River and throughout New York-New Jersey Harbor as a whole. The diluting flow induced by a tidal barrage could reduce East River total nitrogen concentration by approximately 75 percent and reduce concentrations in the

ST. JOHN: IMPACT ON WATER QUALITY

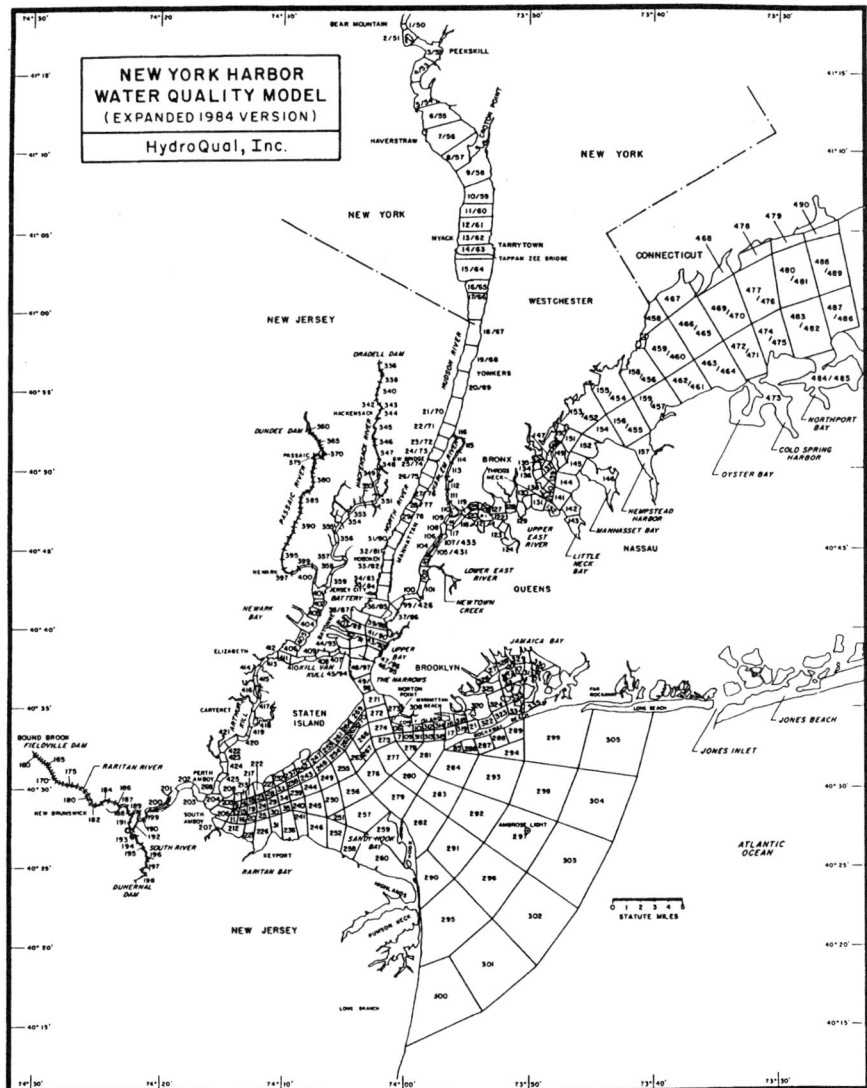

FIGURE 16. New York Harbor 208 Water Quality Model Grid.

Upper Bay and lower Hudson (North) River by as much as 50 percent. Reductions are also calculated in the Kills, Raritan Bay, and Jamaica Bay. Other water quality constituents which behave primarily as conservative substances (*e.g.*, toxic metals) would be affected in a similar manner.

FIGURE 18 presents results for dissolved oxygen. The improvement of approximately 2.0 mg/l of dissolved oxygen in western Long Island

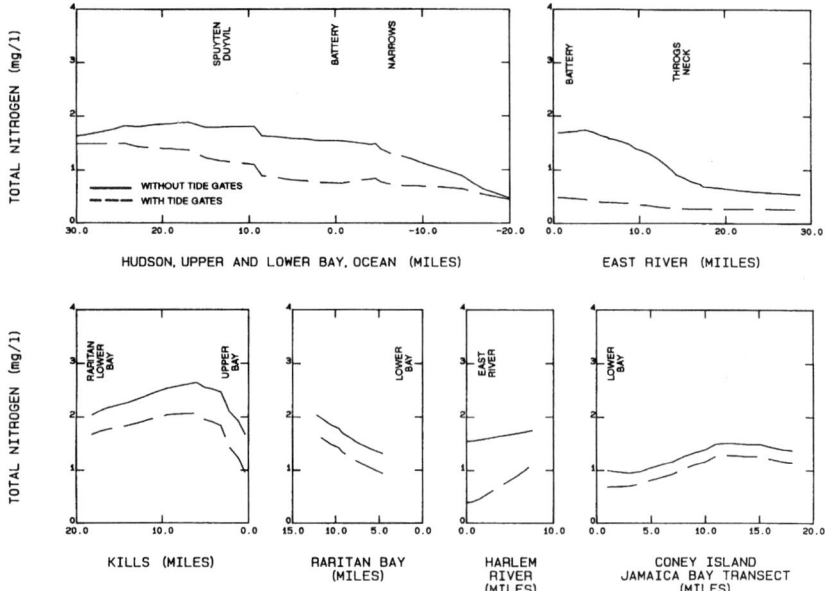

FIGURE 17. Calculated total nitrogen profiles.

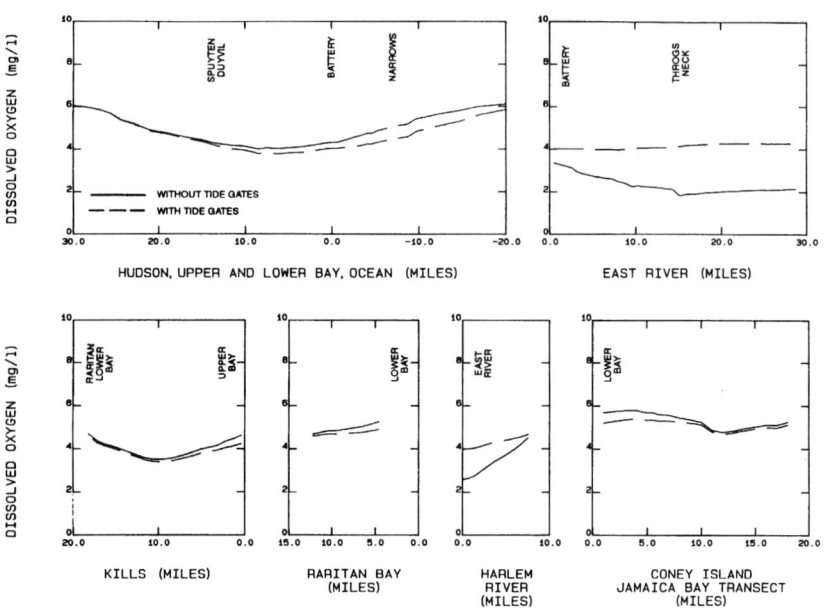

FIGURE 18. Calculated dissolved oxygen profiles.

Sound produced by the tide gates as calculated with the LIS2.0 Model carries into the East River with the larger induced dilutional flow improving conditions to the Battery. Dissolved oxygen conditions in the Harlem River are also improved. However, some reduction in dissolved oxygen of a few tenths to 0.5 mg/l is calculated in the lower Hudson River, Upper and Lower Bays, the Kills and Raritan Bay.

FIGURE 19 presents results for total coliform bacteria, which result primarily from combined sewer overflows and stormwater runoff in New York and New Jersey. Reduced total coliform bacteria concentrations throughout all of the East River are calculated for the tide gate conditions: the reduction is as much as 50 percent in the upper East River. However, it is observed that tide gate operations are calculated to increase total coliform bacteria concentrations in the Upper and Lower Bays on the order of 1,000 MPN/100 ml.

FIGURES 18 and 19 indicate that, while tide gate operations are calculated to improve water quality conditions for dissolved oxygen and total coliform bacteria in the East River and Harlem River, some degradation in quality for these variables may occur at other locations in New York-New Jersey Harbor. In contrast to conservative substances, the concentration distribution for which in estuaries is determined entirely by dilution and tidal exchange, the concentration of reactive substances such as BOD and coliform bacteria is strongly influenced by

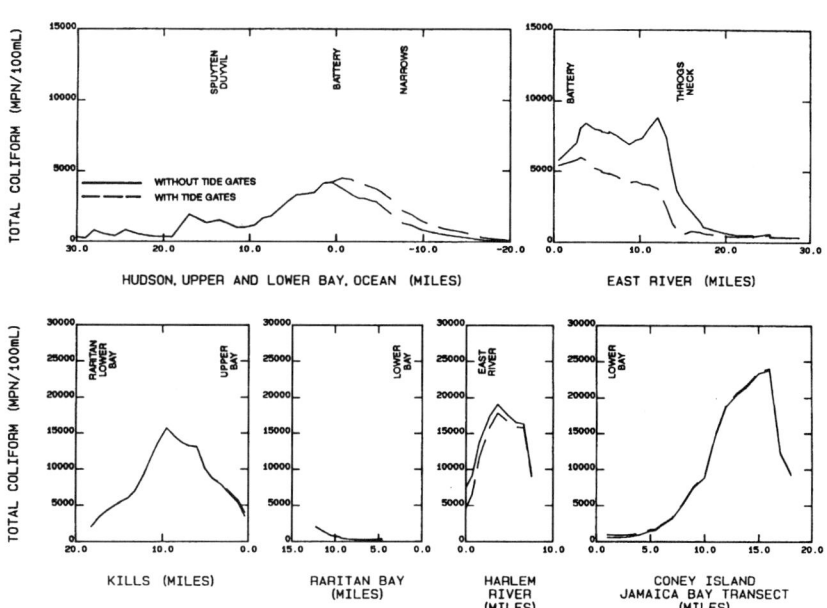

FIGURE 19. Calculated total coliform profiles.

environmental reactions and decay. The results indicate that, in the East River, the mass of BOD/coliform bacteria which decays with time is more important than dilution/tidal exchange as the sink of material which primarily affects concentration values. Hence, the large increase in induced flow produced by tide gates is less effective in reducing concentrations for these variables than for conservative substances (*e.g.*, total nitrogen). In addition, as the residence time of these substances in the East River is decreased by the increased dilution flow, less decay occurs and more mass is transported from the East River into the Upper Bay of the harbor. The increase in dilution flow does not fully compensate for the increased mass and the resulting degradation of quality occurs.

FIGURE 20 presents results for salinity. In this simulation, salinity concentrations at the open boundaries of the 208 Model were assigned at 29 and 34 parts per thousand (ppt) in Long Island Sound and the New York Bight Apex, respectively. The reductions in salinity throughout the system as calculated for existing conditions are caused by dilution from freshwater sources (tributary inflows, waste inputs). Tide gate operations and the large induced tidally averaged flow in the East River are expected to increase salinity to approximately that in mid-Long Island Sound. Salinity in the Hudson River at the Battery is also increased by approximately 1 ppt for the conditions simulated. Salinities in the Lower

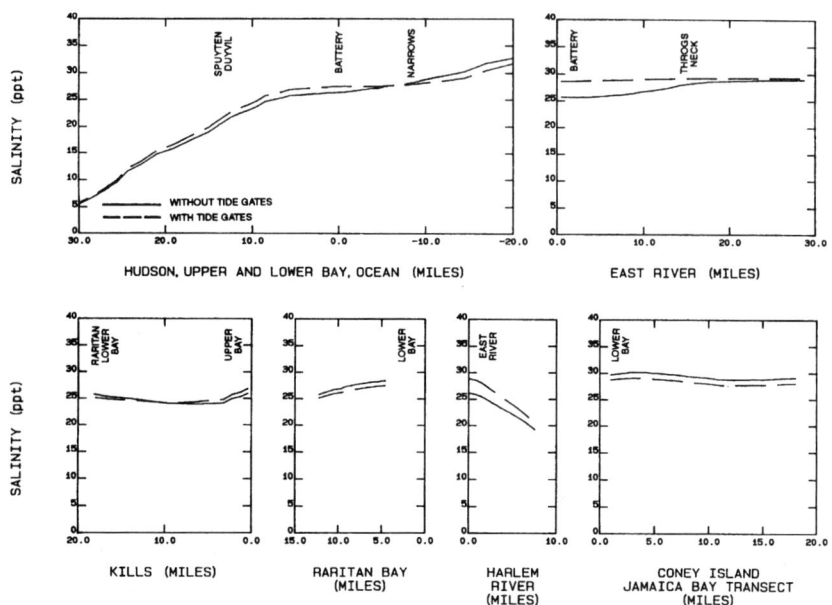

FIGURE 20. Calculated salinity profiles.

Bay to the ocean decrease somewhat as the increased flow with lower salinity concentration tends to dilute intruding oceanic salinity.

It is to be noted that the salinity results are strongly related to the boundary values and freshwater flow inputs (summer conditions) specified for the example. Other input conditions can be expected to produce different results. Salinity analyses should be performed using a system-wide model over an annual cycle.

OTHER CONSIDERATIONS

As shown, operations of a tidal barrage in the East River can significantly affect water quality conditions in western Long Island Sound, the East River, and to a somewhat lesser extent, New York-New Jersey Harbor. Tide gates are calculated to significantly reduce nutrient concentrations in western Long Island Sound while increasing dissolved oxygen. While the increase in the latter parameter is desirable from a general ecological point of view, the sharp reduction of nutrients in the western sound could reduce primary productivity with attendant negative impacts to fisheries yield.[15] To minimize such potential adverse impacts, tide gate operations could be seasonal, limited only to that time of the year (*e.g.,* summer) when operations would produce the most benefit with the least adverse impact.

Time limitations did not permit an analysis to be specifically conducted for New York Bight though appropriate models are available.[6] The increased rectified flow through the sound-harbor system will add nutrient mass to the New York Bight Apex. However, although preliminary indications are that the additional diluting flow, while increasing the nutrient mass flux, will reduce concentration values such that nutrient impacts (hypoxia) on bight waters may be lessened to some degree, a detailed analysis should be performed.

FINDINGS OF THE PRELIMINARY ANALYSIS

For conditions as simulated by the various models used in the preliminary analysis, the following observations are presented.

1. Tide gate operations increased high water elevations by as much as approximately 20 cm at the Battery. Minimal changes in high water levels were calculated at Willets Point.
2. Low water elevations increased by approximately 20 cm on the west side of the tidal barrage and decreased by 25 to 30 cm on the east side of the tide gates.
3. Maximum tidal current velocities in the Hudson River at the Battery were calculated to decrease on the order of 10 cm/sec on flooding tide as a result of tide gate operations.
4. Volume flux (tidally averaged flow) through the East River in-

creased from 128 m³/sec to 3,544 m³/sec as a result of the rectified tidal currents produced by tide gate operations.
5. Elimination of the effects of waste inputs located to the west of the tidal barrage reduced nutrient concentrations and algal biomass in western Long Island Sound by factors of 3 to 4 and increased bottom water dissolved oxygen by approximately 2.0 mg/l.
6. Tide gate operations reduced total nitrogen concentrations in the East River and in the Upper Bay-lower Hudson River area by as much as 75 percent and 50 percent, respectively. Dissolved oxygen throughout the East River increased to approximately 4 mg/l. Total coliform bacteria decreased in the East River by as much as 50 percent.
7. For reactive substances, the induced flow in the East River is calculated to transport increased pollutant mass out of the East River and into the Upper Bay due to decreased retention and reaction times. This results in decreased dissolved oxygen of 0.5 mg/l and increased total coliform bacteria of 1,000 MPN/100 ml in certain areas of the harbor beyond the East River.
8. Tide gate operations increased salinity in the East River to a value approximating that in Long Island Sound. Salinity in the Hudson River at the Battery increased approximately 1 ppt while salinity values toward the ocean decreased somewhat for the conditions simulated.
9. Tide gate operations will significantly reduce nutrients, primary productivity and possibly fisheries yield in western Long Island Sound. Consideration can be given to seasonal operation of tide gates to maximize positive benefits (increased dissolved oxygen) and to minimize potentially adverse impacts (water elevation alterations, increased salinity intrusion, reduced primary productivity). Management of the ecosystem in this manner would benefit from a detailed operations analysis using modeling technology.

LIMITATIONS OF THE ANALYSIS

As noted previously, the perfect modeling tool is not yet available to analyze the hydrodynamic and water quality ramifications of an East River tidal barrage. The purpose herein was to use readily available modeling technology to place some initial perspective on potential impacts; it was more of a sensitivity analysis to deduce the approximate order of impacts and their general consequences—potentially positive or negative. When reviewing results, the following limitations should be noted:

1. The System-Wide Hydrodynamic Model, while producing realistic results, has not yet been rigorously calibrated.
2. The LIS2.0 Model application did not include the expected increase

in volume flux through Long Island Sound from the Race to the Battery and potential attendant changes in vertical density structure.
3. The New York Harbor 208 Model application did not include a rigorous reanalysis of harbor hydrodynamics (*e.g.*, changes in Hudson River estuarine circulation, changes in vertical density,) and the increased volume flux was added simply as dilutional flow.
4. Neither water quality model directly simulated the opening and closing of the tide gates so that the effect of periodic, short-term reductions in advection in areas immediately adjacent to the structure was not directly analyzed.
5. Calculated changes in system salinity distributions are strongly influenced by assigned boundary conditions and freshwater flow inputs.
6. No analysis of potential impacts in the New York Bight Apex has yet been performed.

RECOMMENDATIONS FOR FURTHER ANALYSIS

The calculations performed for this analysis used three separate modeling frameworks. It is recommended that any additional quantitative analysis which may be performed to analyze the consequences of the tidal barrage concept consist of a single comprehensive modeling framework constructed in a manner to eliminate the limitations cited above. Initially, the spatial domain of the model may be that of the 208 Model. The model should be a coupled hydrodynamic and water quality model of the region of interest; it should be three-dimensional, fully time varying and incorporating modern eutrophication kinetics for the dissolved oxygen balance. The initial model should be calibrated with existing data. The technology for such a Harbor Eutrophication Model is readily at hand. Ultimately, the analysis should incorporate New York Bight and a System-Wide Eutrophication Model should be constructed and validated using the grid of the System-Wide Hydrodynamic Model.

ACKNOWLEDGMENTS

The analyses presented in this paper were a collaborative research effort of many individuals at HydroQual, Inc. Alan F. Blumberg, Principal Scientist, supervised hydrodynamic computations performed by Levsiri C. Munasinghe, Engineer. LIS2.0 Model computations were performed by Thomas L. Newman, II, Project Engineer. New York Harbor 208 Model computations were performed by Charles L. Dujardin, Senior Project Manager. Advice of Dominic M. Di Toro, James J. Fitzpatrick, and William M. Leo, Principal Engineers, is gratefully acknowledged.

The application of the extended New York Harbor 208 Water Quality Model was developed for the New York City Department of Environmental Protection and the LIS2.0 Model developed for the Long Island Sound Study is gratefully acknowledged.

REFERENCES

1. BOWMAN, M.J. 1976. Tidal locks across the East River: An engineering solution to the rehabilitation of Long Island Sound. *In* Estuarine Processes. M. Wiley, Ed. Academic Press.
2. BOWMAN, M.J. 1977. Nutrient distributions and transport in Long Island Sound. Est. and Coastal Mar. Sci. **5**: 531-548.
3. LONG ISLAND SOUND STUDY. 1993. Comprehensive conservation and management plan (draft).
4. BLUMBERG, A.F. & G.L. MELLOR. 1987. A description of a three-dimensional coastal ocean circulation model. *In* Three-Dimensional Coastal Ocean Models. Coastal and Estuarine Sciences, Vol. 4. N.S. Heaps, Ed.: 1-16. Washington, DC: American Geophysical Union.
5. HYDROQUAL, INC. 1993a. Task report: Open waters modeling—Inner Harbor Combined Sewer Overflow Facilities Planning Project. Hazen and Sawyer, P.C. for the New York City Department of Environmental Protection.
6. HYDROQUAL, INC. 1993b. Status report on New York Bight nutrient modeling (draft). New York Bight Restoration Plan, U.S. Environmental Protection Agency, Region II.
7. HYDROQUAL, INC. 1991. Water quality modeling analysis of hypoxia in Long Island Sound. Long Island Sound Study.
8. LONG ISLAND SOUND STUDY. 1990. Status report and interim actions for hypoxia management.
9. HYDROQUAL, INC. 1978. New York City 208 Study: Task report—seasonal steady-state modeling (PCP 314). Hazen and Sawyer, P.C. for the New York City Department of Environmental Protection.
10. HYDROQUAL, INC. 1993c. Evaluation of transport patterns, Task 8.0, City-Wide Floatables Study (draft). New York City Department of Environmental Protection.
11. MOODY, J.A., B. BUTMAN, R. C. BEARDSLEY, W.S. BROWN, P. DAIFUKU, J.D. IRISH, D.A. MAYER, H.O. MOFJELD, B. PETRIE, S. RAMP, P. SMITH & W.R. WRIGHT. 1984. Atlas of tidal elevation and current observations on the northeast American continental shelf and slope. Bulletin 1611. U.S. Geological Survey. U.S. Department of the Interior, 1984.
12. GODIN, G. 1972. The analysis of tides. Toronto, Canada: University of Toronto Press.
13. PRITCHARD, D.W. 1964. Dispersion and flushing of pollutants in estuaries. J. Hydraulics Div. ASCE **95(1471)**: 114-121.
14. HYDROQUAL, INC. 1993d. The transport through the East River from data and three-dimensional modeling analysis—addendum (in progress). Long Island Sound Study.
15. NIXON, S.W. 1990. Quantifying the relationship between nitrogen input and the productivity of marine systems. Ecological Management of the Marine Environment Proceedings of the Eighth Marine Technology Conference, Tokyo.

DISCUSSION OF THE PAPER

QUESTION: How long would you expect the altered conditions of decreased dissolved oxygen and increased coliform in New York Harbor to last?

JOHN P. ST. JOHN: We would expect it to occur as long as the tide gates are in operation.

QUESTION: You don't see that as an initial flushing event?

ST. JOHN: No, those were steady state computations. What the model is forecasting is the conditions as they would occur after the system achieves a new equilibrium with the tide gates in operation.

QUESTION: What is the sensitivity of this program in terms of the hydrodynamics and so forth of the location of the tide gates from, let's say, Willets Point down to Brooklyn Bridge?

ST. JOHN: That's a very good question. I hate to guess on things that we haven't calculated, but I'll give you an opinion. I think that the net flow that is induced through the East River—the additional dilution flow—will probably remain the same. And I think that the hydrodynamic impacts would probably remain more or less the same. We'll have to take a careful look at what will be going on in the Harlem River, which I really didn't discuss with you today. I think as far as the water quality impacts are concerned, probably the optimal location would be in the position that I showed as far as preventing the impacts of wastewater discharged into New York-New Jersey Harbor from reaching the critical location in the western Sound. If the tide gates were located farther downstream in the East River between Manhattan and Brooklyn, for example, I think that some of the discharges from East River treatment plants located now to the north or east of the tide gates would enter Long Island Sound on falling tides in that system and have some effect on the water quality conditions in the western Sound. So it is something that would have to be looked at very carefully.

Sedimentation Associated with an East River Tidal Barrage

HENRY BOKUNIEWICZ
Marine Sciences Research Center
State University of New York
Stony Brook, New York 11794-5000

INTRODUCTION

A tidal barrage across the northern reach of the East River will essentially halt the flow in this tidal strait for half the tidal cycle. In response, the balance among resuspension, sediment transport and deposition will readjust. In this article, I will discuss how that readjustment might occur. The potential for shoaling is a particular concern. If shoaling is excessive, a tidal barrage may bring with it a permanent commitment for additional dredging to maintain navigable waters. I intend to show that shoaling deserves further study since the changes have the potential to increase shoaling but that the predictions necessarily contain large uncertainties, which can only be partially reduced by more sophisticated modeling.

CHARACTERISTICS OF SEDIMENT TRANSPORT

Tidal flows through the East River are controlled primarily by water level differences between Willets Point and the Battery and, in part, by differences between Spuyten Duyvil and Hell Gate, through the Harlem River. The predictable, astronomical tides drive water through the East River at maximum velocities of about 0.9 m/sec, although meteorological tides which cannot be predicted in advance can substantially alter this flow. During the summer of 1981 a set of 15 stations were sampled along the axis of the East River to describe the distribution of salinity and suspended sediment concentrations. Salinity was measured with a Beckman salinometer and suspended sediment concentrations were measured by filtering through preweighed 0.45 micrometer nucleopore filters (D. Hirshburg, MSRC, personal communication). The water column was well-mixed north of the Brooklyn Bridge and the tidal stream carries with it suspended sediment at concentrations of about 8 mg/l (FIG. 1). Based on calculated flows from 39 years of tide-gage records,[1] it seems that sediment is sent through the strait from the Sound into the Upper Bay of New York Harbor at a rate of 71,000 metric tons/year.[2]

The northern reach of the River, between Hell Gate and Willets Point, is relatively broad and fringed by embayments. The bottom sediments

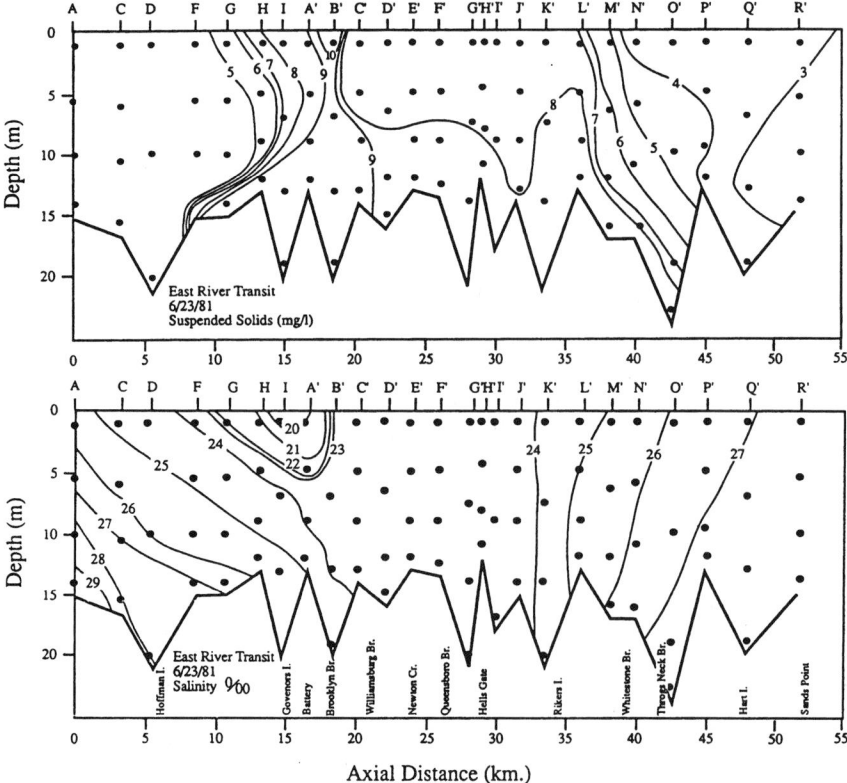

FIGURE 1. Axial sections of the suspended sediment concentration and salinity from the Lower Bay of New York Harbor (on the left) through the East River to Sands Point in Long Island Sound. These data were collected on 23 June 1981.

are primarily silty sands but both the sediment type and the channel morphology have been substantially altered by human activity (Tavelaro, 1992, U.S Army Corps of Engineers, personal communication). Little is known about the sediments in the narrow strait along the Manhattan shore, but silty sands and gravels are found near the Battery[3] and the bathymetry suggests a rocky sea bed.

To improve navigation, however, rocks at Hallets Point were removed in 1876 and Flood Rock in Hell gate in 1885. The latter explosion "exceeded six-fold the greatest charge ever previously fired in the world" (*Engineering News and American Contract Journal* as reported by Klawonn[4]). Little maintenance dredging is done, however, in the East River. The sediments that are dredged are predominantly fine-grained from fringing embayments and creeks. Schubel and Sumner[5] reported that 35,000 cubic yards of muddy sediment had been removed from the

East River annually. On the basis of 42 years of dredging records, Conner *et al.* calculated a higher figure of about 100,000 cubic yards per year, but the disparity is probably explained by the annual variations. The channel presents an area of about 7.6 million square yards so the average deposition rate is about 1.1 cm/yr. This is a modest rate of deposition for dredged channels where values in excess of 10 cm/yr may not be uncommon.

The sands and gravels on the floor of the East River attest to the ability of the present currents to prevent the deposition of fine-grained sediment. However, fine-grained suspended sediment is available for deposition and, where the currents allow, fine-grain sediments and associated contaminants accumulate at fairly rapid rates.

In principle, deposition within the channel is the difference between the flux of particles settling to the sea floor and the rate at which sediment is resuspended. The settling flux is the product of the concentration of suspended sediment at the sea floor and the settling speed of those particles. Measurements have not been made in the East River, but sediment traps have been used to estimate the settling flux in Long Island Sound.[7] At a site in 20 m of water in the center of the Sound north of Hempstead Harbor, long-term average flux of about 15 mg/cm^2/day has been measured, corresponding to a flux of 3.8 mg/cm^2/half cycle (FIG. 2). This flux exhibits a seasonal cycle as settling speeds increase with warmer water temperatures. The suspended sediment concentrations at this location were about 5 mg/l. We might expect similar values in the East River.

Particles that arrive at the sea floor may be resuspended by the currents to be redispersed in the water column or they may be incorporated into permanent sediment deposits. If the dredging records can be used as a guide, the average deposition amounts to 1.1 cm/yr corresponding to 3.0 mg/cm^2/day or about 0.8 mg/cm^2/half-tidal cycle.

IMPACT OF THE TIDAL GATES

The closing of the tidal barrage will greatly reduce the flow velocity through the East River over half of the tidal cycle. Instead of sending water from the Harbor to the Sound on flooding tides south of a tide barrage situated near Hell gate, the water level in the East River will rise in a tidal prism containing less than about 14 million m^3 of water. Ignoring any effects of the Harlem River,[1] the maximum flow speed should be reduced only be about 0.18 m/sec at the Battery and zero at the barrage when the gates are closed. For all practical purposes, the particles that settle to the River floor will not be resuspended during this period so the accumulation rate would be expected to be about 15 mg/cm^2/day or about 3.8 mg/cm^2 while the barrage is closed. This could represent a threefold increase in deposition or a maximum annual total of about 270,000 cubic yards. Whether or not this rate of deposition

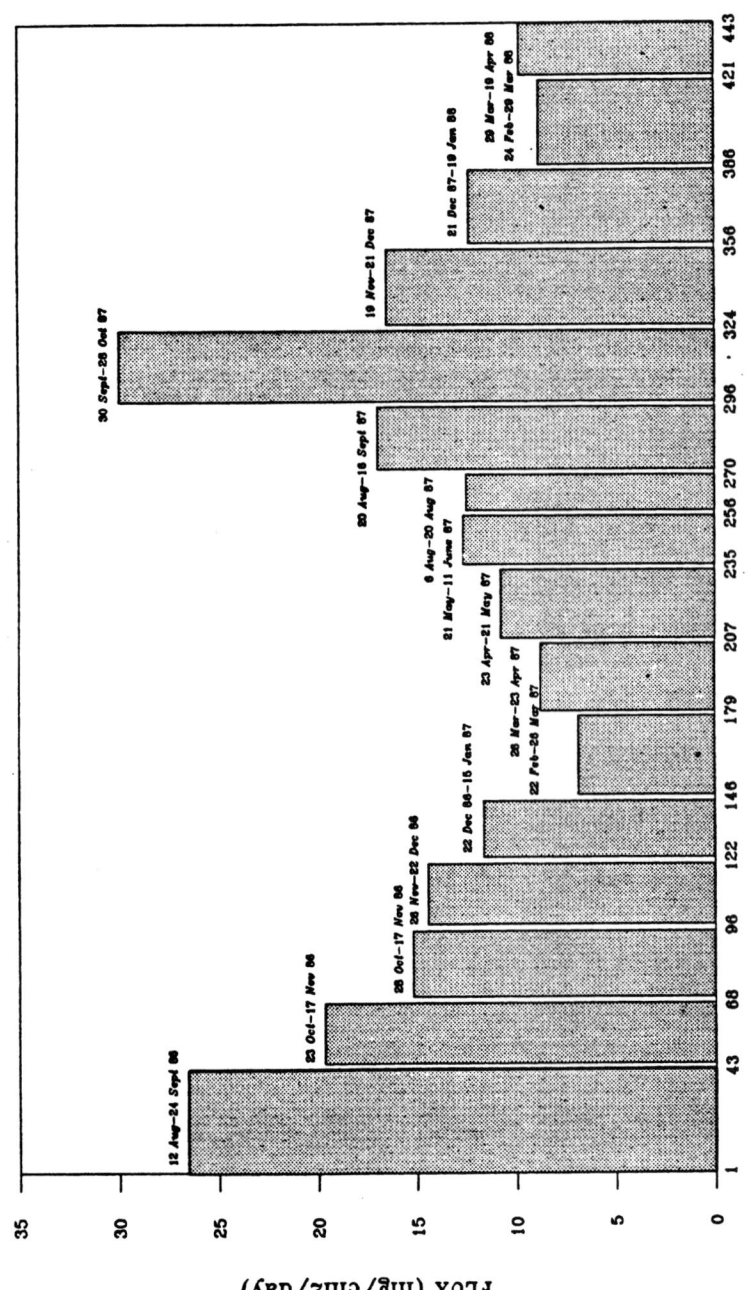

FIGURE 2. Mean flux versus time. Suspended sediment settling fluxes measured using sediment traps one meter above the floor of Long Island Sound at approximately 40°57.4'N; 73°35.0'W.

is realized, however, depends on the ability of the currents when the gates are open to resuspended material that was deposited when the gates were closed.

DISCUSSION

There is no widely accepted method to accurately predict the rate of resuspension of fine-grained sediments. In principle, the rate of resuspension can be related to the shear stress imposed on the bed by the overlying flow, but two principal difficulties arise. First, the relationship is highly non-linear so that small uncertainties in the flow velocities can produce large uncertainties in the calculated rate of resuspension. Second, there are no generally applicable relations between the physical properties of the sediment and the resuspension rate at a given stress level. As a result, direct measurements of the resuspension rates are necessary.[8] When these are available, the resuspendability of fine-grained sediments should be expected to vary widely over a broad spectrum of time period; it is strongly influenced, for example, by biological activity which undergoes strong seasonal cycles.

Although predictions of resuspension may be difficult, the first step would require an accurate forecast of the currents. Even when the tidal barrage is closed, there will be some currents in the East River as the water level rises south of the gate to the tide level at the Battery. In addition, if the barrage is north of the Harlem River, the flow through the Harlem River will be controlled by the difference in water level elevation between Spuyten Duyvil and the Battery. The flow through the Harlem River may have an enhanced impact when the gates are closed.

CONCLUSIONS

Enhanced deposition should be expected to be associated with the operation of the tidal gates. Shoaling rates will increase on both sides of the locks but the increase in shoaling in the lower East River will be limited by tidal flows through the Harlem River.

REFERENCES

1. JAY, D. A. & M. J. BOWMAN. 1975. The physical oceanography and water quality of New York Harbor and western Long Island Sound. Marine Sciences Research Center, State University of New York, Stony Brook. Technical Rep. **23**: 71pp.
2. BOKUNIEWICZ, H. J., L. McTIERNAN & W. DAVIS. 1991. Measurements of sediment resuspension rates in Long Island Sound. Geomarine Lett. **11**: 154-161.
3. COCH, N. K. 1986. Sediment characteristics and facies distributions. J. N.E. Geology **8**: 109-129.

4. KLAWONN, M. J. 1977. Cradle of the Corps: A history of the New York District, U.S. Army Corps of Engineers 1775-1975. Washington, D.C.: U.S. Government Printing Office. 309 pp.
5. SCHUBEL, J. R. & R. M. SUMNER. 1985. Volume 1, Dredging and dredged material disposal in the Port of New York and New Jersey: A case study and an assessment of alternatives. Marine Sciences Research Center, State University of New York, Stony Brook. Special Rep. **60:** 125 pp.
6. CONNER, W. G., D. AURAND, M. LESLIE, J. SLAUGHTER, A. AMR & F. I. LAVENSCROFT. 1979. Disposal of dredged material within the New York District: Volume 1, Present practices and candidate alternatives. Mitre Tech. Re. MTR-7808. McLean, VA: The Mitre Corp.
7. BOKUNIEWICZ, H. J. 1988. Sedimentation of fine-grained particles in Long Island Sound: A review of evidence prior to 1987. Marine Sciences Research Center, State University of New York, Stony Brook. Special Rep. **83:** 47pp.
8. BOKUNIEWICZ, H. J., & L. MCTIERNAN & W. DAVIS. 1991. Measurements of sediment resuspension rates in Long Island Sound. Geomarine Lett. **11:** 154-161.

DISCUSSION OF THE PAPER

QUESTION: Do you have any sense of ecological effects of changes in sediment transport?

HENRY BOKUNIEWICZ: Well, certainly they would change. The substrate might change; that would be the major effect. Certainly, the types of benthic communities that you have are very sensitive to the sediment character. If you are replacing sandy bottom by mud deposits, the composition of the benthic community would change. I can't say much more than that. That is something that would have to be looked at by a biologist.

CHARLES RICH: To what do you attribute the principal problem with capturing sediment in the East River? Is there anything preventing those kinds of studies from being done? I am under the impression that the currents are so strong that that's prohibitive.

BOKUNIEWICZ: Right now it is, that's right. Most of what settles to the sea floor will be resuspended when the currents pick up again. The question is: If you turn half of that current off, will what settles stay there or will it be resuspended? That's what I can't answer, but one that would have to be addressed.

RICH: Have you thought about how to address that?

BOKUNIEWICZ: Well, it's straightforward, but not simple. The idea is that you can predict the currents, so you can predict the stresses on the bottom. Then, the trick is if you know how much material is resuspended at different levels of stress, you can calculate how much the resuspension will be. But that's the tricky part.

Effects of Tide Gates on the Fish Community of the East River

PETER M. J. WOODHEAD
Marine Sciences Research Center
State University of New York
Stony Brook, New York 11974-5000

INTRODUCTION

The fish community living in the lower estuary system of the Hudson River, which includes the East River, is large and dynamic. Although there is severe pollution of the estuarine environment from a variety of urban, industrial and agricultural sources, the fish community is very diverse,—more than eighty species of finfish have been reported caught in the lower estuary of the Hudson and New York Harbor.[1-3] The large community of fishes inhabiting the estuary comprises a viable and valuable fishery resource,[4] and the Hudson River Estuary Management Act of 1987 notes that this is "the only major estuary on the east coast to still retain strong populations of its historical spawning stocks."

The community of fishes living in the East River is a part of the larger community inhabiting the lower Hudson estuary system; it is also connected to the community inhabiting the western reaches of Long Island Sound, of course. Some of the important migratory species referred to in the Hudson River Estuary Management Act have been caught in the East River at some stages of their life cycles.

The operation of a tidal barrage to rectify the tidal flow of the East River will have environmental effects and ecological consequences beyond the bounds of the river itself, in the lower Hudson estuary system and in Long Island Sound. Such changes are likely to affect the fish communities of these water bodies.

In this paper I will limit consideration to two important aspects of the ecology of the fish community in relation to the proposed construction and operation of the tidal barrage in the East River. They are, a) composition and structure of the fish community in the lower estuary system of the Hudson, and b) fish movements.

THE FINFISH COMMUNITY OF THE EAST RIVER

Species Composition

Sampling fish adequately in the East River presents unusual difficulties; nevertheless fishing surveys have shown that the finfish community is quite diverse. Fishery surveys made in the river over the last ten years have taken more than fifty species of finfish.[5-7] Marine species predominate making up about 70% of the community; estuarine and migratory (anadromous/catadromous) species each form about 15% of the total number of species; no freshwater fish occur commonly in the East River. Despite the relatively large number of species recorded, the community is dominated by a smaller number of abundant species; most species were caught in only small numbers or in occasional catches on the surveys.

Fish eggs and larvae have been taken with tow-nets in the East River. Most abundant were the eggs of the bay anchovy, cunner, and windowpane flounder. However, the ichthyoplankton collections were from a small number of stations with relatively few samples and it is not clear whether significant spawning had actually taken place within the East River itself, or whether the fish eggs and larvae had simply been carried into the river from neighboring bodies of water.

Similarity to Neighboring Communities

The species composition of the finfish community in the East River, reported over the last ten years, is listed in TABLE 1; the common and scientific names, together with the species' codings, are given in TABLE 2. Also listed in TABLE 1 are the fish species that were caught during the same period on fisheries surveys of the inner New York Harbor and the west-central Long Island Sound. The species listings for the communities of the three waterbodies may be compared. There is considerable similarity between the composition of the community in the East River and those of both neighboring communities. Nearly all of the species caught in the East River occur in both of the neighboring bodies of water, and the abundant and commoner species are the same in each. In all three communities, marine species are dominant forming 70 to 80% of the fish community, while estuarine and migratory species each form about 10 to 15% of the species total. A notable group of marine species apparently missing from the East River is the cartilaginous dogfishes, skates and rays (elasmobranchs), which probably avoid the lower salinities there.

More fish species were caught in both the inner Harbor and in the Sound than in the East River. However, nearly all of the additional species were taken in low abundances, and many were uncommon or rare. The records of greater numbers of uncommon species in the Sound and upper Harbor are likely to be explained, in part, by the fact that they are both larger, with a wider range of salinities and a greater diversity of habitats. Also, both were sampled on larger scales than the East River during the decade.

The East River is undoubtedly very heavily polluted, but conditions

TABLE 1. Fish Community Reported in the East River

	Inner Harbor	East River	Long Island Sound
Marine			
BAY_ANCH	1	1	1
RED_HAKE	1	1	1
WEAKFISH	1	1	1
WINDOWPN	1	1	1
WN_FLND	1	1	1
BLUEFISH	1	1	1
FLUKE	1	1	1
GRUBBY	1	1	1
SMM_FLND	1	1	1
SPT_HAKE	1	1	1
STR_SEARB	1	1	1
AT_MENHD	1	1	1
A_SILVER	1	1	1
BUTTERF	1	1	1
CUNNER	1	1	1
SCUP	1	1	1
SPOT	1	1	1
4SP_FLND	1	1	1
TAUTOG	1	1	1
BL_SEABS	1	1	1
N_SEARBN	1	1	1
SEAHORSE	1	1	1
SL_HAKE	1	1	1
RCK_GUNN	1	1	1
SM_DOGF	1		1
AT_HERRG	1	1	1
CREV_JCK	1		
FN_CUSKL	1		1
LOOKDOWN	1		
N_PUFFER	1		1
POLLOCK	1	1	1
TOADFISH	1	1	1
N_GOBY	1	1	1
N_KINGF	1	1	1
GRY_SNAP	1		
AM_SANDL	1		1
RH_SCAD	1		1
SEA_GOBY	1		
TR_ANCH	1		1
WT_HAKE	1	1	
4_RCKLG	1	1	1
AT_MACKR	1		1
AT_MOONF	1	1	1
AT_NEEDLE	1		
LIZARDFS	1		1

(continued)

TABLE 1. *Continued*

	Inner Harbor	East River	Long Island Sound
Marine (*cont.*)			
LN_SCULP	1	1	1
N_STARGZ	1		1
SP_BUTFL	1		
CL_SKATE			1
CON_EEL	1	1	
LI_SKATE			1
N_SENNET			1
OCN_POUT			1
PL_FILEF	1		1
RND_HERR			1
SEA_RAVN			1
WH_MULL	1		1
AT_CROAK	1	1	
COD	1		
GOOSEF			1
HRD_TAIL			1
LAMPREY			1
OR_FILEF			1
PINFISH	1		
SH_BIGEYE	1		1
SL_PERCH	1		
SMT_FLND	1		1
SP_DOGF			1
ST_CUSKL			1
W_SKATE			1
F_BLENNY	1		
GS_FLND			1
BND_RUDDER			1
HALF_BK			1
AT_BONITO			1
BEYE_SCAD			1
GRY_TRIG			1
RED_GOAT			1
RUDDERFISH			1
SP_MACK			1
YL_JACK			1
YT_FLND		1	1
Total Marine Species	58	36	70
Estuarine			
HOGCHOKR	1	1	1
PIPEFISH	1	1	1
WT_PERCH	1	1	1
3_STICKL	1	1	1

	Inner Harbor	East River	Long Island Sound
Estuarine (cont.)			
MUMMICHG	1	1	1
I_SILVER	1		
STR_KILL	1		1
WT_CATF	1		
4_STICKL			1
ST_MULL	1	1	1
T_SILVER	1	1	
SHEEP_MINN		1	1
RNW_KILLI			1
9_STICKL		1	
Total Estuarine Species	10	8	10
Migratory			
ALEWIFE	1	1	1
BB_HERRG	1	1	1
AM_SHAD	1	1	1
AMER_EEL	1	1	1
STR_BASS	1	1	1
TOMCOD	1	1	1
RW_SMELT	1	1	1
AT_STURG	1		1
HCK_SHAD	1	1	1
Total Migratory Species	9	8	9
TOTAL NUMBER FINFISH SPECIES	77	52	89

in the river have been improving slowly in recent years. For the fish community, it is particularly notable that there has been a general trend of increasing dissolved oxygen content of the waters.[8] The fish community is sensitive to pollution stresses, which may affect community composition, diversity and species' abundances. In general, the composition of the community sampled in the East River was not different from communities in its neighboring waters. In the East River, the most abundant species were the same dominant species as in adjacent bodies of water, and the proportions of different ecological groups of fish species, marine, estuarine and migratory, in the community were also similar. Nevertheless, improved water quality with the operation of tide gates to

TABLE 2. Fish Species Names from New York Harbor—Long Island Sound

Species Code	Common Name	Taxonomic Name
3_STICKL	Threespine stickleback	*Gasterosteus aculeatus*
4SP_FLND	Fourspot flounder	*Paralichthys oblongatus*
4_RCKLG	Fourbeard rockling	*Enchelyopus cimbrius*
4_STICKL	Fourspine stickleback	*Apeltes quadracus*
ALEWIFE	Alewife	*Alosa pseudoharengus*
AMER_EEL	American eel	*Anguilla rostrata*
AM_SANDL	American sand lance	*Ammodytes americanus*
AM_SHAD	American shad	*Alosa sapidissima*
AT_BONIT	Atlantic bonito	*Sarda sarda*
AT_CROAK	Atlantic croaker	*Micropogonias undulatus*
AT_HERRG	Atlantic herring	*Clupea harengus harengus*
AT_MACKR	Atlantic mackerel	*Scomber scombrus*
AT_MENHD	Atlantic menhaden	*Brevoortia tyrannus*
AT_MOONF	Atlantic moonfish	*Selene setapinnis*
AT_NEEDLE	Atlantic needlefish	*Strongylura marina*
AT_STURG	Atlantic sturgeon	*Acipenser oxyrhynchus*
A_SILVER	Atlantic silversides	*Menidia menidia*
BAY_ANCH	Bay anchovy	*Anchoa mitchilli*
BB_HERRG	Blueback herring	*Alosa aestivalis*
BEYE_SCAD	Big eye scad	*Selar crumenophthalmus*
BLUEFISH	Bluefish	*Pomatomus saltatrix*
BL_SEABS	Black sea bass	*Centropristis striata*
BND_RUDDER	Banded rudderfish	*Seriola zonata*
BUTTERF	Butterfish	*Peprilus triacanthus*
COD	Atlantic cod	*Gadus morhua*
CON_EEL	Conger eel	*Conger oceanicus*
CREV_JCK	Crevalle jack	*Caranx hippos*
CUNNER	Cunner	*Tautogolabrus adsperus*
FLUKE	Fluke (summer flounder)	*Paralichthys dentatus*
FN_CUSKL	Fawn cuskeel	*Lepophidium cervinum*
F_BLENNY	Feather blenny	*Hypsoblennius hentzi*
GOOSEF	Goosefish	*Lophius americanus*
GRUBBY	Grubby sculpin	*Myoxocephalus aenaeus*
GRY_SNAP	Grey snapper	*Lutjanus griseus*
GRY_TRIG	Grey triggerfish	*Balistes capriscus*
GS_FLND	Gulf Stream flounder	*Paralichthys obligatta*
HALF_BK	Halfbeak	*Hyporhamphus unifasciatus*
HCK_SHAD	Hickory shad	*Alosa mediocris*
HOGCHOKR	Hogchoker	*Trinectes maculatus*
HRD_TAIL	Hardtail	*Caranx crysos*
I_SILVER	Inland silversides	*Menidia beryllina*
LIZARDFS	Inshore lizardfish	*Synodus foetens*
LI_SKATE	Little skate	*Raja erinacea*
LN_SCULP	Longhorn sculpin	*Myoxocephalus octodecemspinosus*
LOOKDOWN	Lookdown	*Selene vomer*
MUMMICHG	Mummichog	*Fundulus heteroclitus*
N_GOBY	Naked goby	*Gobiosoma bosci*
N_KINGF	Northern Kingfish	*Menticirrhus saxatilis*
N_PUFFER	Northern puffer	*Sphoeroides maculatus*
N_SEARBN	Northern searobin	*Prionotus carolinus*
N_SENNET	Northern sennet	*Sphyraena borealis*

Species Code	Common Name	Taxonomic Name
N_STARGZ	Northern stargazer	*Astroscopus guttatus*
OCN_POUT	Ocean pout	*Macrozoarces americanus*
OR_FILEF	Orange filefish	*Alutera shoepfii*
PINFISH	Pinfish	*Lagodon rhomboides*
PIPEFISH	Northern Pipefish	*Syngnathus fuscus*
PL_FILEF	Planehead filefish	*Monacanthus hispidus*
POLLOCK	Pollock	*Pollachius viriens*
RCK_GUNN	Rock gunnel	*Pholis gunnellus*
RED_GOAT	Red goatfish	*Mullus auratus*
RED_HAKE	Red hake	*Urophycis chuss*
RH_SCAD	Rough scad	*Trachurus lathami*
RND_HERR	Round herring	*Etrumeus teres*
RNW_KILLI	Rainwater killifish	*Lucania parva*
RUDDERFISH	Rudderfish	*Seriola zonata*
RW_SMELT	Rainbow smelt	*Osmerus mordax*
SCUP	Scup	*Stenotomus chyrsops*
SEAHORSE	Lined seahorse	*Hippocampus erectus*
SEA_GOBY	Seaboard goby	*Gobiosoma ginsburgi*
SEA_RAVN	Sea raven	*Hemitripterus americanus*
SHEEP_MINN	Sheepshead minnow	*Cyprinodon variegatus*
SH_BIGEYE	Short big eye	*Pseudopriacanthus altus*
SL_HAKE	Silver hake	*Merluccius bilinearis*
SL_PERCH	Silver perch	*Bairdiella chrysoura*
SMM_FLND	Smallmouth flounder	*Etropus microstomus*
SMT_FLND	Smooth flounder	*Liopsetta putnami*
SM_DOGF	Smooth dogfish	*Mustelus mustelus*
SPOT	Spot	*Leiostomus xanthurus*
SPT_HAKE	Spotted hake	*Urophycis regia*
SP_BUTFL	Spotfin butterflyfish	*Chaetodon ocellatus*
SP_DOGF	Spiny dogfish	*Squalus acanthus*
SP_MACK	Spanish mackerel	*Scomberomorus maculatus*
STR_ANCH	Striped anchovy	*Anchoa hepsetus*
STR_BASS	Striped bass	*Morone saxatilis*
STR_KILL	Striped killifish	*Fundulus majalis*
STR_SEARB	Striped searobin	*Prionotus evolans*
ST_CUSKL	Striped cusk-eel	*Ophidion marginatum*
ST_MULL	Striped mullet	*Mugil cephalus*
TAUTOG	Tautog	*Tautoga onitis*
TOADFISH	Toadfish	*Opsanus tau*
TOMCOD	Atlantic tomcod	*Microgadus tomcod*
T_SILVER	Tidewater silverside	*Menidia peninsulae*
WEAKFISH	Weakfish	*Cynoscion regalis*
WH_MULL	White mullet	*Mugil curema*
WINDOWPN	Windowpane flounder	*Scophthalmus aquosus*
WN_FLND	Winter flounder	*Pseudopleuronectes americanus*
WT_CATF	White catfish	*Ictalurus catus*
WT_PERCH	White perch	*Morone americana*
W_SKATE	Winter skate	*Raja ocellata*
YL_JACK	Yellow jack	*Caranx bartholomaei*
YT_FLND	Yellowtail flounder	*Limanda ferruginea*

flush pollutants through the strait, seems likely to allow its use by greater densities of fishes.

Divisions of the Community in the Estuary

The lower Hudson estuary system contains pronounced gradients of environmental properties, most notably salinity but also many other important factors, including sedimentation and turbidity, the extent of tidal exchanges of water masses, contamination/pollution and ecological stress, pelagic and benthic food resources,—to mention but a few. Such environmental factors affect the abundance and distribution of fishes. In response, there are differences in the community in terms of the species composition and the relative abundance of species between various reaches of the lower estuary.[2]

The principal divisions, or structure, of the fish community have been described by multivariate analyses made on fishery survey data collected in different reaches of the lower estuary system, between about 1980 and 1990.[2] Results of the analyses consistently showed two principal divisions in the fish community of the lower estuary system of the Hudson, below the Tappan Zee. The boundary between the two divisions is near the entrance to the Hudson River off southern Manhattan (FIG. 1). The southern division occurs in outer reaches of the estuary, including the upper and lower New York Bays, Jamaica Bay, Raritan Bay, Arthur Kill, Newark Bay, and includes the East River. The second division of the community is confined to the lower Hudson River, off Manhattan, the Palisades and into the Tappan Zee. The principal environmental factor associated with this differentiation of the community is the salinity of the water. The two divisions occur in reaches where annual average salinities near the bottom are respectively above, or below, about 22 to 25%.

Operation of a tidal barrage on the East River would increase the salinity of the water there. Bowman[9,10] projects that average salinities in the river would increase to about 28%. The fish community in the East River belongs to the southern (high salinity) division of the larger community of the estuary system, the increase in salinity would not change that and the composition of the community of the East River would not be expected to changed markedly in response to the higher salinities.

However, the southern entrance to the East River at the Battery is close to the boundary between the two principal divisions of the wider estuarine community. The boundary region (in the Hudson off lower Manhattan) is one of considerable hydrographic and hydrodynamic complexity. Tidal rectification would produce about the same volume flows as at present, of higher salinity water on tides ebbing from the East River; flood tide flows would be reduced or arrested. Such changes in tidal flows might be expected to have effects on the structure and dy-

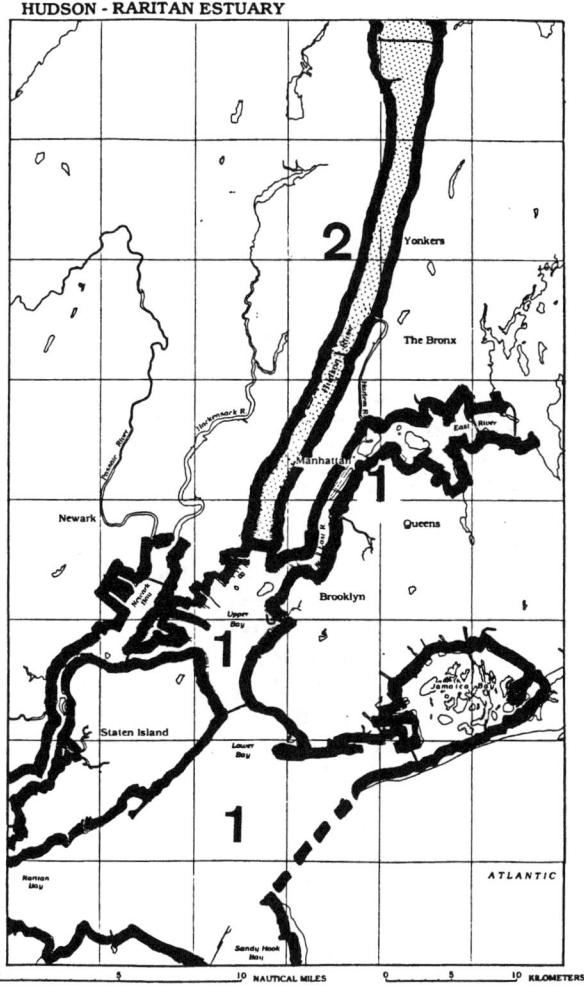

FIGURE 1. Principal divisions 1 and 2, of the fish community of the lower Hudson estuary system.

namics of the water column in this boundary region,[11] they would also locally affect the fish community. Assessments of the details of potential changes and their scale are beyond the considerations of the present paper. Nevertheless, more profound effects on the hydrodynamics of the lower Hudson and on the fish community, might be expected to take place if large volumes of East River water passed through the Harlem River to enter the Hudson at Spuyten Duyvil.

FISH MIGRATION

Movements through the East River

Populations of adult fishes migrate through the lower reaches of the Hudson estuary system *en route* to upstream spawning grounds of the middle estuary. Subsequently, very large populations of growing juvenile fishes resulting from the spawnings, return downstream. The timing of such immigrations and emigrations is quite well known. However, the modes of migration,—how the fish swim through the estuary, and the environmental cues to which they respond in their movements, are not as well known. Large parts of the migrations of such species are made in mid-water, well above the bed of the estuary. The commercial fisheries capture the migrating fish with nets which catch above the bottom: gill nets, drift nets, stake nets. Use of quantitative hydroacoustic methods is required to obtain such information on the behavior of the migrants. They are not sampled very well by ground trawls, which are the most frequently used fishing gears for surveys and sampling in the Harbor and lower estuary.[2]

Several migratory species important to the fisheries and to the ecology of the Hudson River Estuary system, have been caught in the East River (TABLE 1). However, the East River is not a river *per se*, but a tidal strait;[9,10] at both ends it widens into large, open bodies of water, of relatively high salinity. Mature anadromous fish coming from the Bight cannot migrate up the East River to their upstream, low salinity, spawning grounds. Although juvenile anadromous fishes are caught there routinely, the strait may be just another route to higher salinities, and ultimately to the open sea. As a tidal strait, there is no assessment of the relative importance of the East River to the passage of anadromous species through the Hudson estuary system as a whole,—although such assessments might not be difficult to make.

The striped bass is the only migratory species that has been studied in any detail with respect to movements through the East River between the Hudson estuary and the Sound. Annual shallow water surveys made by New York State Department of Environmental Conservation (NYS DEC) catch numbers of juvenile striped bass which are tagged and released into the estuary again. Such releases of tagged fish are made in both the Hudson and in the western bays of Long Island. In the Hudson a majority of the tagged bass are yearlings, in the western Sound most tagged fish are two-year-olds, followed by yearlings.[12,13] Recaptures of tagged bass released by NYS DEC surveys show movement of juvenile fish from the Hudson to the East River and the Sound. Juvenile bass tagged in western bays of the Sound also move to the East River and the Hudson.

The New York State Power Authority (NYSPA) has released hatchery-reared young-of-the-year bass into the Hudson River, and from 1985 to 1989 these young-of-the-year were tagged with small magnetically coded wires. In six years, only two of the tagged hatchery-reared fish from the Hudson were caught in the Sound, although some wild young-of-the-year bass are caught in late summer by the NYS DEC inshore surveys of western bays in the Sound.[13,14] The NYSPA, in conjunction with the Hudson River Foundation, also has a program tagging striped bass in the lower Hudson River, and every year some of these fish have been recaptured in the western reaches of the Sound.[13,14]

Summarizing results of the tagging programs for striped bass, it is clear that some juvenile striped bass from the Hudson move into the Sound and it appears that the route for such movements is through the East River. The movements of the young-of-the-year appear principally restricted to the Hudson Estuary, though some have been caught in the western Sound. Few hatchery-reared tagged fish have been caught in the Sound. The movements of the one and two-year-old bass are more extensive. Numbers of these juveniles migrate from the Hudson into the western Sound, and also from the Sound to the Hudson. At present it is unclear whether there are regular patterns in timing and direction of these migrations of the juvenile fish. Older bass from the Hudson migrate widely along the northeastern seaboard, with a northern bias in their distribution. It is not known what proportion of these older fish pass through the East River, but the majority of bass may leave the estuary through the Verrazano Narrows.

There is no information equivalent to the studies on juvenile striped bass for the alosid river herrings: the American shad, alewife, blueback herring and hickory shad. The juvenile populations of all the species of river herrings leave the estuary in great numbers as young-of-the-year fish. As such, some river herrings appear in the East River in fall-winter, during their emigration from the estuary system.

The Atlantic sturgeon had a large spawning stock in the Hudson during the nineteenth century but the population has now declined dramatically, so that there is management concern for the conservation of the stock. Atlantic sturgeon migrate between the Hudson and the Atlantic, but almost nothing is known about factors orienting migratory behaviors of sturgeon in the Hudson. Few sturgeon, if any, have been caught in the East River.

A tidal barrage would periodically arrest tidal flows, and stop the passage of fish. Periods of closure will alternate with open gate periods and that may be sufficient to allow adequate passage of the fishes. However, if the gates are found to interfere with fish movements, there are possibilities to minimize interference through innovative management of tide gate operations. During important periods, "windows of time" for the passage of fish through the East River can be established. Tide gate operations are potentially adaptable, and at such important times it should be possible to modify the operations of the barrage to offer least impediment to fish movements.

REFERENCES

1. LAKE, T. & C. L. SMITH. 1992. A list of fish species in the Hudson estuary. Unpublished ms.
2. WOODHEAD, P. M. J. 1992. Inventory and characterization of habitat and fish resources, and assessment of information on toxic effects in the New York-New Jersey Harbor estuary. Report in 6 sections to US EPA, concerning Tasks 3.2, 5.1 and 5.3 of the Harbor Estuary Program. 210pp.
3. WOODHEAD, P.M. J. The fish community of New York Harbor: Spatial and temporal distributions of major species. In Proceedings of the Conference on the Impacts of New York Harbor Development on Aquatic Resources. Hudson River Foundation for Science, New York, September, 1987. In press.
4. SMITH, C. L. 1988. Introduction. In Fisheries Research in the Hudson River. C.L. Smith, Ed. The Hudson River Environmental Society. Albany, NY: SUNY Press. 407pp.
5. ENERGY AND ENVIRONMENTAL ANALYSTS, INC. 1985. East River Landing development. A report to New York City Public Development Corp., New York, NY, October, 1985.
6. ENERGY AND ENVIRONMENTAL ANALYSTS, INC. 1991. East River Landing aquatic environmental study. Final Report to New York Public Development Corp., New York, NY, April, 1991.
7. PARRISH AND WEINER, INC. 1989. River Walk, 23rd St. at the East River, New York, NY. Draft Environmental Impact Statement. Vol.2, Dec., 1989.
8. KELLER, A. A., K. R. HINGA & C. A. OVIATT. 1990. New York-New Jersey Harbor Estuary Program Module 4: Nutrients and organic enrichment. Final Report to US EPA's NY-NH Harbor-Estuary Program.
9. BOWMAN, M. J. 1976. Tidal locks across the East River: An engineering solution to the rehabilitation of the western Long Island Sound. In Estuarine Processes. M. Wiley, Ed. New York: Academic Press.
10. BOWMAN, M. J. 1993. Tidal gates and their effect on water quality. East River Tidal Barrage Symposium, Columbia University, New York, NY, 29 April, 1993. 16pp.
11. ST. JOHN, J. P. 1993. Hydrodynamic and water quality impacts of the proposed East River tidal barrage. East River Tidal Barrage Symposium, Columbia University, New York, NY, 29 April, 1993. 35pp.
12. MCKOWN, K. A. 1993a. An investigation of the 1991 Hudson River striped bass spawning success. In A Study of the Striped Bass in the Marine District of New York. VI. NY State Department of Environmental Conservation, pp. 3–53.
13. MCKOWN, K. A. 1993b. An investigation of the movements and growth of the 1990 Hudson River year class. In A Study of the Striped Bass in the Marine District of New York. VI. NY State Department of Environmental Conservation, pp. 150–207.
14. MCKOWN, K. A. & M. PENSKI. An investigation of the movements and growth of the 1991 Hudson River year class. In A Study of the Striped Bass in the Marine District of New York. IV. NY State Department of Environmental Conservation, pp. 65–68.

Tide Gates and the Estuarine Environment

Rapporteur's Comments

M. LLEWELLYN THATCHER[a]

Department of Civil Engineering and Engineering Mechanics
Columbia University
New York, New York 10027-6699

The presentations by M. J. Bowman, J. P. St. John, H. Bokuniewicz and P. M. J. Woodhead have set the stage for a dramatic approach to the demanding need to reduce pollution of our local waters. There are certainly objections that will be raised, and should be raised. However, the tidal barrage proposal has the remarkable feature that most pollutant concentrations would be dramatically reduced *both* in Western Long Island Sound and in New York Harbor. Yes, there are exceptions, and these need to be examined further. For example, the predicted slight increase in salinity in the New York Harbor could present a threat to water supply intakes in the Hudson River (such as at Poughkeepsie). But the project does not specify that one-way flow must always be the rule of operation. Careful design can permit flexibility so that the gates could allow bidirectional flow at certain times such as when the Hudson salinities are high and at times pertinent to the migration of fish.

This "rapporteur" believes that our community of universities, public agencies, design firms, consultants, environmental groups and others would well serve our planet and its populations by keeping an open mind to proposals such as this one. The savings of such a plan might well outweigh its shortcomings. Cost and benefits need to be evaluated, including the often neglected aspects of "costs to whom" and "benefits to whom."

In an effort to place the proposed project in perspective in terms of the scale of its proposed modification, we can examine some historic changes. Through recent participation in the EPA-sponsored New York/New Jersey Harbor Estuary Project,[1] we had the opportunity to examine some of these physical changes in our harbor estuary. FIGURE 1 shows the hydrography of Upper New York Bay as digitized from the 1845 and 1989 National Ocean Service (formerly Coast and Geodetic Survey) charts.

The changes are indeed significant. Water surface areas have decreased about 30%, and water volumes have increased about 15%. The evidence of dredging and filling is prominent. The few charts that can be

---

[a]Address for correspondence: Thatcher Research Associates, Inc., 47 Washington Spring Road, P.O. Box 596, Palisades, NY 10964; Tel: (914) 359-3047.

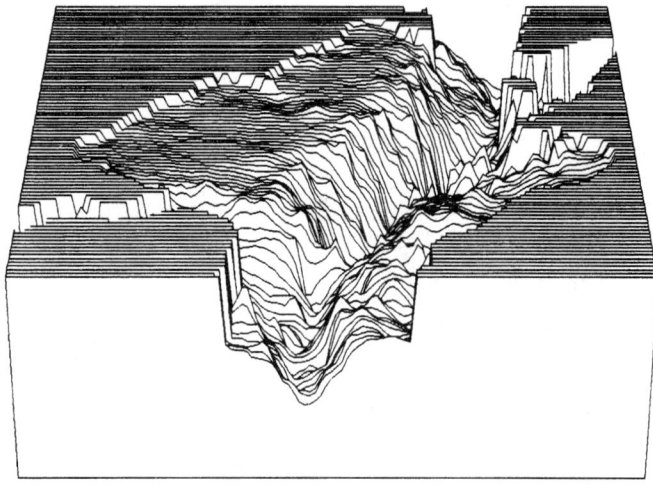

Upper Harbor 1845

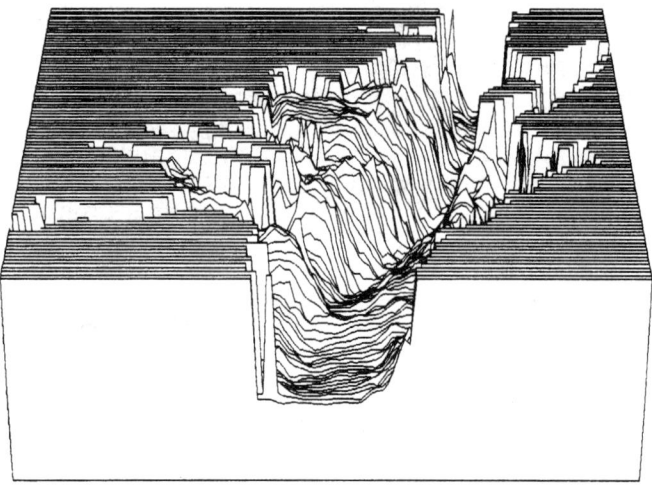

Upper Harbor 1989

FIGURE 1. Significant changes have been made to the hydrography of Upper New York Bay as indicated by those made between 1845 and 1989.

found before 1845 show that even greater modifications took place in the 1700s and in the early 1800s. Another example of a prominent physical change is the Harlem River Canal. This canal has opened a connection between the Hudson River and the East River that did not exist before the early 1900s.

The proposed tidal barrage provides a control mechanism (a valve) that would permit the regulation of the direction of flow in the East River. Compared with the above-mentioned historical changes, it does not stand out as so radical.

Finally, I wish to express some questions which have come as a result of the presentations.

1. In terms of the model results from the 208 Harbor Model, I find it difficult to reconcile the calculated salinity profile (St. John's Fig. 20) showing less salinity from the Narrows to the Ocean for the "with Tide Gate" case versus the "without Tide Gates" case. The Tide Gates seem to raise the salinity in the Hudson and Upper Harbor. But the resulting salinity in the ocean is less than for the "without Tide Gates" case. Is this possible, or is it a result of the 208 model's limitations in a predictive mode?
2. What would be the advantages and disadvantages of the tidal barrage structures in terms of extreme events such as hurricanes and northeasters such as those we have recently experienced? It seems to me that careful planning and design could make the structures beneficial tools for storm surge control, and could have the significant effect of ameliorating problems of scour and sedimentation that are often related to extreme events.
3. Although total nitrogen concentrations are reduced throughout the region by this scheme's increased tidal flushing, the mass of total nitrogen transported into New York Harbor and eventually into the New York Bight will be increased. Are there any detrimental effects related to this increased mass?

REFERENCES

1. THATCHER, M. L. & C. MENDOZA. 1991. Module 6: Hydrologic Modifications. Report to the New York/New Jersey Harbor Estuary Program. Department of Civil Engineering and Engineering Mechanics, Columbia University, New York, July 15, 1991.

Tide Gates and the Estuarine Environment

Rapporteur's Comments

ROBERT WILL

New York District
U.S. Army Corps of Engineers
26 Federal Plaza
New York, New York 10278-0090

Thank you for the opportunity to provide the Corps' initial environmental comments on this proposal. In all likelihood, a Federal Environmental Impact Statement (EIS) would be required for a project of this nature and scope. Thus, I will direct my remarks to those environmental and social issues that would need to be addressed to generate an adequate EIS that complies with National Environmental Policy Act guidelines.

Our initial reaction is that the major potential impact of this project seems to be on the hydrodynamics and salinity distribution of the Hudson and Long Island Sound estuaries, primarily because placement of a barrage on the East River could potentially result in a significant alteration of estuarine circulation.

An unprecedented amount of study may be needed to bring this concept to fruition. Critical information gaps in our knowledge of the affected estuaries need to be filled to the extent possible. Many of the tools needed to address potential impacts are state of the art, for example, advance numerical hydrodynamic and water quality models, and physical circulation models, and even full utilization of state-of-the-art tools will not answer all relevant questions.

At a minimum, we suggest that the following questions need to be addressed for an EIS:

1. How does the East River function, both in terms of hydrologic interaction with the Hudson and Long Island Sound estuaries, and as a biological conduit between these two water bodies? Specifically, we need to have a much better understanding of water movement through the Harlem as well as the East River, and we need to know the extent of dependency of migratory fish on these rivers, along with the role these rivers play in dispersing eggs, larvae and yearlings of important species of fish from spawning to nursery and feeding areas. In short, we need to understand the contribution of these rivers to the estuaries they are connected to.

2. What is the overall effect on both the Hudson and Long Island Sound estuaries, given the predicted changes in salinity? Even small

changes in salinity in an estuary could have profound effects on benthic and fish communities. How different will estuarine circulation be in Long Island Sound when one of the sources of lower salinity water, the East River, is cut off? In the Hudson River, will migrating fish be able to decide on the correct path to their spawning grounds, given the new salinity and current regime? To what extent will the barrage itself physically hinder the passage of migratory fish and the dispersal of larvae? Will a restocking program be necessary to compensate for losses? If the gates are operated to allow for passage of eggs and larvae during certain critical time periods (possibly for several months), wouldn't this reinstate a two-way flow and defeat the purpose of the barrage to some extent? Intuitively, our initial reaction to the scope of all these impacts is that they may be confined to the harbor and Long Island Sound, but this would need to be studied.

3. What are the impacts of introducing oceanic water of greater clarity into Long Island Sound and the harbor? With light penetrating deeper into the water column, will algae production be increased, potentially diminishing or negating the effect of nutrient dispersion? Also, since estuaries are naturally turbid, how will organisms react to less turbid conditions in terms of predation avoidance, finding food and other modifications in behavior?

4. How will wetlands be affected? Will tidal prisms be changed in Long Island Sound resulting in a reduction of intertidal and marsh habitat? Will a shift in the general salinity gradient of Long Island Sound result in a localized shift in the ranges of some species that could significantly reduce their habitat? Will increased salinities in Long Island Sound result in the introduction of greater numbers of marine predators, such as starfish and oyster drills? This could have a significant effect on shellfish populations, which could simultaneously be under a great deal of stress because of increased salinities. Also, increased salinities could inhibit growth of larval and juvenile marine organisms, increasing their vulnerability to predation for longer periods.

5. Increasing dissolved oxygen concentrations in the water column has negative as well as positive impacts. For example, will wood borers increase their activities, resulting in a more vigorous attack on submerged wooden structures? Will this require an increased commitment on the part of the Corps of Engineers to pick up driftwood?

6. What will be the effect of this project on the spread of the zebra mussel? The southward spread of the mussel in the Hudson River could be either inhibited or encouraged depending on the nature of the new salinity regime in the Hudson.

7. Would dredged material disposal practices in Long Island Sound be affected? If bottom currents are increased, will this affect the stability of capped mounds? Will contaminants, which are now bound to buried sediment particles, be exposed to marine organisms as a result?

8. Will there be increased salt water intrusion in Long Island Sound that might affect fresh water aquifers?

9. How will this project affect environmental restoration efforts currently under way or planned for this region? For example, will plans to restore historical anadromous fish runs, such as shad, be negatively affected? Or will these efforts actually be enhanced by improvements in water quality?

10. Since a man-made structure will be controlling the hydrodynamic and salinity regime in a large portion of the region, what would be the environmental and social impact of a debilitating mechanical or structural failure?

11. Public perception of this project will be a major factor in determining its viability. Some people might perceive this project as an attempt by the mostly affluent communities around western Long Island Sound to utilize New York Harbor, a relatively polluted body of water, as a relatively inexpensive diluting agent for their municipal waste. Thus, those who have a stake in cleaning up the New York/New Jersey harbor would need to be convinced that there would be a worthwhile improvement in water quality in the harbor as well.

An EIS for this project would also need to address several other issues, including the synergistic and cumulative effects of this project:

A. For example, Congress has authorized a program to decontaminate and remediate contaminated sediments in the New York/New Jersey harbor area. There would be little point in cleaning up an area that would later be affected by negative changes induced by implementation of the barrage.

B. Special consideration needs to be given to threatened and endangered species, such as sturgeons, to comply with the strenuous requirements of the Endangered Species Act. Also, several species of endangered sea turtles are known to inhabit this area during warmer months of the year. Their degree of dependence on the Hudson and Long Island Sound estuaries is poorly understood.

C. A rigorous alternative analysis would be needed. One of the alternatives would undoubtedly be upgrading of sewage treatment to various levels, in lieu of, or in combination with the barrage. Cost alone is not the deciding factor in selection of an alternative, but a balance of factors, including environmental impacts, that are in the public interest. Upgrading to tertiary treatment may cost more, but it could have few or none of the impacts of the barrage.

Also, what alternative modes of implementation are being considered to minimize impacts? For example, is it possible to gradually phase in the changes in salinity in the estuaries over several years to give living resources (particularly sea run anadromous fish) a better chance to acclimate to changing conditions? This approach would also have the benefit of allowing time to analyze the accuracy of model predictions and take remedial action, if necessary.

D. An EIS needs to refine the probabilities of an impact to some reasonable level, recognizing that the degree of negative impact is only partially predictable. Application of a worst case scenario to unknown impacts thought to be important would probably be necessary. However, a reasonable worst case scenario for the various impacts will be difficult to identify.

In summary, we need to understand the system we are dealing with, what will be lost from that system upon implementation of this project, and determine whether that loss is acceptable to society. Further, given the improvements in water quality that have been brought about in New York Harbor over the past few decades, we need to ask ourselves whether we want to change the affected estuaries to something quite different from what they are now to achieve limited water quality improvements. It is assumed that there would still need to be an upgrading of sewage treatment to meet the water quality goals of the region. There is a danger that projects like this, no matter how innovative, might be used as a substitute for what some may feel needs to be done, that is, to reduce nutrient and contaminant inputs at their source. Finally, we need to learn from the experience of others who have substantially modified their estuaries, and how difficult and costly it could be to reverse decisions that involve massive man-made structures.

Thank you for your attention. We hope that these comments will be helpful in planning this project.

Tide Gates and the Estuarine Environment

Rapporteur's Comments

LYNN MARIE BOCAMAZO
New York District
U.S. Army Corps of Engineers
26 Federal Plaza
New York, New York 10278-0090

On the basis of the previous presentations and other thoughts, I will make a few brief statements on the hydrodynamic, storm surge impacts, and navigational aspects of the conceptual design of a tidal barrage constructed in the East River to improve water quality in western Long Island Sound. These comments are made to raise issues which should be taken into consideration during further investigations of this conceptual design.

In terms of hydrodynamics, or where the tidal water will go, both the system-wide changes in New York Harbor, Long Island Sound and the New York Bight, and the site-specific changes in the East River, Harlem River, Hudson River and Upper New York Bay need to be examined closely with the best scientific and engineering tools available, including numerical and physical models, to determine more conclusively how a barrier will affect the tidal flow.

Among issues that must be examined is the transfer of the dynamic hydraulic head, which is due to the differences in the tidal phase in Long Island Sound and the Battery, into a static hydraulic head adjacent to the tidal barrage. The change in the tidal regime and the possible increase in the mean high water elevations may cause changes in the shoreline along the East River and Long Island Sound. The gates, as well as other structures such as locks, may adversely impact the flow in the East River, even when the tidal gates are open, due to frictional forces. The structure may cause stagnation of the water immediately adjacent to it. If the structure caused tidal channel velocities to increase, damaging erosive forces could impact shoreline structures.

A high-resolution numerical model grid of the East River could contain sufficient resolution to examine impacts of the proposed tidal gates and navigational locks, but it could not examine the details immediately around such structures. Here, an undistorted-scale physical model is suggested as the best method for evaluating structure impacts on the hydrodynamics, such as friction effects on the tidal flow. These data would be essential to properly represent the structures' characteristics in numerical hydrodynamic and water quality models, and to calibrate and validate the numerical models to the structures. Corps studies, which have combined the use of physical and numerical models, have been developed for a tidal control structure on the Saugus River, north of Boston, Massachusetts, and for the tide gates on Lake Pontchartrain in Louisiana.

The existing New York Harbor physical model at the Corps' Waterways Experiment Station is distorted and at a scale that could not accommodate the specific, detailed testing needs of this project. The tidal boundary at Willets Point in the present physical model is too close to the Upper East River for proper boundary conditions. A new, undistorted physical model could give qualitative information on the effects of turbulent flow through the structure on bottom sediments.

The Corps has developed a three-dimensional system-wide hydrodynamic and water quality model of the New York Bight, Long Island Sound and New York Harbor, which has been calibrated to some extent. This tool, with some modifications, is ready for use in evaluating the impacts of the tide gates. An expanded higher resolution model is proposed for New York Harbor, the Bight Apex, the East River, western Long Island Sound, the Hudson River and all the tidal estuaries. This expanded model would be nested with the system-wide model, to obtain boundary conditions sufficiently far from the Harbor and estuaries.

The impacts of storm surges from either northeasters or hurricanes would need to be addressed in the design and operation of a tidal barrage on the East River. Storm tides converge in western Long Island Sound, typically giving higher total water elevations here than in any other location in the Harbor or Long Island Sound. Significant impacts from the December 11, 1992 northeaster were felt on the Franklin D. Roosevelt Drive, at Rikers Island, and La Guardia Airport, all on the East River, and at City Island in western Long Island Sound. Hurricanes, owing to their counterclockwise rotation, also have a large effect in western Long Island Sound, if their path is over Long Island or to the east. Effects of the tidal structures and their operations during storms should be examined carefully to evaluate potential flood problems and the need for emergency operating procedures.

As discussed by Dr. Bokuniewicz, further sedimentation studies would be required to address changes in the sediment regime. The readjustment of the currents and the tidal prism in the East River may result in the increase of shoaling in the River, which may cause the need for increased maintenance dredging of navigation channels adjacent to the East River, such as Newtown Creek, the Brooklyn Navy Yard, and Buttermilk Channel, or possible relocation of the navigation channels. Sediments deposited in the navigation channels may be contaminated, resulting in increased disposal problems for the Corps. The navigability of the East River may change, due to the impacts of the tide gates on channel currents. Significantly lowering the plane of mean low water in the East River may result in expensive channel deepening. The Federal Navigation Channel is presently at −35 feet mean low water depth, and in some locations, such as Hell gate, the bedrock depth is at −36 ft mean low water.

The East River is part of the Intracoastal Waterway system, and recreational traffic delays, due to the time required to transit the locks, may be unacceptable in the East River. Coast Guard vessels from New London, Connecticut, transit the East River to get to the Brooklyn Navy Yard, and the East River may be used by the Coast Guard and Navy for strategic naval requirements.

Appropriate market studies may need to be undertaken to determine the vessel usage of the lock system. It may not be possible for the locks to be financially self-sustaining, and may require some form of governmental subsidies to meet operating expenses. Some vessels which presently use the East River may choose to use alternative routes to avoid the lock operation and the time involved in transitting the lock.

And finally, the location of the structure should be placed primarily for the water quality goals in western Long Island Sound. If another location along the East River is chosen to provide additional features, the modification to the water quality goals would need to be addressed.

Tide Gates and the Estuarine Environment

A New York City Perspective

EDWARD O. WAGNER
*Director, Bureau of Clean Water
New York City Department of Environmental Protection
96-05 Horace Harding Blvd.
Corona, New York 11368*

The purpose of today's symposium is to assess both the utility and feasibility of using tide gates on the East River to improve western Long Island Sound water quality. This innovative proposal will have potentially wide ranging effects on water quality, aquatic resources, habitat, capital spending and transportation, and deserves a holistic, in-depth analysis from many viewpoints.

On the surface, the proposal for an East River Barrage may appear to have broad and immediate appeal. If it is true that such a structure would greatly improve water quality in the western Sound, many of the proposed point and non-point source controls and lifestyle changes throughout New York City, Westchester, Long Island, and Connecticut could be avoided. There are those who believe that the Long Island Sound's problems are primarily caused by New York City discharges, so, to them, having the solution in New York City may be logical and equitable as well. Indeed, the concept of an East River barrage has a "magic bullet" feel to it, that is, by building this one structure, a host of very complex water quality problems currently plaguing this valuable water body can be solved. While we at the Department of Environmental Protection encourage the development of innovative approaches, we are cautious when single solutions are proposed to solve complex, regional water quality problems which have in fact arisen from many sources.

Significant improvements in dissolved oxygen (DO) concentrations over the past 50 years in most areas of the Hudson-Raritan estuarine system have been extensively documented.[1-3] These improvements are associated with the regional construction and upgrading of water pollution control plants to secondary treatment. Since 1960, raw sewage discharges to the East River have declined from 400 mgd to less than 1 mgd, and TSS and BOD loads have declined by 68% and 66%.[4] Total nitrogen loads have declined by approximately 5%. These declining loads have resulted in average summer DO increases in the East River approaching 60% saturation, a level last achieved in 1909. Similar improvements have been observed at most other stations monitored by the City's Harbor Survey Program, except for stations in the western Long Island Sound.[5] That is, despite the elimination of raw sewage discharges, and major decreases in BOD and TSS loads not only along the East River but also from all communities tributary and adjacent to the Sound, DO in the western Sound appears to have become worse. It is believed that excessive nutrient inputs are the primary cause of the observed hypoxia. However, elevated water column nitrogen concentrations have been observed for decades, but severe sustained hypoxia appears to be a recent phenomenon.

The premise supporting an East River barrage is that the East River has a significant impact on the western Sound. But how then are decreasing East River pollutant loads and greatly improved East River water quality reconciled with declining Long Island Sound water quality? Such a linkage is counterintuitive, and suggests that our understanding of pollutant fate, transport, and effects in this area is very incomplete. Our inability to understand recent changes in loadings and water quality in the Sound undermines confidence in our ability to predict the future, especially with the many unforseen impacts which a barrage might bring.

A similar decline in minimum bottom dissolved oxygen values has also been observed elsewhere in the harbor, such as northeast Jamaica Bay, Raritan Bay, and the Arthur Kill, suggesting that broad scale meteorological or oceanographic effects may be involved. Alternatively, some have hypothesized that the hypoxia in the western Sound may be occurring not in spite of, but because of the recent construction and upgrading of regional wastewater treatment plants. If so, it is certainly an unpredicted effect, and indicates that other predictions need to be considered with great care.

Stepping back for a minute from the proposal's technical issues, the concept of building a tide gate which would so radically disrupt the natural flow of this major estuarine system is somewhat jarring. Solutions to man-made problems should strive to support and augment natural features of a system. The East River barrage concept is contrary to this principle because of the degree to which it intrudes upon and disrupts the natural system. Society's efforts at massive engineering efforts to control natural forces are often futile and counterproductive. In this region, physical changes in many cases have had greater and more lasting impacts than pollutant loads themselves. For example, dredging has changed Jamaica Bay's mean depth from 3 to 16 feet, and the residence time has increased from 11 to 35 days. These physical alterations have diminished the bay's ability to both absorb and flush out contaminants. Harborwide, of the 27,600 acres of wetlands in 1900, nearly 90 percent was destroyed by 1969. The East River has itself already been subject to massive physical alterations since European settlement, including loss of wetlands and streams, modified shorelines, blasting of reefs and rocks, and dredging and filling. Although these changes occurred incrementally over many years, if our predecessors had the tools and understanding of the water quality effects of these intrusions, they may not have gone as far.

Other examples where massive engineering solutions are being rethought include in the Netherlands, where it was recently decided to restore natural conditions by opening dikes to allow the sea into previously reclaimed areas.

The Long Island Sound Study has identified five major areas of concern: hypoxia, toxics, pathogens, floatables, and living marine resources. A Comprehensive Conservation and Management Plan (CCMP) is being developed to address use impairments in the system.

There are many misconceptions about the sources of water quality problems in this region. In discussions about the Sound's quality, some correctly express concern about those beaches which are now chronically closed, and that there are areas where shellfishing is restricted or permanently prohibited. The implication in this context is that the barrage will change all that.

But the Long Island Sound Study has documented that all beach closures between 1986 and 1990 were within embayments or tributaries, and most were associated with rain and local runoff.[6] Therefore, a tidal barrage will not open those beaches. Similarly, restricted and prohibited shellfish beds in the western Sound are primarily designated as such owing to their proximity to inputs, especially runoff. Thus the barrage is unlikely to result in significant shellfish bed openings. Neither will the barrage stop wetland loss and upland habitat destruction, overfishing, and problems with persistent toxics.

The draft Comprehensive Conservation and Management Plan of the Long Island Sound Study correctly recognizes that improving the water environment in the Sound will require reduction and control of a variety of conventional and toxic contaminants from point and non-point sources throughout the region as well as restoring habitat and rethinking land use practices. I am concerned that some will see the tide gate solution as an excuse not to address the very difficult but critical problems of population density, development, unabated non-point sources, and habitat loss throughout the Sound's watershed.

The barrage proposal has two underlying assumptions: 1) that control of pollutant loads from the East River will fix water quality problems in the western Sound, and 2) increased dilution and transport can supplement pollutant control and removal. However, as recent analyses of historical pollutant loading and water quality data have shown, reductions in East River loadings did not automatically translate into improvements in the Sound.

Other aspects of the ecosystem's response are similarly unclear. For example, from Dr. Woodhead's presentation, present patterns of fish migration and plankton transport through the East River are not well understood, and so predictions of tidal barrage impacts are necessarily speculative. Indeed a good, recent comprehensive assessment of the health and status of the region's aquatic biota does not currently exist. Without such a database, future impacts to these communities will be impossible to accurately predict.

Similarly, those participating in the Long Island Sound Study have witnessed net flow estimates from the Sound to the East River vary from 100 to 380 cms, depending on which group of professional oceanographers have modeled it most recently. This example is not intended to question the skill of the modelers, but rather it highlights the hydrodynamic complexity of the system. Again, given our present limited understanding of the system, it is difficult to predict what a tidal barrage might cause.

In conclusion, while we at the Department of Environmental Protection welcome innovative solutions to difficult problems, we are necessarily cautious in our view of this engineering solution. A single project designed to change the natural circulation so dramatically will, in a single stroke, have far-reaching hydrodynamic, water quality, habitat, biotic, and public policy impacts, many of which are unseen and beyond our present capability to assess.

We must resist the temptation to embrace this proposal as a panacea for the water quality problems of the Long Island Sound. Furthermore, great effort will be required to fully evaluate its impact on estuarine circulation, the health of aquatic biota and their habitat, and the impact on regional wetland and littoral areas.

Listening to Robert Will's comments about what would be required for an environmental review of such a project, I recall the comment of one of my staff people who said, "This is a half-billion dollar project with a billion-dollar environmental impact statement."

I would suggest that these resources might be better spent at this time on efforts to achieve a better understanding of the past and present relationship between pollutant loadings and water quality problems and to advance the additional comprehensive research and planning called for in the Long Island Sound Study's CCMP. While the approach in that plan may not satisfy the impatient, it has, in my opinion, the greatest likelihood of leading to a balanced and integrated program for restoring and preserving our natural environment.

REFERENCES

1. O'CONNOR, D. 1990. A historical perspective engineering and scientific. In Proceedings of Cleaning Up Our Coastal Waters: An Unfinished Agenda. Manhattan College, Riverdale, NY, March 12-14, 1990.
2. WAGNER, E.O. 1992. Water quality trends in New York Harbor. Presented at the Fifth Water Environment Federation/Japan Sewage Works Association Joint Technical Seminar on Sewage Treatment Technology, Yokohama, Japan, June 24, 1992.
3. NEW YORK CITY DEPARTMENT OF ENVIRONMENTAL PROTECTION. 1993. New York Harbor Water Quality Survey, 1991-1992. NYCDEP Marine Sciences Section, Wards Island, NY. NTIS No. PB93-213577.
4. SWANSON, R.L., A. WEST-VALLE, M. BORTMAN, A. VALLE LEVINSON & T.E. ECHELMAN. 1991. The impact of improved sewage treatment in the East River

on western Long Island Sound. *In* The Second Phase of an Assessment of Alternatives to Biological Nutrient Removal at Sewage Treatment Plants for Alleviating Hypoxia in Western Long Island Sound. Coast Institute of the Marine Sciences Research Center, State University of New York, Stony Brook, NY, November 21-22, 1991.
5. BROSNAN, T. M. & A. I. STUBIN. 1992. Spatial and temporal trends of dissolved oxygen in the East River and Western Long Island Sound. *In* Proceedings of the Long Island Sound Research Conference. UCONN/CT Sea Grant, Storrs, CT, October 23-24, 1992.
6. CHIARELLA, L. 1993. LISS Comprehensive Conservation and Management Plan Support Document: Pathogen Contamination, Assessment of Conditions and Management Recommendations. New York State Department of Environmental Conservation, Stony Brook, NY.

Tide Gates and the Estuarine Environment

General Discussion

R.L. SWANSON: At this point, we would like to get some response from the audience. But first I'd like to give the opportunity to speakers earlier this morning if they would care to react to anything the panel has raised or commented on. Malcolm, John, Peter, Henry: do you have any reaction to concerns with what has been raised with potentially legitimate issues?

M.J. BOWMAN: Not at all. I think that the panelists have presented a fascinating series of questions that should be addressed. I can't really take issue with any of those. But I would question whether we have the capability of addressing some of those unanswered questions. I think that with the modern scientific tools we have available we can make an intelligent and informed prediction of the future. So we must learn from the past, but we still have to look to the future. That's a sort of philosophical comment.

J.P. ST. JOHN: I agree, generally. I think that the positions that were given by the various panelists were certainly well thought out. Without any question, they raised a number of issues that certainly should be answered. I think that to proceed with the concept of the tidal barrage in the East River would require many, many detailed investigations to respond to all of the questions that have been raised by the various rapporteurs.

I would say that in general I have a somewhat more optimistic viewpoint about the utility of mathematical modeling in forecasting conditions that would be affected by major engineering structures. I would say that as far as water quality conditions of the East River are concerned that the reduction in waste loadings that are brought about by improvements in wastewater treatment in the East River and elsewhere—in New York Harbor, for example—were estimated to produce the improvement in water quality just about in terms of what has been observed. The reason for that is that the pollutants that have been removed by increased wastewater treatment are primarily organic materials which are oxidized primarily in the East River. It was never anticipated that the improvements in the East River wastewater treatment in terms of removing organic pollutants would significantly improve water quality conditions in Long Island Sound. So I think that the results of what has been observed in that regard are quite consistent.

Nevertheless, I would certainly support the concern that Ed Wagner has expressed that we have not yet had the opportunity to evaluate at any level of detail the variations that have occurred in water quality in western Long Island Sound over long periods of time. I support the notion that before major engineering structures are considered for control of water quality in western Long Island Sound—or any other solutions for that matter—be fully implemented that an analysis and full understanding of variations in water quality in western Long Island Sound should certainly be conducted.

H. BOKUNIEWICZ: I don't have any comments that are any different from what anyone else has said, although it seems to a little disturbing that we seem to be getting into a position where we can't afford to study a problem—to study a solution—so that it has to be put back on the shelf.

P. M. J. WOODHEAD: I have rather more optimism about the things we can do about these problems in terms of looking at them. I think that there is quite a lot of data already available to make some first cuts and come up with more focused answers, not complete answers. I thought Ed Wagner's address was a fair way of looking at things. Surely, we have done so much damage to the environment in headlong fashion, that we must take a more measured pace. Try to know what we are doing. But I do have some optimism that we can come up with better answers about these things. I do agree with Henry that it seems premature at this workshop, looking at some drafts, to step away from the project. We should take it a little further in sharpening up the answers, sharpening up the questions before saying... I love the comment about a half-billion project with a billion dollar environment impact statement. That's the New York way of doing things, of course. I don't think it has to be that way. A result of having a somewhat a wider experience is that one learns that it isn't always done the New York way.

SWANSON: Peter, I was pleased to know that there is such a thing as an optimistic fisheries scientist. I'd like to open up the questions to the panelists and also to the speakers of earlier this morning.

D. BURLEY: I am here representing the New York State coastal management system. One comment that I'd like to argue is perhaps indirectly related. I spent two days earlier this week up on Lake Ontario dealing with people whose coastline property is being eroded rather seriously, a problem that we deal with and the Corps of Engineers deals with. The point I want to make here is that the property that is being eroded there is being eroded because of certain things involving the Great Lakes, much beyond these people's control. The other thing that I wanted to say is that the coastal management program of the State of New York stands for a number of policies that relate to a number of things that were mentioned today: water quality certainly among them, the effects of habitat, the effects of species, also maritime commerce and a number of other issues. So I guess one reason I am standing here is that as this project progresses, I would like to alert you that we would like to work with you as early as possible so that you don't surprise us at the last minute. Because we, like the Corps of Engineers, will be concerned about the effects ultimately due to this.

GERALD LIEBER (*Roosevelt Island Operating Corporation*): Roosevelt Island is obviously vitally interested in anything affecting the East River.

GENERAL DISCUSSION

As you probably know, we have ground water on the island, we had some flooding, we have storm sewer systems, and in fact we have had sea wall construction for the last eight or nine years. One of the concerns I have is the comment of John St. John's about a 20 centimeter rise which I think translates to about 20 percent increase in elevation over a four to five foot normal high tide. Now does that translate to the entire East River? In other words, at Roosevelt Island, which is midtown rather than at the Battery—and we do get high tides as much as nine feet in very high astronomical situations—what will be the increase in tide levels?

St. John: We have the results that you are asking for back at the office. I don't have answers right on the top of my head. But it looks as though what would happen is that there is approximately an 8-inch increase at the Battery that would decrease through the East River to about an inch immediately to the west of the tide gate. At Roosevelt Island, I would guess we would probably be talking about something like perhaps 5 or 6 inches. So that's about what I can tell you from our modeling estimates of water elevation. The impact of that on shoreline structures, for example, I am not competent to talk about. That's why I didn't make any comments. It is a potential issue.

Tadeusz Marchaj: I would like to ask Mr. Wagner: he mentioned that someone hypothesized that the hypoxia that is occurring in western Long Island Sound may be occurring not in spite of but due to the recent construction and upgrading of regional wastewater treatment plants. I would like to hear who the author of this hypothesis is, because maybe we have to stop building the wastewater treatment plants.

Wagner: The speculation about the conundrum about the reduction in the pollutant loadings and the decrease in water quality in Long Island Sound has spurred a lot of creative juices and a lot of creative thinking among a lot of people. The particular comment that I made there was made from two possible perspectives. One is that the form of the nutrients that is now being discharged from the secondary treatment plants as opposed to what was being discharged either raw or with lower levels of treatment may in fact be enhancing or encouraging greater algal blooms, greater algal development. The other possibility that was advanced is that the reduction in the suspended solids load on the river reduces turbidity which might increase light penetration and also exacerbate the production of algal biomass. The one thing that still remains a mystery is what exactly triggers the development of algal biomass. What is the relationship there? The modelers have the models, but as I pointed out, the threshold level for algal blooms occurs throughout the entire region, and we don't always have algal blooms, and so that's one of the questions that we would raise.

Question: With regard to the models that we were discussing, how much of an impact if any do these have on the tides and currents predictions by the National Oceanic and Atmospheric Administration?

St. John: The question is: how reliable are the models? I assume that you are talking primarily about the hydrodynamic model that we constructed, and the answer to that is that model is basically uncalibrated. As a matter of fact, it was put together as a research effort at HydroQual primarily to address this particular issue in terms of very, very preliminary assessment. We did a skill assessment of the model, looking at comparisons of water elevations throughout New York Bight into New York Harbor and throughout Long Island Sound. I would have to say that as far as water elevations are concerned the model and predicted tide elevations compared reasonably well. As a matter of fact, I would almost say very well. Tidal current velocities are a different matter. We didn't have a lot of information by which to compare model results, so that is an area that is still an open question.

MARY GASTRICH (*New Jersey Department of Environmental Protection*): There were some fascinating presentations today and I enjoyed the comments that everyone has made, but I wanted to add to what was said on further exploring the right questions, the kinds of questions, and getting some additional answers. I would like to speak for New Jersey. We are part of the ecosystem here, although the conversation was mainly about New York State waters. I would like to encourage everyone here that is involved in the planning and research for this tidal barrage to extend their thinking to some of the effects that occur in New Jersey that we are concerned with. Various speakers this morning raised questions that, in my mind, New Jersey is very interested in. We would like to extend your thinking to the entire region, especially the New York Bight, the shoreline, and the harbor. I'd like to thank you for your attention.

SWANSON: In case everybody couldn't hear that, Mary's comments were basically a plea to work with the people who are concerned with moving forward with the tidal barrage but also to take due consideration of impacts that may potentially affect New Jersey's coastline in New York Bight and also in the harbor.

I want to thank all the speakers this morning for their thought-provoking papers.

Part II
THE TIDAL BARRAGE AS A BRIDGE

Another East River Crossing?

LUCIUS J. RICCIO[a]

Commissioner, New York City Department of Transportation
New York, New York 10013

Generations of New Yorkers have been frustrated by the lack of access between Manhattan, the surrounding islands and the mainland. The Harlem River, earlier known as Spuyten Duyvil Creek, posed only minimal problems given the narrow crossing, and accordingly New Yorkers spanned the creek beginning in 1693.

The East River, of course, posed more monumental tasks. In the early 19th century, engineers, carpenters and jacks of all trades proposed everything from suspension bridges to dikes as ways to link Manhattan and Brooklyn. In 1810, Thomas Pope, a New York craftsman, dreamed of and designed a "Flying Pendant Lever Bridge" that would have spanned 1,800 feet and climbed to a height of 223 feet above the water.

Of course the only serious plans for the East River began in 1867 with the formation of the New York Bridge Company and John Roebling's plans for what would become the Brooklyn Bridge. It is all the more appropriate that we are discussing the possibility of an additional structure now because May 24 will mark the 110th anniversary of the opening of the Brooklyn Bridge.

The Brooklyn Bridge, and the bridges constructed rapidly in the years after, met capacity and were quickly saturated. The important lesson, however, is not that there was almost immediately the need for additional structures, but rather the East River Bridges were built primarily for public transportation. In 1907, the peak year, the Brooklyn Bridge carried nearly 450,000 people a day along two vehicular lanes and four rail tracks, compared to the 178,000 who use the bridge today in vehicles. Similarly, the Williamsburg Bridge carried 505,000 people a day in 1924 along six rail tracks and four vehicular lanes, compared to about 250,000 today.

Despite the diminished transit use of the East River Bridges, they are still critical links on important subway lines. Subways carry sixty percent of the people crossing the Manhattan Bridge and thirty percent of those crossing the Williamsburg Bridge. Hopefully, more trains will return to the bridges in the future. To make that possible, we have included in the reconstruction designs for the Williamsburg and Queensboro measures that will allow for additional trains down the line.

The question before us today is not whether more trains should utilize the East River bridges, though that answer is yes. But rather, do we need an additional East River crossing? The answer is maybe, depending on use. We do not need, nor will we entertain an idea for, a new

[a]*Present address*: Manuel Elken. Co., 419 Park Avenue South, New York, NY 10016.

crossing for vehicles. With nearly one million vehicles entering Manhattan daily we are already at saturation levels and any steps to encourage more vehicles would be foolhardy. While we are interested in entertaining ideas for high-occupancy vehicle (HOV) lanes, any structure that accommodated just car-pooling or buses would open up additional lanes for vehicles on the already existing structures. We would prefer, and are developing plans for, turning some of the lanes on the East River bridges to HOV lanes already.

The benefits of any new structure depend, of course, on the location.

THE BRONX WHITESTONE BRIDGE LOCATION

If the tidal barrage were built close enough to the Bronx Whitestone Bridge to provide easy connections with its approach ramps, two or three motor vehicle lanes could be built on top of it. They would effectively add more lanes to the bridge. We would, in this case, entertain the use of these lanes for buses and other commercial vehicles in order to help speed their trips between the Bronx and Queens. The lanes could be operated by the Triborough Bridge and Tunnel Authority, with regular tolls charged to support public transportation.

The tidal barrage would not function well in this location as a rail link. Existing rail lines in the Bronx and Queens are not near the shore here. The Hell Gate Bridge already provides a good rail connection between Queens and the Bronx for freight and Amtrak trains.

THE EAST RIVER/MIDTOWN LOCATION

As with the Whitestone location, a structure could be built with vehicular lanes to supplement the Queens-Midtown Tunnel but as I mentioned above even if these were dedicated to HOV's, the end result would be more capacity for cars.

There are, however, other possibilities for this area. The City is currently in the final stages of preparing to construct a trolley along 42nd Street. The trolley, which will run from the Javits Center, along 42nd Street, to the United Nations, will be built and operated by a private company. We are hopeful that construction will begin in 1994 and be completed in 1996. The barrage could allow us to carry the trolley across the East River to Long Island City, although with the subway connection planned by the Metropolitan Transportation Authority between the upper level of the 63rd Street line and the Queens Boulevard line, additional capacity is not necessary.

The barrage could also supplement the Port Authority's planned people mover, which will provide transportation between Manhattan and LaGuardia and Kennedy Airports. The tidal barrage could be used as a second river crossing for the automated ground transportation

(AGT) system, enabling it to reach a new terminal site just north of the 34th Street heliport or on land made available by the closing of Con Edison's obsolete steam plant at 38th Street.

THE EAST RIVER/LOWER MIDTOWN LOCATION

The tidal barrage, I am told, would also work from a water quality perspective if it were built to Brooklyn from a point in Manhattan north of the Ferry Terminal. But its use for transportation facilities is more difficult because of the need for higher ship clearances than at other locations. This either means a drawbridge, which would disrupt transportation while open, or a very high structure. With these limitations, there are still a few transportation options we could explore.

Building the Second Avenue Subway may not be justified if it does not run through to Brooklyn and connect with the Fulton Street IND line, which was the original concept in 1920. Because it was never implemented, the Fulton Street line's local trains lack independent access to Manhattan and must share tracks with express trains to cross the East River. This effectively reduces the line's passenger capacity by 50 percent during peak periods.

A new tunnel for the Brooklyn connection would be very expensive. The tidal barrage could be used as the connection at a lower cost. The engineering, land use, and socioenvironmental problems of bringing the Second Avenue Subway above ground in lower Manhattan and getting it onto a high enough structure on the tidal barrage would, to say the least, be formidable.

So do we need a new East River Crossing? From a transportation perspective the answer is yes and no, depending on use. Before we even contemplate building a new structure from a transportation angle, we should evaluate how better to use the structures that we have, to increase public transportation on them and limit the number of vehicles that are entering Manhattan.

Like our predecessors, we all want to leave our mark on our city. And what better way than building a structure that improves water quality and enhances transportation? My concern is that the facilities we have are already sufficient if used properly. While not as sexy as a new bridge, it is our responsibility to see that what we have is rebuilt and maintained—and returned to public transportation.

DISCUSSION OF THE PAPER

QUESTION: Last summer I had a preliminary meeting with the Port Authority, and they were considering part of the Queensboro Bridge landing just west of the Manhattan tram station as an alternative to another landing in Queens at the train yards. Is that dead?

LUCIUS RICCIO: No. I can't take all credit for this, but I did argue for the connection to Manhattan, and I proposed the outer roadways of the Queensboro Bridge as the mechanism. If you look at the Queensboro Bridge approaches, they are spectacular structures. There was a plan for the structure between First Avenue and York Avenue called Bridge Market, but because of the recession and the downturn in the real estate market that has lain fallow, you might say. There is nothing going on there. Well, if you look at the grand arches of this structure, it would be a wonderful airline terminal—like the old East Side bus terminal. It would be a wonderful airline terminal that you could bring the trains down and around and into, and you could have cab turnarounds, and it could be fed from First Avenue and York Avenue. The Port Authority looked at that, and then they proposed this other concept where the trains would come off the bridge and use the little plaza area where the tramway comes in. That's also do-able. The difficulty is designing the transportation in and out of that, because you already have—especially in the evening rush hour—a tremendous confluence of many, many vehicles trying to get off. As a matter of fact, that is one of our worst locations in the evening rush hour for getting people out of Manhattan. So if you add to that an additional I don't know how many hundred cabs, trying to get people to that it might be difficult. It might be better to move them off First Avenue or someplace away from there. That is still alive, and I like the idea of using the outer roadway. As a matter of fact, this coming year the construction on the lower level of the Queensboro Bridge, which is being conducted by New York State Department of Transportation, should be completed, at which point there will be more lanes—more roadways open up on the Queensboro Bridge—than there have been since World War II. That bridge will be in the best shape it's been in in fifty years. The only thing left to build will be the outer roadways. What I have asked my engineers to do is to design the outer roadway reconstruction to be able to take trains. Now, by the way, you should also know that we are rebuilding the Williamsburg Bridge in a way that will give future generations the choice of putting more trains back on that bridge. It will be built with the structural integrity to be able to support that. So that is still a very viable plan, but as I said, it might not be the ideal place to have a lot of cars coming in. There might be a better location down near the United Nations which currently does not have a bridge and does not have the evening rush hour pushing a hundred thousand or so vehicles through the city streets. We could have a terminal area, quite frankly, near the old bus terminal. It might be better, and the tidal barrage might be able to give us that access across the river.

QUESTION: Ray Ruggieri of the New York Metropolitan Transportation Commission has spoken recently of how the concept known as NIMBY (Not In My Backyard) has been replaced by a new one which

Ray referred to BANANA, standing for Build Absolutely Nothing Anywhere Near Anything. What I want to ask you is what do you think could be done to be sure that this project doesn't succumb to BANANA?

RICCIO: Actually, we had one case which astounded me. If I may digress for a second, we wanted to build an asphalt plant in Queens to go into direct competition with the private asphalt producers to force the price of asphalt down. And that community board for some reason liked the idea. They saw the virtue in what we were doing, and they voted in favor of it. That was the first known recorded case of what I call YIMBY—Yes, In My Backyard. We rewarded them by not having them built it there. American logic here. The contractors were in such shock. They figured that no community would ever want another asphalt plant, and they brought their price of asphalt down. The price of asphalt now is about $21 per ton; it was about $30 per ton just two years ago. We are saving tens of millions of dollars on that. The contractors are still doing OK as best I can tell, and the taxpayers are saving millions. But that story never gets in the papers, but, you know, that's New York.

Bud Griffis could probably talk for hours on how you approach the legal system and the political system to try and get a project done, even one that is so clearly—I don't know enough about the tidal barrage—but even with so clearly a public benefit, it is still always difficult to get things through. Quite frankly, adding a transportation dimension to this will add to the complexity of getting through the legal system tremendously, because you will have to have approaches and hook-ups at either side, and there will be transportation consequences of traveling to and from, and so it's almost mind-boggling to conceive of all the hurdles and the leaps one will have to take to actually make this thing happen. And I guess that the only way things work, really, is that you get forced into doing something.

One of the great advantages of the link between environmentalism and transportation is that the environmentalists have been tremendously helpful to us in being able to have some control over traffic. If it weren't for environmentalism, we wouldn't have any control over traffic. We wouldn't have any ability to stop the addiction to automobiles, and particularly the addiction to dirty automobiles. I just got back from Europe. I mentioned earlier that we allow our automobiles to go just about anywhere. Our automobiles are much cleaner than European automobiles. You stand next to a European automobile, and you think you are in an incinerator. Are you using low-grade garbage as your fuel in this thing? I don't know, it was just horrible, the regular cars. But they then restrict where cars can go. So we have no restrictions on cars, but our cars are cleaner. Their cars are filthy, but they can't go everywhere. I don't know what the smart thing is. If someone could figure out a strategy which because of the water dirtiness and for environmental reasons something has to be done, and you get a judge to order the city that you have to do something: like how about a tidal barrage? And then you are forced into doing it.

Part III

CONCEPTUAL DESIGNS OF THE EAST RIVER TIDAL BARRAGE

F. H. ("BUD") GRIFFIS, *Chairman*

East River Tidal Barrage

MICHAEL J. ABRAHAMS AND ALEX MATLIN
Parsons Brinckerhoff Quade & Douglas
One Penn Plaza
New York, New York 10119

INTRODUCTION

This paper presents an engineering solution that addresses, at a conceptual level, the configuration of a barrage that would serve to prevent northward flow of water in the East River while at the same time allowing it to flow south. The purpose of this modification to flow in the East River is to improve water quality in Long Island Sound, the East River, and New York Harbor. It is recognized that such a structure and subsequent water flow change would affect the marine environment and that issues such as marine life, sedimentation, and river hydraulics need to be evaluated as part of any such project. These very important issues have not been addressed in this paper and need to be considered by others.

In this paper we have identified the physical characteristics of the East River and, based on those characteristics, developed a solution that we believe will minimize the impact of such a barrage on the river and surrounding area. With that approach in mind, we have avoided a solution that includes any other features, such as a bridge or hydroelectric plant.

Recognizing that marine navigation on the East River plays an important role in the New York economy, we have established the level of activity on the river and have incorporated features in our study to accommodate navigation. Nevertheless, it is recognized that such a barrage would affect navigation and, if the development of a tidal barrage is to proceed, a careful study must be made of its effect on navigation and the features that will be needed to accommodate shipping.

SITE DESCRIPTION

The East River is about 16 miles long. The main channel is 40 feet deep at mean low water and 1,000 feet wide from upper New York Bay to the former Brooklyn Navy Yard. North of this point to Throgs Neck, the channel varies in width from 550 to 1,000 feet.

The average tidal range varies from 4.4 feet at the Battery to 7.1 feet at Throgs Neck. FIGURE 1 shows tidal charts for April 29, 1993 and for the next spring tide (May 6) at the Battery and at Willets Point immediately east of Throgs Neck. Extreme high tide ranges from 10.6 feet above mean low water at the Battery and 15.5 feet above mean low water at Throgs Neck to extreme low tide of 3.8 feet below mean low water at both locations. Thus the extreme tidal ranges are 14.4 feet at the Battery and 19.3 feet at Throgs Neck. This does not include other influences on water level such as waves and storm surge.

There are seven anchorages along the length of the East River: Anchorage No. 6 on Hammond Flats near the Throgs Neck Bridge; Anchorage No. 7 between Whitestone Point and Willets Point Wharf; Anchorage No. 8 near the Bronx Whitestone Bridge; Anchorage No. 9 near College Point; Anchorage No. 10 in Flushing Bay; Anchorage No. 11 near Rikers Island; and Anchorage No. 14 in Hallets Cove. These anchorages are used for both barges and ships.

Twelve bridges and tunnels whose clearances affect the East River are listed in TABLE 1.

According to the U.S. Corps of Engineers publication *Waterborne Commerce of the United States, 1989,* 10,363,739 short tons were carried on the river, including 3,299,703 tons of residual fuel oil, 1,112,267 tons of distillage fuel oil, and 4,670,895 tons of waste and scrap during a one-year period. Other products carried include bananas; coffee; crude petroleum; sand, gravel and crushed rock; sugar; lumber; gasoline; jet fuel; kerosene; and cement. The bulk of this traffic was local, with the remainder being foreign or domestic shipments.

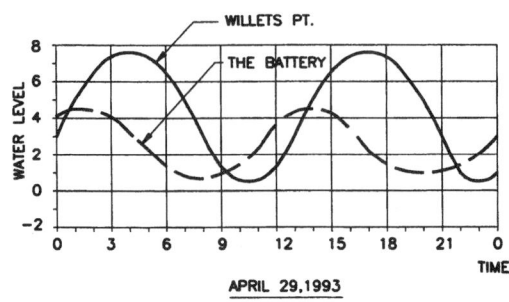

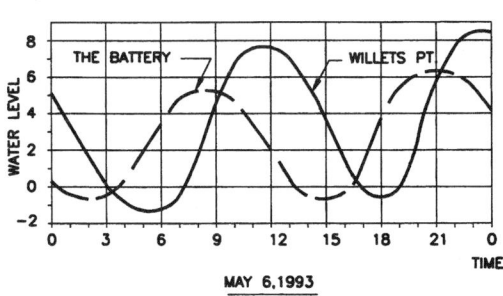

FIGURE 1. Tidal charts at ends of East River.

TABLE 1. Bridges and Tunnels across the East River[a]

Miles Above Mouth	Location and Name	Clearance (feet)		Remarks
		Horizontal	Vertical[b]	
0.8	Brooklyn Bridge	1,350	127	
1.1	Manhattan Bridge	1,200	134	
2.3	Williamsburg Bridge	1,536	133	
5.5	Queensboro Bridge	900	131	West Channel
5.5	Queensboro Bridge	760	133	East Channel
5.6	Roosevelt Is. Cable Car	850	135	West Channel
5.8	E. 63rd St. Tunnel	—	—	45' West Channel
5.8	E. 63rd St. Tunnel	—	—	45' East Channel
6.4	Roosevelt Island Bridge	403	40-99	Vertical Lift/E. Channel
7.8	Triborough Bridge	1,070	138	
8.2	Hell Gate Bridge	830	134	Railroad
10.7	Rikers Island Bridge	125	52	Rikers Island Channel
13.8	Bronx-Whitestone Br.	2,265	135	
15.8	Throgs Neck Bridge	1,711	138	

[a]There are a number of other utility and subway tunnels under the East River that are not included in the above listing.
[b]At mean high water (MHW).

MARINE NAVIGATION

Marine traffic on the East River consists mainly of barges, tugboats, ferries, pleasure boats, and other small craft. While large vessels are also present, they are much less frequent.

Barges are towed, pushed, and self-propelled. They carry various types of cargo such as bulk cargo, oil and other liquids, general cargo, containers, construction equipment, *etc*. Barge lengths vary from 65 feet to 300 feet. Considering the strong currents in the river, which are especially swift at Hell Gate, practically all barges and tugs schedule their trips so they travel with the current. While accurate statistical data on barge and tug traffic is not available, it can be approximated from discussions with persons having maritime interests, as well as field observations. For the purpose of this conceptual design, it can be assumed that an average of four to six tugs and barges per hour pass along the East River in the vicinity of Hell Gate.

Large ships are normally cargo vessels that enter New York Harbor via the East River, bound for Red Hook, Stapleton, the Brooklyn Navy Yard, and other terminals. They include mostly bulk carriers, tankers, container ships, general cargo ships, and roll-on/roll-off (ro/ro) vessels.

Statistical data on large ships are available through the Maritime Association of the Port of New York and New Jersey. An analysis of this data for the last 18 months indicates the following:

- The number of ships travelling the East River normally varies from 25 to 40 per month.
- Seasonal changes have no noticeable effect on the number of ships travelling the river.
- Ship lengths generally vary from 200 to 1,000 feet, but more than 80% of the ships are within the range of 400 to 700 feet, and about 92% of all ships are 700 feet long or shorter. Diagrams of normal and cumulative distributions of overall ship lengths are shown in FIGURE 2.
- Ship widths generally vary from 40 feet to 140 feet, but about 80% of the ships are 70 to 110 feet wide, and 98.7% of all ships are 110 feet wide or narrower. Diagrams of normal and cumulative distributions of ship widths are shown in FIGURE 3.
- Statistical data on the actual draft of ships travelling the East River was not available.

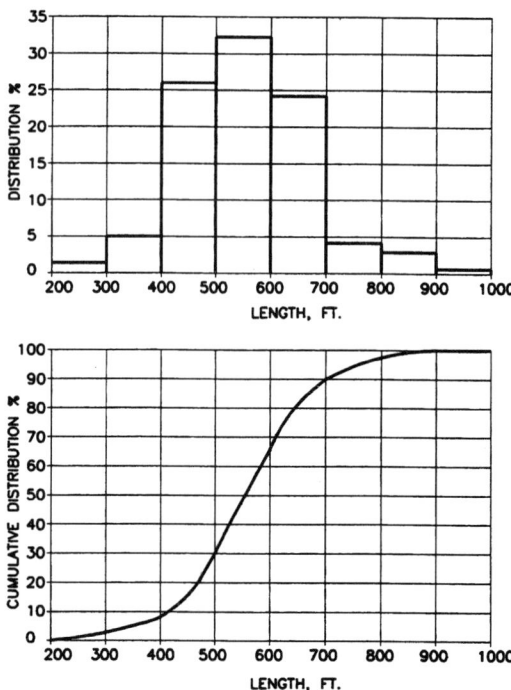

FIGURE 2. Distribution of ship lengths on the East River.

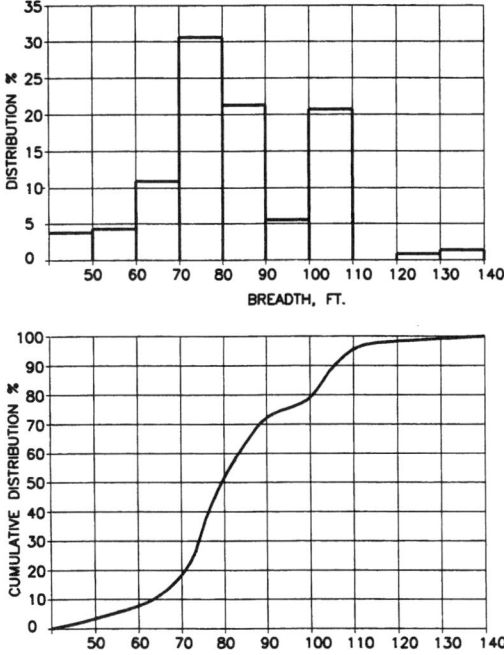

FIGURE 3. Distribution of ship widths on the East River.

GEOLOGY OF THE EAST RIVER

The formation of the East River resulted from a complex sequence of changes in the geologic history of New York City dating back to early Paleozoic time. The bedrock along the East River consists of units from the New York City Group, such as the Manhattan Schist, Inwood Marble, Fordham Gneiss, and undifferentiated schists and gneisses. These units were once sedimentary sequences that have since undergone complex and extensive metamorphic changes, primarily intense folding, faulting, and intrusion by granitic-type magmas.

Subsequent uplift and erosion continued and developed an erosion surface, upon which sediments from more geologically recent deposition occurred. The rock units of the New York City Group make up the Manhattan Prong of the New England Upland Physiographic Province. Uparching of the erosional surface created differential erosion along planes of weakness in the rock mass (primarily fault zones), thus resulting in much of the present day topography in the New York metropolitan area. The East River flows along a fault zone situated east and west of Roosevelt Island. After glacial action during the Quaternary period, depositional and erosion effects altered the topography. Glacial

Lake Flushing which developed over Manhattan, Queens, and Brooklyn left remnants of varved lake deposits throughout the area. As glaciers receded, the lake drained and some upwarping occurred. Following the upward movement, some subsidence occurred and submerged old valleys, such as the East River, which is considered an estuary.

OTHER BARRAGES

Recently a number of tidal barriers have been proposed and, in some cases, built. These barriers have served various purposes, including protection of low lying areas from flooding and hydroelectric power generation. Several of these projects were reviewed as part of this study, among them the Thames River Tidal Barrier, the Venice Project, the Mersey River Barrage, and the Eastern Scheldt Storm Surge Barrier.

Perhaps the best known of these projects is the barrage constructed across the Thames River to protect low lying parts of London from flooding. The barrage is 550 feet long and consists of a series of hydraulically operated gates that can be activated to prevent flooding. A feature of the gate design is that it can be raised for servicing and is used only during periods of anticipated high water. Normally the gates are kept in their retracted position, allowing free use of the river by navigation.

While not yet built, the proposed tidal barrier under development in Venice is also well known, as are Venice's problems with flooding due to high water. The scheme being developed in Venice is quite different from that completed in London; the gates are operated using only the buoyancy of the hollow gate section to resist a hydraulic head differential. We understand that at the present time a test section has been built and is undergoing development. When completed, the barrier will be 1,200 meters (3,937 feet) long and is expected to be used about three or four times a year.

Other barriers, such as the Mersey Barrage or the barrage in the river Hollandsche Ijssel near Rotterdam, utilize a lock and movable barrier to permit the passage of navigation while the barrier is in place.

SITE SELECTION

The main river parameters in selecting an East River location, such as water depth and width, vary a great deal over its 16-mile length, and not all locations are suitable for construction of the tidal barrage. Using a minimum water depth combined with a reasonable width as controlling criteria, three locations have been considered as potential barrage sites:

- The Williamsburg Bridge
- Roosevelt Island, in line with 72nd Street on the Manhattan side and the 36th Street (Roosevelt Island) Bridge on the Queens side;

- Between Wards Island and Queens, immediately south of Lawrence Point and about a mile north of the Triborough Bridge.

Among these three alternatives, the third has been selected as the most suitable tidal barrage site (FIG. 4). It is located in the middle of a 2-mile-long straight stretch of the navigation channel between North Brother Island and the Triborough Bridge, providing straight approaches at least 1 mile long to the site from either direction.

The river is approximately 1,500 feet wide at the proposed site. The water depth at mean low water is about 36 feet over most of the river width, with the exception of a narrow (approximately 100- to 150-foot-wide) trench 70 to 75 feet deep. This trench, apparently a geological fault or highly decomposed zone in the rock, is located closer to the Queens side and is parallel to the shore. A section across the river at the proposed site is shown in FIGURE 5.

The land areas on both sides of the river are not residential areas, and the waterfronts are not developed. The Queens side is the site of a Con Edison power plant. The Wards Island side is a park area owned by the City. A photographic view of the site is shown in FIGURE 6.

The general geology at the proposed site is fill and glacial deposits overlying bedrock. The overburden consists of manmade miscellaneous fill on top of possibly glacial lake deposits and glacial moraine deposits. Below the glacial moraine, bedrock is typically decomposed from the surface of the top-of-rock to a variable depth depending upon the degree of weathering. The top-of-rock elevation may vary from 40 to 80 feet below the ground surface. The bedrock consists of undifferentiated crystalline rocks of the New York City Group, such as schist, gneiss, and granodiorite.

The river currents at the proposed site, which is located next to Hell Gate, are very strong. Direction of the current changes approximately every six hours following the tidal cycle. The maximum current velocities under normal tidal conditions are about 4 knots from south to north, and about 5 knots from north to south.

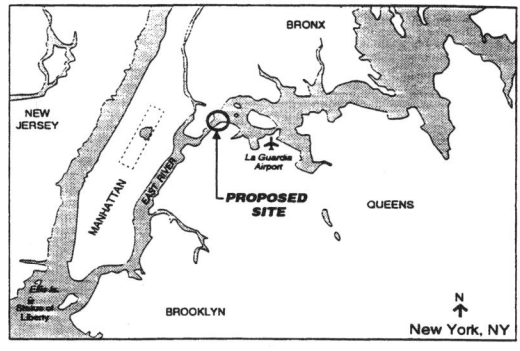

FIGURE 4. Proposed location of tidal barrage.

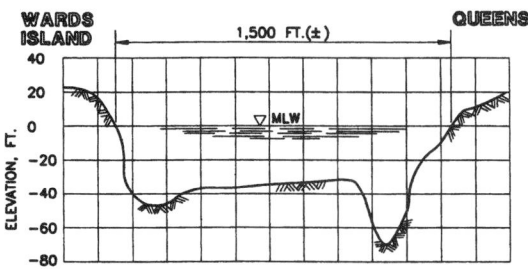

FIGURE 5. Section across East River at proposed site.

PROPOSED BARRAGE LAYOUT

The barrage needs to serve two functions. First, it must prevent northward tidal flow and second, it needs to accommodate marine traffic. So, it is proposed that the tidal barrage consist of two elements: the gates and the navigation lock. The gates will control the river current by opening to allow the river flow and closing to prevent flow in the other direction. The navigation lock will allow ships and/or small craft to pass the barrage when its gates are closed.

Two types of navigation locks have been considered: a large vessel (or ship) lock and a barge lock. The basic dimensions of each lock chamber

FIGURE 6. Photographic view of proposed site.

(length, width, and controlling water depth) have been established so that the locks can accommodate most (90 to 95 percent) ships or barges currently travelling on the East River. These dimensions are presented in TABLE 2.

As mentioned above, the current changes direction approximately every six hours, *i.e.* four times a day. The barrage gates may be operated in different regimes: they may be kept closed either every south-to-north current cycle (two times a day), every other cycle (once a day), or even every fourth cycle (once in two days). The less frequently the gates are closed, the more time will be required to flush the river.

Since large vessel traffic on the East River is quite infrequent, only one or two ships per day, it may be expedient to compromise between the frequency of the gate closing cycles and considerations of ship traffic. Consequently, two alternative concepts of the barrage arrangement have been considered as described below.

Alternative 1. The barrage includes one ship lock and one barge lock. These two can accommodate all barges, tugs and small craft, and 90 to 95 percent of the ships. For those few northbound ships whose length or width exceeds the ship lock clearance, the gates will have to be kept open when required. There may be only two or three such ships per month. This alternative will allow the gates to close for almost every south-to-north current cycle.

Alternative 2. The barrage includes one or two barge locks and no ship lock. These can accommodate probably 90 to 95 percent of all barges, tugs and small craft travelling on East River. Large northbound vessels, as well as barges exceeding the lock clearance, will have to travel when the gates are open. This alternative will allow the gates to be closed once a day (every other cycle) and will require ships and barges to adjust their schedules accordingly.

The two alternatives of the proposed barrage layout are shown in FIGURES 7 and 8.

PROPOSED CONCEPT FOR THE GATES

The gates will cover about 80 percent of the river width, or approximately 1,200 feet. As opposed to the other known flood barriers, which are raised occasionally (perhaps two or three times a year) such as those on the Thames River and in Venice, the East River gates will be operated

TABLE 2. Suggested Dimensions of Navigation Lock Chamber

Type of Lock	Length	Width	Water Depth
Ship Lock	750	115	35
Barge Lock	400	70	18

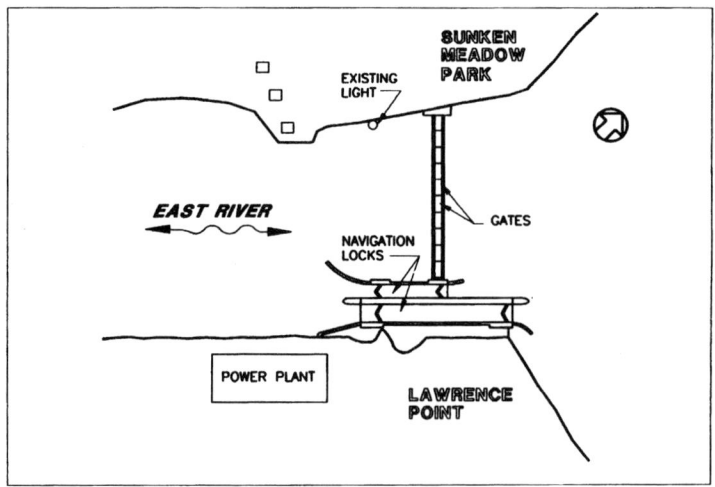

FIGURE 7. Proposed barrage layout, Alternative 1.

on a regular basis. Depending on the selected scheme, they may be raised and lowered daily or even twice a day. This imposes certain requirements on the gate concept: they should be simple, reliable, easy to operate, and easy to maintain.

Among all possible schemes for the lifting mechanism, the concept of a buoyant gate appears to be the simplest and most reliable. The idea is

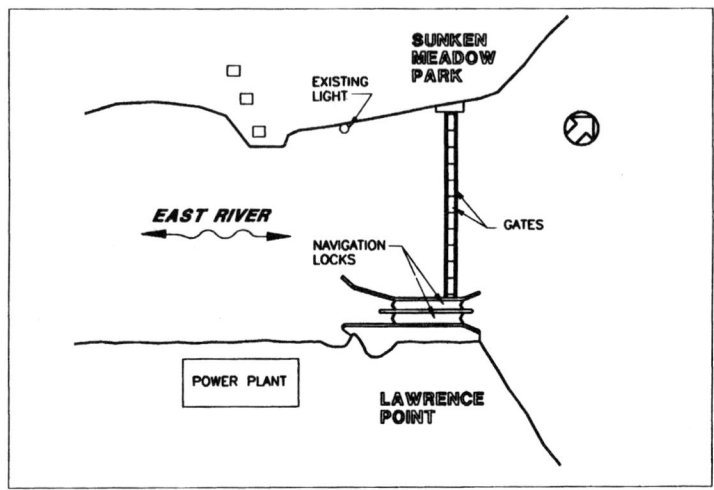

FIGURE 8. Proposed barrage layout, Alternative 2.

to raise the gate by pumping air into the hollow gate body filled with water, displacing the water in it, thus making the gate float. To lower the gate, the air is released, and the gate sinks under its own weight. With this concept, there is no need for lifting motors, gears, or other mechanical elements which are subject to extensive maintenance and failure. All that is required for a buoyant gate is an air compressor, piping, and valves. Two concepts of buoyant gates have been developed as shown in FIGURES 9 and 10.

Alternative 1. This gate alternative is the same as that being developed for the Venice Project (FIG. 9). The gates, or rather sections of a continuous barrier, lay flat on the bottom when open. There are no piers or other structures extending above the bottom, so when the gates are open the river looks like it did before any construction. When floating, the gate sections, which are assumed to be 100 feet long are sealed at overlaps with rubber gaskets for water tightness. In the raised position, the gates float at an angle of approximately 45 degrees above horizontal. This angle may be controlled, if necessary, by the amount of the ballast water that is left inside the gate. A clear advantage of this scheme is that it would eliminate any river obstruction in the lowered position and would be fail safe in the raised position. The gate foundation would be constructed using immersed caissons floated into position and installed on a gravel bed in a screeded trench. This type of construction has been used to build a number of structures, including the 63rd Street Tunnel under the East River and the IRT tunnels under the Harlem River. A similar technique is currently being evaluated by the Corps of Engineers to construct a replacement lock in New Orleans, Louisiana.

Alternative 2. The second gate alternative, shown in FIGURE 10, is more conventional and somewhat similar to the Thames Barrier, except

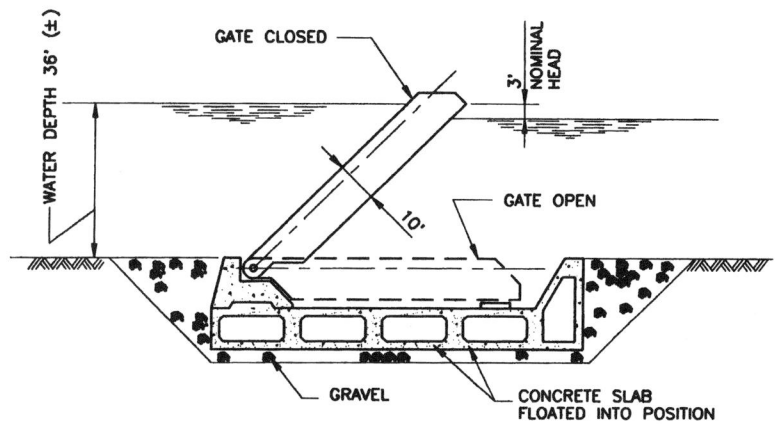

FIGURE 9. Section of proposed gates, Alternative 1.

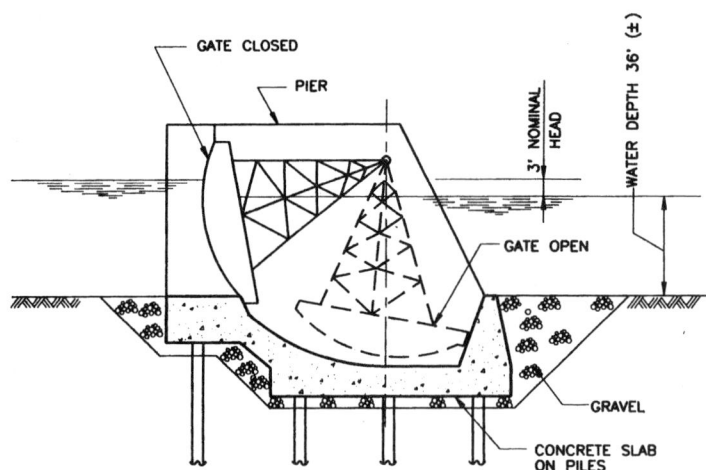

FIGURE 10. Section of proposed gates, Alternative 2.

that the gates are buoyant. Each gate, assumed to be 200 to 250 feet long, spans between piers. It has a segmental cross-section and is attached to the piers with steel trusses. The gates rotate around a pivot point that is located above the water level. This alternative seems to be easier to maintain and operate but may be more costly, since the piers will have to be constructed inside a cofferdam. Also, the presence of the piers spaced at 200- to 250-foot intervals across the river poses an apparent impediment to navigation. Therefore, preference is given to Alternative 1.

It is recognized that a problem with both alternatives is the potential for silt and debris accumulation to affect their operation. The method of silt and debris removal will need to be solved as part of the project design process.

SUMMARY

An evaluation has been made of the possible location and configuration of a tidal barrage across the East River for the purpose of changing the water quality in the river, as well as in Long Island Sound and New York Harbor. It has been concluded that a possible site is located between Wards Island and Queens. The proposed barrage would need to include a navigational lock to accommodate marine traffic and would generally consist of a series of movable gates. The gates would operate using compressed air and could operate on a daily basis.

REFERENCES

Bowman, M.J. 1976. Tidal locks across the East River: An engineering solution to the rehabilitation of western Long Island Sound. New York, Academic Press, Inc.

Bowman, M.J. 1976. The tides on the East River, New York. Journal of Geophysical Research. March 20, 1976.

Eastern Scheldt Storm Surge Barrier. 1982. Proceedings of the Delta Barrier Symposium, Rotterdam, Netherlands. October 13-15, 1982.

Gilbert, S. & R. Horner. 1984. The Thames Barrier. London: Thomas Telford, Limited.

Il Sistema Informativo Territoriale del Progetto Venezia. 1984. Consorzio Venezia Nuova Serivizo Informativo, Concessionario del Ministero del Lavori Pubblici Magistrato, Alle Acque di Venezia, Interventi per la Salvaguardi di Venezia, legge, N. November 29, 1984. 798.

Modulo Sperimental Elettroneccanico: Mose. 1984. Consorzio Venezia Nuova Serivizo Informativo, Concessionario del Ministero del Lavori Pubblici Magistrato, Alle Acque di Venezia, Interventi per la Salvaguardi di Venezia, Legge, N. November 29, 1984. 798.

Schubel, J.R. 1991. The second phase of an assessment of alternatives to biological nutrient removal at sewage treatment plants for alleviating hypoxia in western Long Island Sound. Coast Institute of the Marine Sciences Research Center, report of a workshop, November 1991.

Thames Barrier Design. 1977. Proceedings of a conference held in London, England. October 5, 1977.

Tidal power: Trends and Developments. 1992. Proceeding of the 4th Conference on Tidal Power, March 19-20, 1992. Organized by the Institution of Civil Engineers. London: Thomas Telford, Limited.

Tide Tables. 1993. 1993 High and low water predictions. East coast of North and South America. National Oceanic and Atmospheric Administration.

Waterborne Commerce of the United States, 1989. Calendar Year 1989, Part 1. U.S. Army Corps of Engineers, WRSC-WCUS-89-1, New Orleans.

DISCUSSION OF THE PAPER

Malcolm Bowman: What is the point about a nominal head of three feet? If you look at your first graph, it shows the tidal elevations at the Battery being much greater than that.

Alex Matlin: Those charts show present tidal charts—actual—at the Battery and at Willets Point. Once we close the gate, it doesn't mean that the water on the Battery side will be level all the way up at the level of high tide and the other side will be all the way at the lower level. And this morning's speaker explained to us that the expected change of water level is about eight inches. So three feet is probably on the conservative side. Again, this is an assumed number. We haven't done any hydraulic studies.

BOWMAN: You should look at that carefully because what John St. John said was that a 20 centimeter rise is above present high tide levels.

MATLIN: All right. But I don't believe that you can have four feet, five feet of water here if that is the difference between the Battery and Willets Point. It will be the slope of the water surface, and anyway this is beyond our scope. This is only shown pictorially. The gate can be designed for two feet, it can be designed for five feet as well.

QUESTION: Roosevelt Island was mentioned as a potential site. It appears to me that there is a fifty percent solution possible by increasing reliance upon the west channel, and leaving the east channel open, thereby having partial navigation at all times. I have some calculations here, and the calculations show that fifty percent of the net flow postulated earlier would still go forward. Is this something you have considered?

MATLIN: We have not considered this alternative. In other words, what you are saying is that the navigation lock will not be necessary at all. The channel will be open all the time and the job will be done by closing about two-thirds of the cross-section. We did not consider that. That sounds a little bit scary to me because you are closing the main channel first. Right now, the main channel is the west channel, it's not the east channel. Secondly, by doing that you will increase velocities in the east channel—I don't know how much, but it may be a substantial increase—how much?

QUESTIONER: Fifty percent.

MATLIN: A fifty percent increase is substantial, and we don't know how much that would affect the scour of this channel or what would happen. But it is certainly something to be considered if the studies are done.

DONALD HILL: Alex, have you gotten as far as estimating how much it would cost to build this?

MATLIN: Yes. The cost was roughly estimated—or I would rather say evaluated—and it can be built at a cost now estimated between four and five hundred million dollars, in other words, below half a billion, including navigation locks, based on the alternative with the two smaller locks and the gate of alternative number one, without piers—the Venice tide gate.

General Concepts for and Design Issues Related to an East River Tidal Barrage

JOHN J. SZELIGOWSKI,
HARRY EKEZIAN, AND LYLE H. HIXENBAUGH

*TAMS Consultants, Inc.
655 Third Avenue
New York, New York 10017*

INTRODUCTION

The primary focus of this morning's symposium session has been the environmental implications of constructing a tidal barrage across the East River estuary. Impacts of such a structure on river hydraulics, water quality, sediment transport, and aquatic ecology were addressed and needs for further environmental analyses were identified. In order to fully evaluate the barrage concept, however, it will also be necessary to consider its specific configuration, the methods used to construct and emplace it, and the monetary costs of the undertaking.

This presentation addresses, in a general way, some of the engineering issues associated with the tidal barrage concept. As with the environmental issues discussed this morning, considerable analysis, including some fundamental development work, would be needed before it would be possible to feel comfortable with any specific design for the barrage. That effort alone would last several years and has not yet been initiated.

However, using information available from projects completed elsewhere, and given an understanding of the fundamental principles that would be applied to design of any tidal barrier, we can obtain some sense of the physical characteristics of an East River facility. The ideas presented here are a result of combining extensive engineering expertise with good common sense, over a very short time frame, to generate preliminary concepts for structural elements of the barrage. The illustrations and information provided here may raise numerous questions with regard to the project's feasibility; in fact, a conceptual engineering investigation is supposed to do just that. Thus, while listening to or reading this presentation, and formulating questions on its content, it should be remembered that the preparers themselves have raised many of the same matters and are also looking forward to the responses.

LOCATION

Among the numerous factors that would be evaluated during the search for an optimal tidal barrage location are whether the site would:

- Accomplish the project's water-quality objectives;
- Minimize negative environmental impacts;
- Avoid severe hydraulic, geologic, and morphological conditions;
- Maintain waterborne traffic; and
- Achieve the project's multiple use goals.

We have identified two possible places for the device, one at the transect from Clason Point, Bronx, to College Point, Queens. Another is midtown Manhattan (FIG. 1). We give a certain amount of emphasis to the midtown location, simply because it does offer some alternate or multiple use options. The first important point, however, is that the location must meet the water quality objectives of the project. There is some uncertainty as to whether the midtown location would do that because of the tendency for the water to flow around Manhattan Island through the Harlem River and into the Hudson River. That aspect of location is, of course, the most important.

Then we must consider engineering implications of alternative locations. First, the midtown location obviously has more severe river currents than the College Point-Clason Point transect (FIG. 2) The hydro-

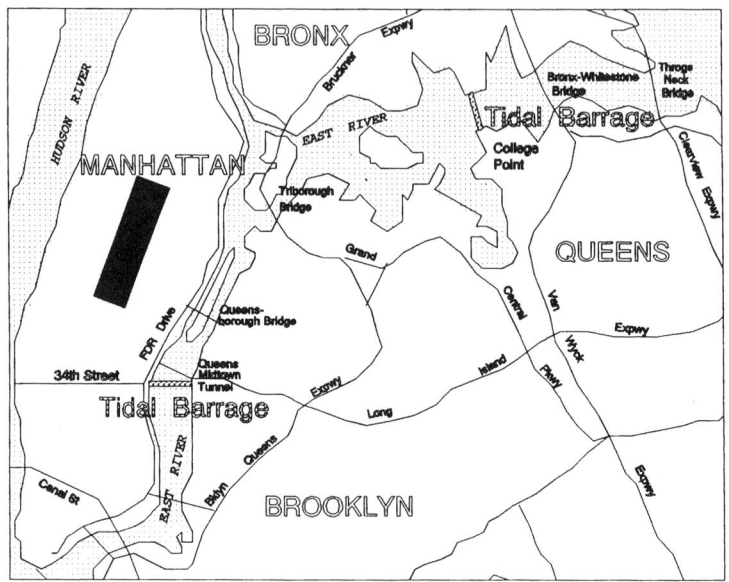

FIGURE 1. Possible locations of tidal barrage.

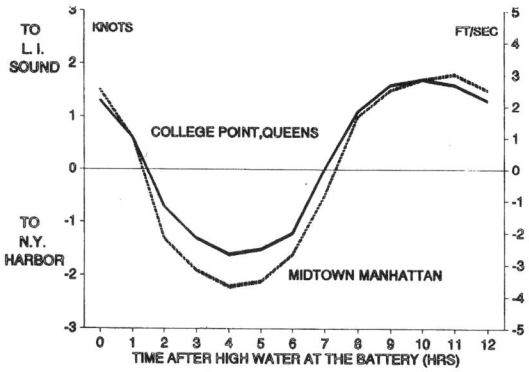

FIGURE 2. Current velocity profile. Predictions for spring high tide at the channel center by the National Oceanic and Atmospheric Administration.

dynamic forces implied by that factor will affect the constructability of the device. In addition, currents will cause scouring and potentially other impacts on structures near the barrage.

An important engineering consideration is that the barrier must be founded on competent bearing surface. At the midtown location, the top layer of the bottom material is sand and clay, probably glacial material, overlaying the basic rock. Any silty material would have to be removed. If a competent bearing surface is not found once the bottom material has been prepared and leveled, it would be necessary to use a pile-type foundation or other supporting mechanisms.

GATE AND GATE STRUCTURE

Concepts Used in Other Applications

Major tidal structures have been constructed at several locations in Europe. Experience with these structures establishes a starting point for selecting an East River system.

In England, across the Thames River, there is a barrier that can be closed when London is threatened by high tides. An interesting feature of the Thames Barrier is that the gates between the fixed piers can be rotated. They are normally submerged so as not to interfere with river navigation, but they can be rotated 90 degrees to create the tidal barrier, and another 90 degrees to an overhead position for maintenance. Another barrier has been constructed across the Hull River in England.

In the Netherlands the Delta works were constructed across the Oosterschelde. Another barrier has been built near Rotterdam, similar to the one across the Hull River in England. Like the Thames Barrier, the storm barrier across the Oosterschelde is intended to operate infrequently. It has very massive vertical gates that move up and down between piers. There are two interesting things here for us. One is that the roadway atop the Oosterschelde barrier is an example of multiple use. The other is the history of the project.

The original design for this storm protection device was a fixed dam. Of course, if a dam were placed at the discharge point of the Rhine and the Maas and the Schelde Rivers, the estuary behind the dam would be converted from a brackish condition into a fresh-water lake. The fishery interests and the environmental interests in Holland in the late 1970s and early 1980s apparently balked at that possibility. This forced the government to change the design from a dam to a gate-type system where the gates are almost always raised. This parallels some of the thoughts and concerns over environmental factors expressed this morning.

Of course, a situation like that occurred at a number of other places in Holland, for example, the conversion of Ijssel Lake to fresh water. The northern Enclosing Dike in the Netherlands includes gates that operate to release water when the level of the North Sea is lower than the fresh water behind the gates.

A storm barrier has been proposed to enclose the Venetian Lagoon. This is intended to protect the lagoon, St. Mark's Plaza, and the other historic places from the Adriatic Sea. The Italians have a great flair for design. In the recessed or seated position, the Venetian gate is full of water so that it submerges, and waterborne traffic can pass over it. Aside from the storm safety aspects, a principal design objective was aesthetics; don't have a pier showing. In its operative position, water is driven out by air being pumped into the chamber, and the gate becomes neutrally buoyant. Aside from a test structure, this concept has not yet been implemented.

Gate Systems

Characterizing gates as either active or passive is one of several ways in which such systems can be viewed:

- An active gate system is one that requires supplied motive power for its functioning, and
- A passive system would be operated by the available tidal hydraulic forces.

Perhaps the most critical elements of the East River barrage are the controlling gates which must operate daily, throughout the year, for the system to have its intended water quality benefits. At this point in the planning process TAMS has selected a passive concept upon which to base further discussion of the barrage. If the passive system described here were ultimately selected it would offer significant advantages in construction costs, construction time, and ease of maintenance. As already noted, however, final selection of a gate concept must be based on detailed analysis, including hydraulic modeling, and prototype testing. Such investigations have not yet begun.

The passive gate system we discuss would have the following design and construction features:

- The gates would be neutrally buoyant and open when the river flows from Long Island Sound to New York Harbor;
- Gates would be approximately 13 by 21 feet in area and would be arrayed in three tiers within a supporting structure;
- A gantry crane would be available to pull the gates for maintenance;
- A typical gate structure would be constructed of reinforced concrete and could house four gate sets;
- The gate housing structures could be built in graving docks such as those found at the Brooklyn Navy Yard; and
- Once a gate structure has been completed, it would be floated into place and founded on a prepared level bed of crushed stone or sand.

The three-tiered system of neutrally buoyant gates is shown in FIGURE. 3. Water trying to go to Long Island Sound, from left to right, closes the gate. Water moving from Long Island Sound to the East River side of the barrier opens the three-tiered gate system, and allows the flushing action to occur. This sketch shows the principal structural elements of the gate system. There is a base that is founded on prepared bottom material, crushed stone. The design would be different if the underlying material were not sufficiently competent to handle these weights and loads. On either edge is fairly lengthy armoring to avoid scouring below the gate structure, a very serious concern. The basic concrete frame of the gate structure is shown with two maintenance roadways on top and a grating covering the space through which the gates would be pulled for maintenance. This is a key element because the gates would have to be maintained regularly to operate day-in and day-out. Perhaps in a storm emergency the top gates would be pulled to allow the water level on each side of the gates to equilibrate.

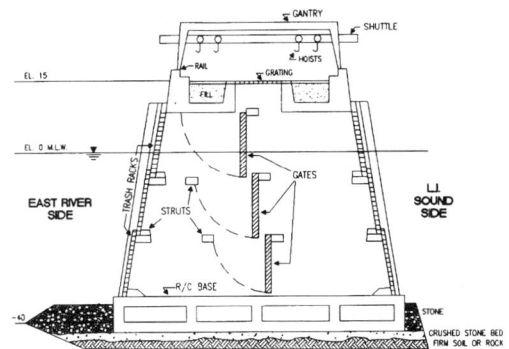

FIGURE 3. Typical cross section of gate structure.

A single module of the gate housing structure is shown in FIGURE 4. The module consists of five reinforced concrete piers in which four sets of gates would be mounted. The structure is about 100 feet in length and about 40 feet high. Since the crossing might be 3,000 feet at the midtown Manhattan location, it could take 20 or 25 of these, allowing some room for the ship locks and other features, to complete the barrier system. An important feature is obviously constructibility. To the extent that these modules can be constructed off-site at the Brooklyn Navy Yard and not on-site, project costs would be dramatically reduced.

Here is the tidal barrage at the midtown location (FIG. 5). The first thing to note here is that there are several submarine crossing interferences in New York Harbor. Here there are two railroad tunnels and an automobile tunnel. By threading the barrier between those, it would touch the Queens side around Hunters Point and would extend to the Manhattan side at 37th Street. We are illustrating this location because it offers some of the multiple use opportunities that Commissioner Riccio spoke about. First and foremost, however, attention should be given to the project's water-quality objectives which have not been studied for this location.

NAVIGATION LOCKS

The East River is an active navigation channel. It is used at times by relatively large oil tankers and routinely by barges and coastal freighters. In addition, during the summer months, and particularly at times of holiday celebrations, the river is visited by large numbers of private

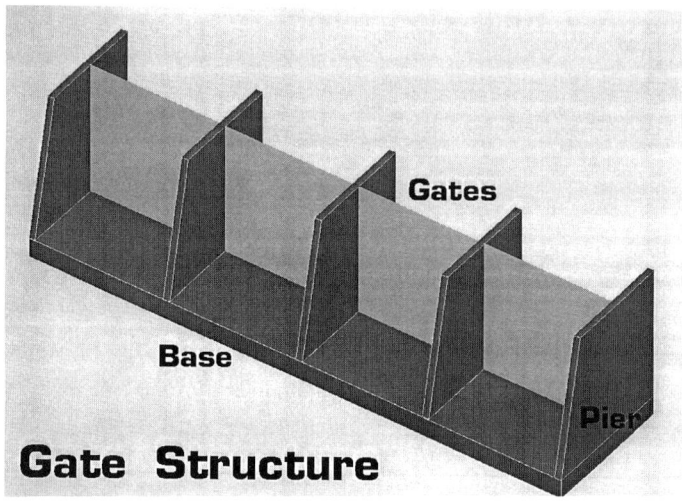

FIGURE 4. Gate structure module.

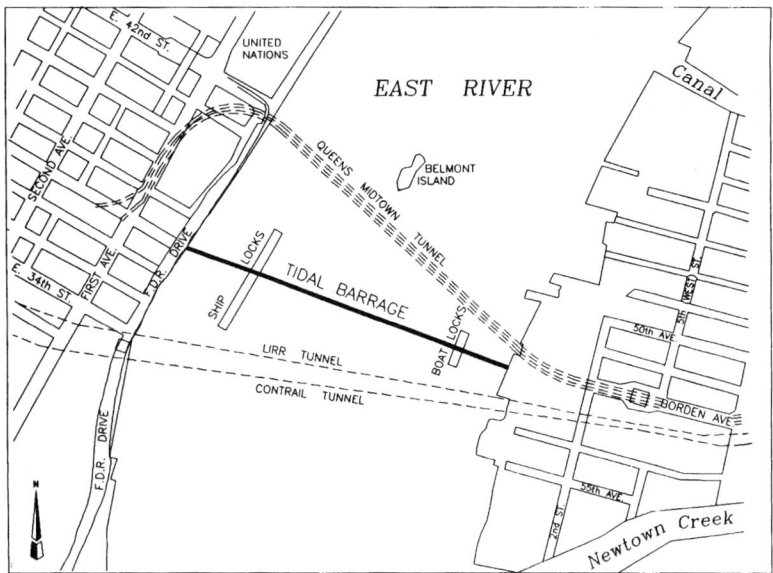

FIGURE 5. Possible mid-Manhattan location of the tidal barrage.

boaters. Maintenance of water-borne traffic, consequently, is a major consideration for design of an East River barrage.

Two pairs of locks are provided for navigation of vessels through the barrage; one pair for ships and the other for boats. The ship locks would be 80 feet wide and 1,000 feet long, and their related structures would consist of reinforced concrete caissons or cells. As in the case of the barrage structures, the caissons would be prefabricated off-site, floated to the project site, sunk and filled with sand to offset buoyancy. At the ends of the locks, temporary cofferdams will be built and the lock chambers would be dewatered to permit construction in the dry of the lock floor and the sills for the lock gates which will be held against hydrostatic uplift by piles or rock anchors. Stone will be placed along the exterior side of the lock walls for protecting the base of the structure against scour.

The boat locks would be 25 feet wide and 325 feet long, and their walls would consist of epoxy-coated steel-sheet pile cells filled with sand. Such cells would also be constructed at the ends of the locks to support a prefabricated reinforced concrete sill structure for the lock gates. The depth of water at the site of the boat locks will be considerably greater than the depth required for their navigation so that no floor would be constructed within these locks.

The smaller set of locks would be used frequently by barges and pleasure craft. The large ship locks are intended for the large tankers that come through intermittently and would not be required to operate very often. Here is what the system might look like (FIG. 6). The barrage extends from Hunters Point, Queens, to the Manhattan side, and includes two sets of ship locks and two sets of boat locks. The figure shows a ship, a barge, and some of the Manhattan skyline.

CONSTRUCTION COSTS AND SCHEDULE

The cost of construction entailed in the passive gate barrage concept is estimated to be on the order of one billion dollars. Implementation of the project, encompassing environmental evaluations, permit application processes, and engineering would take at least four years; the time frame for subsequent construction is estimated at about five years.

The most significant factors that will affect cost of the passive concept are actual conditions found at the selected crossing location including factors such as river width, soils, and shoreline configuration. If the passive system described here could not be adopted, costs of actively operated alternatives would be expected to be greater.

OTHER POTENTIAL BENEFITS

Should it be decided that the water quality benefits of the barrage warrant its construction, it would then be possible to consider additional

FIGURE 6. General view of tide gates and navigation locks at the midtown location.

applications for the resulting new East River crossing. Of course, additional uses for the barrage would be dependent upon its final location. At this time it appears that a mid-Manhattan location offers interesting multiple use options:

- Esplanade at either location considered here;
- Airport connector at mid-Manhattan location; and
- Light rail (trolley) connection from Long Island City to mid-Manhattan.

For illustration, we show an airport link starting near La Guardia Airport, moving down along some highway or railroad corridor to the Sunnyside railroad yards, and down the rail freight corridor to the Queens waterfront, over the barrage, and to a terminus around 34th Street (FIG. 7).

What might that look like on the barrage? The next illustration is of a monorail on the barrage structure (FIG. 8). The structure is fairly massive. In some ways you might say that the monorail or the rail connector or whatever kind of transit vehicle is envisioned gets a free ride; however, in our estimate we did not consider the cost of this additional feature.

And when you put it all together, there is a monorail going to midtown Manhattan on the barrage (see Frontispiece).

Just a few points. In our thinking, there is a fixed bridge over the

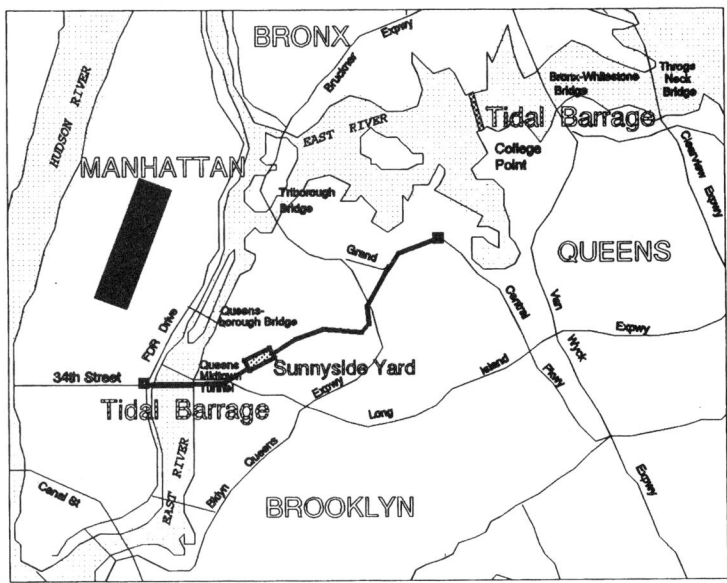

FIGURE 7. Route of airport transit link on the barrage.

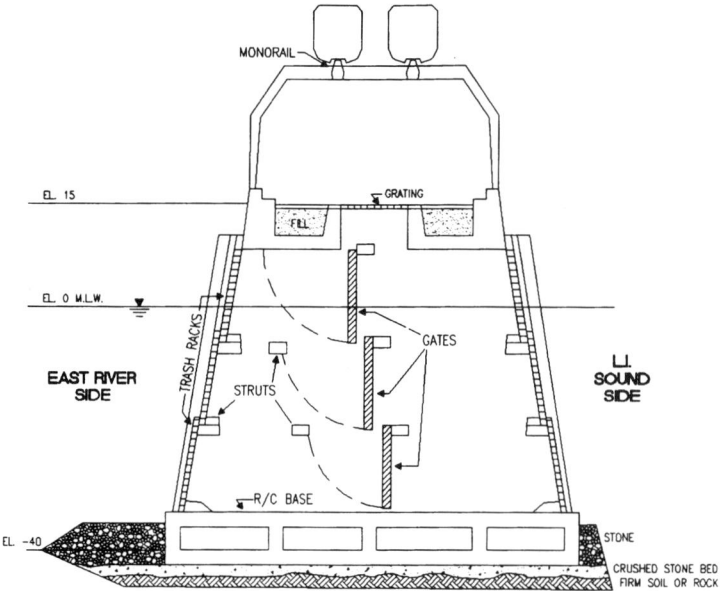

FIGURE 8. Typical cross section of gate structure with monorail.

small-boat locks. That is why there are small-boat locks in the first place. There would be sufficient clearance to keep that a fixed structure. You would need some kind of swing bridge over the large ship lock, because those vessels would be enormous. And finally there is a terminus shown here alongside or over the Franklin D. Roosevelt Drive for the rail service.

SIGNIFICANT DESIGN ISSUES

As has already been suggested, many design issues would have to be resolved before a preferred barrage system concept could be established. Some of these are listed here:

- An operating cycle must be determined which reflects both the intended water-quality benefits and constraints imposed by conditions within the East River;
- A preferred location must be established; location in turn will dictate design variables related to foundation and hydraulic conditions;
- The gate system must be selected based on detailed analysis including hydraulic and physical modeling; and
- A precise evaluation of river traffic must be conducted so that design parameters for ship and boat locks can be formulated.

DISCUSSION OF THE PAPER

QUESTION: I wonder if any consideration was given to ice load—wind-driven ice.

JOHN J. SZELIGOWSKI: Yes, we thought about that problem. The problem is ice coming down the river, which hasn't happened that frequently recently, but I can recall a few instances. I travel from Staten Island every day by ferry, and we have bumped into a lot of ice floes. Our structure is sufficiently massive, we think, to take some load from ice, but that would have to be really looked at far more carefully. By the way, this brings to mind one of the things that I promised myself I would do. Harry Ekezian, who has worked with TAMS for about 40 years and is now retired and a consulting engineer, came up with all these sketches and responses to most questions about that gate system, and he is in the audience. At some point, I may ask Harry to answer a question.

QUESTION: Can you describe for me a little about how the lock works? Is it a large structure: how long, how wide?

ALEX MATLIN: I addressed that in my presentation. If we build a lock for large ships, I suggest a chamber 700 feet long, 115 feet wide; for barges and tugs only: 400 feet long, 70 feet wide. That should do the job for ninety to ninety-five percent of the fleet.

SZELIGOWSKI: I don't know if I can add much to that. These locks would have entryways—like doors, essentially—at either end. And vessels would come through at all times. The locks would have to be operated whether the barrage was closed, and therefore blocking river flows, or open and flushing out the system. The ships would have to come through—in our thinking, at least—at all times. Even if you look at the devices that were proposed for Venice, while there are no structures associated with them, when they are up they are in the way. And these, as I guess the both of us understand it, are going to operate day-in and day-out. So they are going to be up half the time.

QUESTION: How would the high-frequency AGT (automated guideway transit) system be compatible with the cycle time for lock operation?

SZELIGOWSKI: Let me paraphrase that so I can answer it. The question really is, is there going to be problem with interference between shipping traffic and rail traffic if this location were adopted? The answer is, yes, it's a problem.

QUESTION: Was there any study made as far as the operating time of the locks?

SZELIGOWSKI: We haven't looked at it in that kind of detail, frankly. So I can't answer your question, I'm sorry.

Part IV

COMMENTARY

CHRISTIAN MEYER, *Chairman*

Infrastructure as Public Place

ANTHONY C. WEBSTER
Graduate School of Architecture
Columbia University
New York, New York 10027

INTRODUCTION

On balance, many infrastructure works have done more harm than good to the urban public realm. Transportation systems in particular have rent the fabric of America's cities, as they have provided efficient conduits for removing urban populations to surrounding rings of diffuse and atomized suburban sprawl. The situation in Boston's Charlestown district at the turn of the century illustrates the problems that trains have introduced into the urban environment. J. Anthony Lucas has captured the deleterious effects of that community's first train line.

> ... Charleston became a drab corridor through which goods and commuters poured in and out of Boston ... many of the passengers were from outlying suburbs, [and] often filled the inbound cabins, leaving no seats for Charlestown residents.
> Then, in 1901 came the elevated railway, which not only quadrupled the traffic passing through Charlestown but put much of it in shadow and split it into fragments on either side of the tracks. From the West End, the El screeched across the bridge to Charlestown's City Square, then up main street toward the suburbs. For long-range commuters, it was a blessing, ... for Charlestown it was a curse, a hissing monster which brought noise, dirt and darkness to the town.... Within ten years of its completion, the El had become an emblem of exploitation.[1]

More recently, making way for the automobile has often meant further dissection of America's urban environments, as well as degrading their air quality and increasing their noise levels. New York in particular has suffered from the "ringing" of its waterfront areas with "parkways" that block pedestrian access to the water. Robert Moses, in proposing the Henry Hudson Parkway on Manhattan's west side, pointed out that the city's residents, being able to drive along the water, would not have to leave town to experience a public amenity unequaled in the world.[2] Today, the roadway's impact seems less beneficial. Along much of Manhattan's upper west side, the elevated structure severs the waterfront from its adjacent neighborhoods, and makes access to the island's shores—except for the fleeting glance of the harried driver—virtually impossible over many long stretches.

The problems that infrastructure projects have created are particularly alarming because of their enduring nature. The location of railways, highways and most other public works are immutable for decades once established, and are a major factor in determining the quality of life for generations of nearby residents.

INFRASTRUCTURE'S MANY ROLES

With this in mind, it is gratifying that our most successful transport-infrastructure projects have a positive overall impact. Instead of dismembering urban environments or rendering a city's natural amenities inaccessible, these transportation-infrastructure projects have become—visually, symbolically, and spatially—some of our most important civic works. John and Washington Roebling's 1883 Brooklyn Bridge is a classic example (FIG. 1). Designed as a crucial transit link between the cities of New York and Brooklyn, the completed structure quickly took on a number of civic functions, which it still serves today. In addition to its role as an "intermodal" armature for auto and pedestrian traffic, the bridge is one of the world's most universally recognized urban icons. The structure is an elegant symbol of both man's technological prowess and the joining of Brooklyn and Manhattan into the whole of New York City. Finally, the bridge is also one of the most important spaces in the city, a destination for both tourists and natives—a place to loiter. At any given moment, the bridge's pedestrian occupants are as likely to be using it as an observatory—viewing the boat traffic below or the flanking skylines—as they are to be simply crossing the river.

In less densely populated settings, America's most interesting infrastructure works are magnets for nearby populations and travellers, cre-

FIGURE 1. Brooklyn Bridge. John and Washington Roebling, New York City. Pedestrian walk. Photo courtesy John Lopez, New York Metropolitan Transportation Council.

ating public islands in the wild. One of the most heroic examples is the Hoover Dam, completed in 1935 (FIG. 2). The structure's immense presence—its downstream face towering more than 220 meters above the Colorado River—restrains enough water to create the 640 square kilometer Lake Meade, and generates an average of 1.3 MegaWatts of electrical power. The dam's size, as well as the inviting body of water it creates, combine to draw an extraordinary number of tourists to an area described by Franklin Roosevelt as "a forbidding desert . . . [and] a cactus covered waste."[3] Despite its arid and remote setting, the dam drew "an astonishing three-quarters of a million visitors in 1935," and is visited by similar numbers of tourists today.

Man's attraction to his interventions in nature is not limited to works of heroic scale. As the modest presence of eastern Long Island's Shinnecock Tidal Barrier shows, even the smallest infrastructure works can draw us to them (FIG. 3). Completed in 1968 to replace a wooden tidal barrage, the 40 foot wide Shinnecock Barrier separates water levels differing by at most one meter, and is barely perceptible from a distance. The structure's tide gates regulate the passage of water between the Shinnecock and Great Peconic bays, and its lock allows the passage of small vessels at all times. Although the Barrier hosts many visitors, its civic aspirations are if anything less pretentious than its construction is modest. The Barrier's portable outhouse is one of its most prominent visual references, and its western waterside esplanade doubles as a parking lot. Despite its out-of-the-way location, simple operation, small

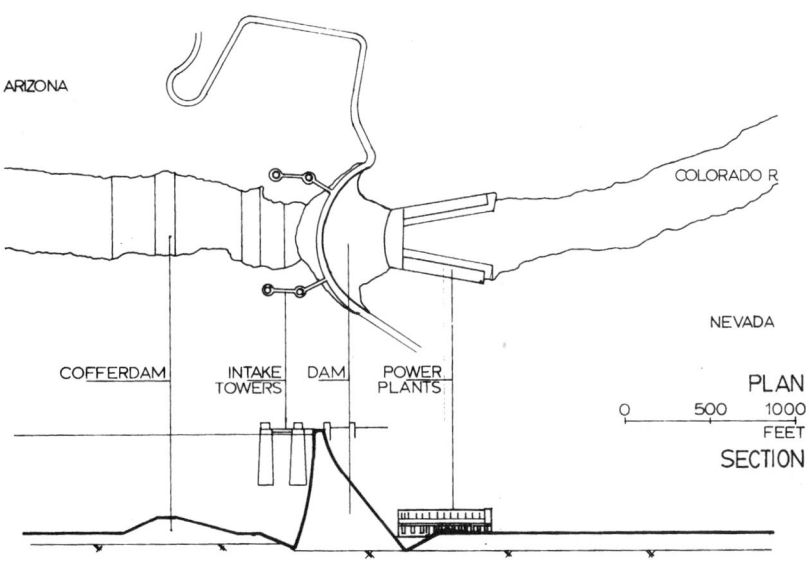

FIGURE 2. Hoover Dam, plan and section.

FIGURE 3. Shinnecock Tidal Barrier, general view.

size, and undesigned public place, the structure draws a fairly constant stream of visitors. Recreational fishermen standing on the Barrier's edge share the presence of man's intervention in nature as much as they share a spot for casting; casual observers evidence our seemingly endless fascination with the machines we use to manipulate the earth's natural forces.

Like the Brooklyn Bridge and the Hoover Dam, the Shinnecock is both a public amenity and a utilitarian object. But unlike these large-scale works, Shinnecock's modest presence belies its enormous usefulness. This unassuming structure is directly responsible for the high-quality water in Shinnecock Bay, and for maintaining the bay's connection to the Atlantic ocean.

As the area surrounding the Shinnecock Bay was developed in the 19th century, its outlet to the Atlantic was sealed off by sand deposits left by shifting tides (FIG. 4). Efforts to reopen the outlet proved fruitless. By 1890, nearby residents reported that the landlocked bay's waters "had become brackish . . . and unfavorable to the health and business of the people living in the neighborhood."[5] Soon after, New York State embarked on an effort to connect Shinnecock Bay with the Great Peconic Bay to the north—both to increase the Shinnecock's salinity and freshness, and to allow the passage of boats from the landlocked bay to Long Island Sound. In 1892, the state completed a two and one half mile canal between the Shinnecock and the Great Peconic Bays. In 1919, the state completed a wooden tide gate and lock system near the canal's mid-length. The tide gates controlled water flow between the two bays caused by tidal water-level fluctuations in the Peconic; the lock was included to allow for the passage of boats through the canal when the tide gates were closed.

In 1938 a hurricane re-opened an inlet between the Shinnecock Bay's Southern shore and the Atlantic (FIG. 4). In an effort to keep the inlet open, authorities manipulated the action of the tide-gates to flush the inlet with high velocity water after each tide.[6] The high tide at the Atlantic Ocean adjacent to the inlet precedes the high tide at the Peconic Bay side of the canal by about two hours. As high tide approached in the Peconic, the gates would be left open, raising the water level in the Shinnecock bay. At the tide's peak, the gates were closed, forcing the water that entered through the canal to exit via the inlet. Because the maximum average tidal difference in water level between the canal and the Atlantic is just less than a meter, water trapped in the Shinnecock by the tide gates would exit through the inlet rather quickly, scouring its edges and acting as a natural hydraulic dredge. The inlet's twice-daily scouring succeeded in keeping it open with almost no additional maintenance. Between the 1938 storm and 1964, about $110,000 was spent on dredging to keep the inlet navigable. Over the same period, $1,200,000 was spent on dredging the nearby Moriches inlet. Despite the large sum spent at Moriches, this inlet was often difficult to navigate or closed due to shoaling.

The post-hurricane manipulation of the Shinnecock tide gates to scour the inlet also ensured that the bay's waters were periodically flushed with clean, salt water from the Great Peconic. As Harrison Weber observes in his 1964 report to the Suffolk County Department of Public works, the beneficial effect on the Shinnecock's marine environment and local residents was dramatic:

FIGURE 4. Shinnecock Tidal Barrier, site plan.

Shinnecock Bay became alive and productive. Clams which previously grew to one half inch diameter before dying now grew rapidly to market size. A man who was willing to work hard could go clamming and earn $50 or more a day and many did. The bay also became [populated by] salt water fish, crabs and scallops.[6]

The 1968 replacement of the Shinnecock Canal's tidal barriers and lock did nothing to reduce their effectiveness. Today the tidal barrier still quietly performs the utilitarian functions of water quality improvement and automated inlet dredging, while acting as a focal point for recreation among the local population.

RECENT TRENDS IN INFRASTRUCTURE DEVELOPMENT

Unfortunately, the lessons of the best infrastructure projects have been largely ignored over the last decade. During this time, the federal infrastructure bureaucracy has seemed intent on—if not its own dissolution—at least the abdication of its roles as strategic planner and advocate of public works. Despite knowing as early as 1979, for example, that one fifth of the nation's auto bridges were unable to safely carry the loads they were designed for and the amount required to repair them was about $26 billion, the amount of federal funding allocated for their rehabilitation was set at $1 billion per year and remained grossly inadequate through the 1980's.[7]

The impotence of the many local governments to move new transportation projects forward during the same period is well symbolized by the decade-long gridlock over New York City's Westway project. The recent development of Donald Trump's Riverside South housing/transportation/park project in the same city underscores the concomitant inability of many local planners to initiate civic improvements. After New York's government did no more than put a stop to Trump's first, overscaled proposal for the site, a coalition of six civic groups worked with Trump to create a manageable plan for the area.[8] Their current proposal envisions re-routing the West Side Highway away from the water's edge and establishing a park extending from adjacent eastern neighborhoods to the waterfront. New York's state and city governments lent the project their support only after this proposal was developed by the private coalition.[a]

A couple of important developments stand in opposition to the general decline of infrastructure planning and design in the United States. Significantly, they also explicitly recognize the opportunities for creating public places that are inherent in many infrastructure projects, and they

---

[a]There is some evidence that New York's administration is currently trying to take a more active role in developing its public realm. Mayor Dinkens recently announced the "New York City Comprehensive Waterfront Plan." The plan includes provisions for redeveloping the city's waterfront, and aims to turn much of it into parkland.

include funding to exploit these opportunities. The "Intermodal Surface Transportation Efficiency Act (ISTEA)," written by Patrick Moynihan and signed into law in 1991, stakes out a forward-looking position for the nation's transportation infrastructure in both technical and civic terms.[9] The bill, which allocates spending of approximately $155 billion over the next six years, funds the development and redevelopment of transportation systems, and helps underwrite the cost of creating new technologies, such as mag-lev trains and intelligent vehicle highways.[10] Equally important, the bill includes funding for civic amenities, including the creation of public places associated with transportation nodes, the construction of bikeways, and the redevelopment of historic public-works-related structures.

Another important trend in infrastructure development is the tendency of public clients to actively solicit design proposals that serve a combination of utilitarian and civic functions. In 1989, for example, the city of Chichester in England capitalized on its need for increased parking to improve the area surrounding its historic, medieval cathedral district. In commissioning a parking structure for visitors to the cathedral district, the city rejected the obvious solution—to build a parking deck on the nearest piece of free land. It chose instead to work with the Royal Institute of British Architects to sponsor a competition for a combined parking/circulation system, to serve the needs and control the access of tourists into and out of the district. The winning design, by architects Birds, Portchmouth Russum, with engineers Ove Arup and Partners, addresses far more than the utilitarian functions of its car-park (FIG. 5). The circulation towers at the north end of the project visually mark four main parking zones with a color-coding scheme; the towers empty onto an elevated walkway that both echoes the medieval ramparts across the green and screens the parking structure from the historic district; the walkway extends over existing streets as a bridge, creating a dedicated pedestrian pathway to the walled city (FIG. 6). Taken as a whole, the Birds, Portchmouth Russum solution solves the utilitarian problem of parking while creating an new civic icon for Chichester, and establishing a new public promenade featuring the city's best view of its cathedral.[11]

The city of Minneapolis has similarly used the creation of its 1988 Whitney Pedestrian Bridge to repair the rent in its city fabric created by interstate I-94, while also creating a new public place (FIG. 7).[12] The bridge, conceptually designed by the artist Siah Armajani, spans over 16 lanes of freeway to connect the Walker Art Gallery's sculpture garden with a city park. In addition to being used as a transportation conduit by workers and museum-goers, the structure attracts "joggers, cyclists, lovers, tourists—everyone uses the bridge".[13] The bridge's benches and periodic outward bowing in plan invite lingering, making it a place to be as well as structure for transportation.

As programs like ISTEA take hold, as cities become increasingly aware of the potential for infrastructure projects to both serve utilitarian

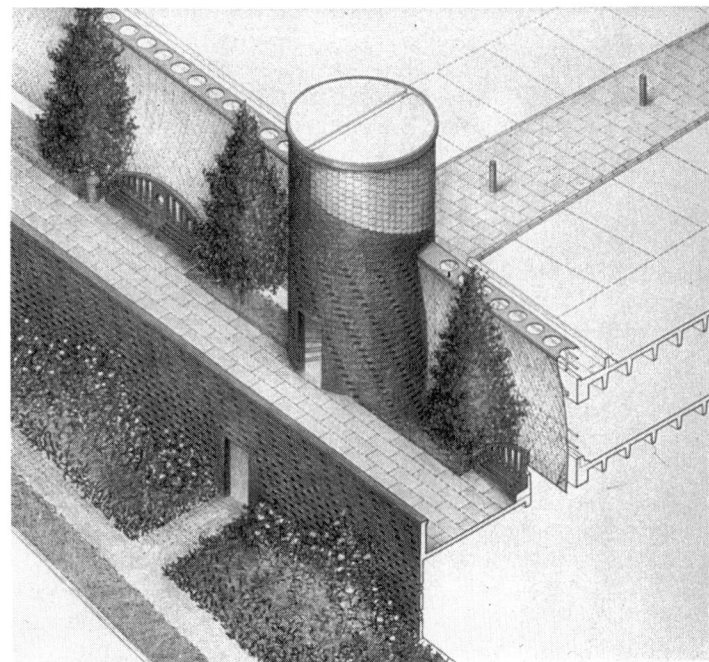

FIGURE 5. Carpark and walkway, Birds, Portchmouth Russum, Architects. Chichester, England. Cutaway view.

needs and to improve the public realm, and as tightened budgets require us to demand more bang from our infrastructure buck, the number of hybrid civic engineering projects will increase. Unfortunately, if past performance is a guide, the engineering community is not well prepared to accept this challenge.

A CRITIQUE OF THE INFRASTRUCTURE-DESIGN PROFESSIONS

Most engineers are trained as specialists and are narrowly focused, which makes it difficult for us to grapple with issues beyond the purely technical. Our narrow focus is largely caused by the increasing complexity of the field, and the wealth of technical information an engineer must master. Because there is so much to learn, it is commonly accepted that a structural engineer's technical education is just beginning when he completes his university studies. As the preeminent German engineer Joerg Schlaich points out: "At the end of his studies, an engineer is happy if he can [design] a beam on three supports in prestressed concrete. If

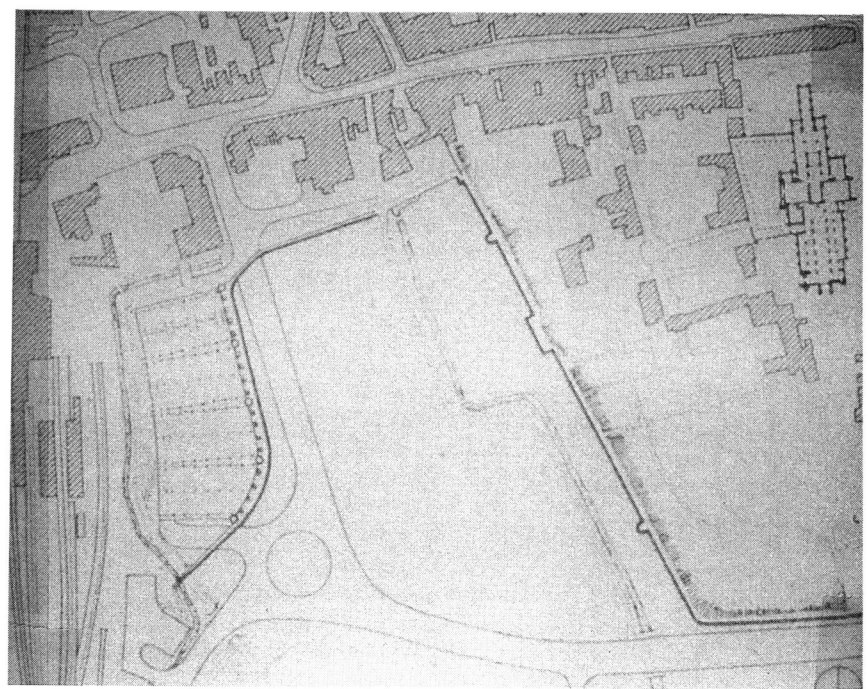

FIGURE 6. Carpark and walkway, Birds, Portchmouth Russum, Architects. Chichester, England. Site plan.

FIGURE 7. Whitney Pedestrian Bridge, designed by Siah Armajani. Gift of the Minneapolis Foundation/Irene Hixon Whitney Family Founder-Advisor Fund, the Persephone Foundation, and Wheelock Whitney, with additional support and services from the Federal Highway Administration, the Minnesota Department of Transportation, the City of Minneapolis, and the National Endowment for the Arts, 1988. Photo courtesy Walker Art Center, Minneapolis.

you introduce a cable or a complicated support, he will be lost."[14] Spending much of our careers mastering the technical facets of design leaves little time to become familiar with larger civic issues of program, casual circulation and formal composition.

Despite its enormous success as both a transportation link and a civic icon, the Brooklyn Bridge's continued failure to provide convenient pedestrian access underscores the problems that permeate even the best of our engineered infrastructure. Though the Roeblings' original design provided barely adequate movement on and off the bridge,[15] subsequent renovation of the bridge's pedestrian paths has made entering Manhattan even more difficult. Currently, there are two ways to descend from the structure to Manhattan by foot: via a decrepit, subterranean subway tunnel or along a concrete traffic island that ends abruptly at Centre Street's busy stream of traffic. This bizarre circulation system makes the processing from one of New York's civic icons to its downtown a confusing—if not frightening—experience. The fact that the structure remains such a popular place shows that man's attraction for heroic machines, civic monuments and great views sometimes overcomes even the most basic architectural design flaws.

If the Brooklyn Bridge epitomizes the engineer's perfunctory treatment of siting and circulation, the design of the 1931 George Washington Bridge shows that the limited participation of architects in civic transportation projects doesn't guarantee better results. The George Washington Bridge was designed by engineer O.H. Ammann, who retained architect Cass Gilbert to help develop the project's aesthetic and programmatic features. Gilbert's primary contributions include proposals for cladding the bridge's towers in granite and creating observatories at their tops. Both schemes were rejected by the Port of New York Authority as too costly.[16] While to present-day eyes the judgment against cladding the towers was lucky, the decision not to exploit the bridge for more than just transit seems unfortunate. Similarly disappointing is the fact that despite Gilbert's limited participation in the bridge's design, access to it by bicycle is—depending on what portion of the structure is being painted at the time—often impossible without mounting a long flight of stairs. Once on the bridge, a cyclist's (and a pedestrian's) experience is somewhat vitiated by the noise and fumes of the adjacent auto traffic. This problem could have easily been solved, as we will soon see, simply by moving the elevation of the bridge's walkways above the roadway. As constructed, the bridge sees a smaller number of recreational visitors than it might (and probably fewer than it should, considering its proximity to densely populated Manhattan neighborhoods), and amplifies its function as merely an armature for transport.

Not all infrastructure projects fall short of their civic potential when designed by engineers. The Spanish engineer Santiago Calatrava (who received a Doctorate of Technical Science from the ETH in Zurich in 1981) is well known for addressing a broad set of concerns in his bridge designs, and for producing works that transcend issues of engineering without disregarding them. In addition to being interesting as structures, Calatrava's bridges are both mega-sculptures and public places, as his double-arch Bach de Roda Bridge in Barcelona (FIG. 8) demonstrates. The 1987 structure was commissioned to bridge the gap in the city fabric cut by a rail line in the 19th century. Calatrava's design meets this goal, but it also goes much further—by using an inventive structural scheme to create a neighborhood focal point and gathering place.

In elevation, the choice of twin arches supporting a roadway by a set of suspender cables presented Calatrava with the structural achilles heel of this form: its susceptibility to buckling. In plan he was given the problem of resolving two arches that cross the train tracks below at a skewed (approximately 60 degree) angle. The buckling problem is often solved by a horizontally oriented truss between the main arches (FIG. 9). This solution applied to the skewed plan would certainly work structurally, but formally it would introduce a competing system, unrelated to the arches. Calatrava's solution to the structural problem was to place

FIGURE 8. Bach de Roda Bridge, Santiago Calatrava, Barcelona. General view.

FIGURE 9. Arched Roadway Bridge, showing lateral bracing system between arches.

secondary arches of equal height next to the main arches on either side of the bridge. The secondary arches lean inward from their base, beyond the bridge's edge, and are connected to the main arches by fins near their apex, thus bracing both arches against buckling. This resolution at once gives the bridge a unique three dimensional form, obviates the need to place a bracing truss between the two main arches, and allows the problem of skew to be solved by simply shifting the arches in plan.

The secondary arches also have a purely architectural purpose. Angled suspenders, lying in the plane of these arches, help support a pedestrian walkway at the roadway level. The walkway's edge is bowed outward in plan, reflecting the arch's elevation while creating a pedestrian plaza at the center of the bridge. The sloped suspender ropes at the walkway's edge and the main roadway suspenders themselves define the limits of the plaza in three dimensions. The concrete abutments of the secondary arches are flanked by concrete stairways, descending from the pedestrian platform to a park below. With the introduction of the pedestrian plazas and circulation system, Calatrava transforms, as Kenneth Frampton notes "the mere commission for a bridge into an occasion for creating a place."[17]

It is important to point out that Calatrava's synthetic ability to address technical, formal and programmatic issues is highly unusual. In addition to his extensive training as an engineer, Calatrava has a B.S. degree in architecture, and has spent years sketching, studying cities from an urban designer's perspective, and making models of his proposed designs. Most engineers and architects do not have the breadth of training, or arguably the talent, to take on the range of issues that Calatrava addresses singlehandedly.

As Birds, Portchmouth Russum's work in Chichester shows, for projects with modest technical requirements, architects and/or urban designers can be very successful in leading a collaborative design team. Similarly, large infrastructure projects with complicated technical requirements can address public functions when designed by a collaborative team led by engineers. London's 1982 Thames Barrier, designed by the engineering firm of Rendal, Palmer and Tritton, and the city's Department of Architecture and Civic Design, illustrates this (FIG. 10). The barrier was envisioned to prevent flooding 45 square miles of greater London, and from a technical point of view was ingeniously designed to meet this goal.[18] The structure includes a set of eight movable flood gates, set between seven piers and two abutments at either riverbank. The gates are shaped as circular sectors in section, and are rotated into open or closed positions by hydraulic pistons located in each pier. The gates' arc-like movement cleverly aides in the maintenance of the system in two ways: first, when partially opened, the gates create high velocity currents that scour the adjacent waterways, obviating the need for dredging; second, the gates can be rotated completely out of the water, which greatly simplifies their repair.

The Barrier's architects also made significant contributions to the project. At the industrial area adjacent to the barrier, they opened the waterfront up to the public. On the south bank of the Thames, the architects established a riverfront park, including a museum, a cafe overlooking the barrier, and extensive parking. The architects' contribution to the barrier itself was to create aluminum hoods set on each pier over the hydraulic pistons and the motors that power them. This decorative gesture makes a strangely mechanistic-yet-picturesque image, which appears as an uncomfortable collage of industrial-revolution-era machinery and Chinese junks.

Possibly despite the decorative hoods, the Thames Barrier has become one of London's civic icons. As Rex Barrow points out, it is considered by many to be "a fascinating addition to the Thames landmarks."[19] Although the barrier is appreciated directly by those visiting it, and celebrated at tourist shops in models and postcards, it is also a monumental reference to those entering the city from the sea. As the first prominent structure passed by boat when traveling up the Thames from the ocean, it is a gateway to London.

Somewhat surprisingly, some recent projects show that large-scale, technically challenging works can be generated successfully in both structural and civic terms when collaborative design teams are led by an

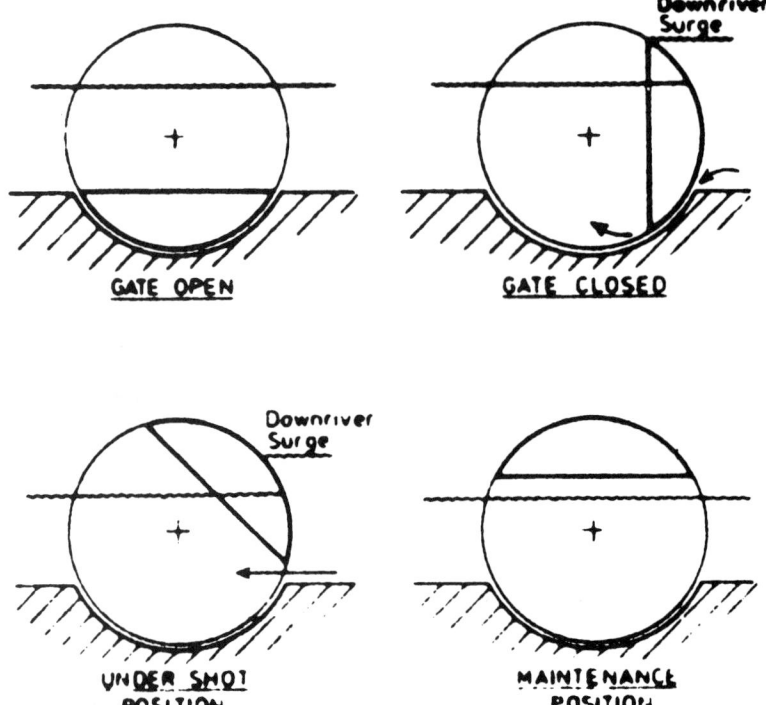

FIGURE 10. Thames Barrier, Rendal, Palmer and Tritton, and London's Department of Architecture and Civic Design. Detailed view and positioning of gates.

architect. An example is currently unfolding in St. Paul, MN in the replacement of the city's Wabasha Street Bridge. After a quick set of interviews, the city invited James Carpenter to design a replacement for the 150 year old bridge, which supports three traffic lanes and a crowded bike and pedestrian path. Carpenter, who trained as an architect at the Rhode Island School of Design before taking a degree in sculpture, has retained Joerg Schlaich to help develop the structure's technical details—including its overall structural system and the materials and forms of its connections—while generating the bridge's circulation system and overall silhouette himself.

Carpenter's proposed cable-stayed bridge would cross the Mississippi river with four lanes of auto traffic, as well as two pedestrian and two bicycle lanes (FIG. 11). The design would separate motorized traffic from pedestrians and bicycles by lifting the latter above the roadway for most of the bridge's length—improving both the air quality and noise levels for pedestrians and cyclists. It also would provide a pedestrian connection to a currently inaccessible island in the middle of the waterway, which is expected to feature riverside promenades and playing fields for various sports. Finally, the bridge's unique form rises high enough above the river and most of the city's monotonous skyline to create a new urban landmark.

By awarding the Wabasha commission to a designer whose strengths

FIGURE 11. Wabasha Street Bridge, James Carpenter and Joerg Schlaich, St.Paul, MN. General view of model.

are in the creation of form and space, St. Paul has implicitly decided to improve not just its transportation infrastructure, but also to create a new civic icon, improve the accessibility of its city to its pedestrians and cyclists, and make better use of its island waterfront. By working with one of the world's pre-eminent bridge engineers, Carpenter in turn ensures that his design will meet its crucial structural needs equally as well as it performs its public functions.

CONCLUSION

As America's infrastructure continues to crumble, as our funds become increasingly limited, and as we renew our interest in the public realm, the potential for civic engineering works to serve as community icons and public places should not go untapped. Some of our best existing infrastructure works give clues as to how we might proceed at this unique moment: the success of the Thames Barrier and the Shinnecock Tide Gates as icons and public-attracting magnets, respectively, demonstrates the large amount of public good to be reaped from a modest infusion of civic provisions; Calatrava's work shows that in suturing the rifts left by earlier infrastructure growth, we can create new urban focal points; Carpenter's and Birds, Portchmouth Russum's projects illustrate that collaborative teams of architects and engineers can produce projects meeting a broad range of utilitarian and civic needs; maybe most importantly (and probably underemphasized in this paper), the Shinnecock Barrier demonstrates that infrastructure development and environmental enhancement are not mutually exclusive.

Proposed projects like the East River Tidal Barrage can exploit all of these lessons in improving America's urban centers. The East River project in particular has the potential to improve the region's water quality, create a new transit link, and increase access to the waterfront along Manhattan's congested shores. For these reasons it deserves to be further explored. If recent history is any indicator, neither the local nor the federal governments can be expected to pursue the project. Similarly, if it is developed by the engineering community alone it stands a good chance of falling short of its civic potential. For the Barrage project to move forward successfully, the engineering profession needs to proactively pursue it, working collaboratively with the architectural, urban design and scientific communities. This process, combined with public debate on the structure's merits, would maximize both the possibility of its realization and the benefits it could provide to New York City.

REFERENCES

1. LUCAS, J. A. 1985. Common Ground. New York: Random House. p. 78.
2. CARO, R. 1974. The Power Broker. New York: Knopf. p.343

3. "PRESIDENT ROOSEVELT DEDICATES BOULDER DAM." 1935. Reclamation Era. October: 1935 *Quoted in* Stevens 1988.
4. STEVENS, J.E. 1988. Hoover Dam: An American Adventure. University of Oklahoma Press.
5. History of New York Canals. 1905. Supplement to the report of the State Engineer and Surveyor—1905. Chapter XII. *Quoted in* Weber, H. 1964. Report on preliminary plans for new Shinnecock Canal locks. Prepared for the Suffolk County Department of Public Works, July 30.
6. WEBER, H. 1964. Report on preliminary plans for new Shinnecock Canal locks. Unpublished report prepared for the Suffolk County Department of Public Works. July 30.
7. ABRAMSON, M. 1979. Deathtrap bridges—a national disgrace. The Bergen Record (New Jersey), January 7.
8. DAVIDOFF, L. 1993. Executive Director of the New York City Parks Council. Phone interview. April 5.
9. PLUNGIS, J. 1992. Transportation's New Deal. Empire State Report. May: 33–36.
10. A Summary: Intermodal Surface Transportation Efficiency Act of 1991. 1992. U.S. Department of Transportation. (a brochure).
11. SWENARTON, M. 1991. City of towers: Birds, Portchmouth Russum at Chichester. Architecture Today. April: 25–30.
12. LASSAR, T. 1990. Bridges as artful spaces. Urban Land. November: 32, 33.
13. TOMKINS, C. 1990. Open, available, useful. The New Yorker, March 19: 48–72.
14. GANS, D. *et al.*, Eds. 1990. Bridging the Gap: Rethinking the Relationship of Architect and Engineer. New York: Van Nostrand Reinhold. p. 162.
15. MCCULLOUGH, D. 1972. The Great Bridge. New York: Simon & Shuster. pp. 543, 544.
16. AMMANN, O. H. 1933. General conception and development of design. *In* George Washington Bridge Across the Hudson River. Port of New York Authority, Eds. American Society of Civil Engineers. pp. 51–56.
17. BLASER, W. Ed. 1989. Santiago Calatrava: Engineering Architecture. Basel: Birkhouser, p. 17.
18. KENDRICK, M. 1988. The Thames Barrier. Landscape and Urban Planning **16:** 57–68.
19. BURROW, R. 1986. Some UK achievements in bridges, buildings and other structures. Concrete. January: 10–14.

DISCUSSION OF THE PAPER

CHARLOTTE FAHN: I represent the Parks Council. I would just like to thank you for calling attention to the connection between parks and infrastructure, because there are fewer and fewer opportunities to create parks and public open space today in the traditional way. The more the engineering community becomes aware of the possibilities, and that there is a whole community of parks people in the city looking to work on this effort, the better for both groups.

ANTHONY WEBSTER: I thank you, and I agree with you, obviously. I think in particular of this ISTEA legislation and the efforts of Richard Schaffer and the planning commission to get the waterfront proposal going. This project has a lot of potential to speak to many civic issues.

Prospects of Tidal Electricity Generation

GEORGE BIRMAN

Consulting Engineer
422 East 58th Street
New York, New York 10022

The New York Power Authority (NYPA) undertook in the early 1980s a research project to harness the kinetic energy in free-flowing waters. The goal was to build a device that could convert the kinetic energy in free flowing water to electrical energy. New York University (NYU) was contracted to design, fabricate and test the device. In essence, the hydro energy conversion system (KHECS) is an underwater windmill where the free flowing water drives a propeller-equipped shaft coupled to an electric generator.

Model tests were conducted at the David Taylor Naval Ship Research and Development Center to find the optimum shape and configuration of the propeller blades. The most promising and efficient blade configuration was a three-bladed axial flow propeller. The tests were conducted at various water velocities. The recorded data were shaft RPM and the corresponding shaft torque at different water speeds. The tests confirmed the "cube law" relationship between the water velocity and the power output (FIG. 1). As the water velocity is doubled, the power output increases eightfold.

Based on the results of the model testing, NYU undertook the design and fabrication of a prototype KHECS. This prototype was intended to be installed in the East River at the Roosevelt Island Bridge (FIG. 2). The output of this prototype device was estimated to be about 30 kilowatts at the tidal river velocity of 6.9 feet per second. Since the tides reverse every six hours, the design had incorporated a special rotary bearing that allowed the device to turn 180 degrees when the tides are reversing.

The design was completed, and the device was fabricated and assembled at a shop in New Jersey. Some preliminary testing was performed at the shop. At this point, some contractual and budgetary problems arose and the project was cancelled. When President Reagan approved the construction of the Superconducting Supercollider, many smaller

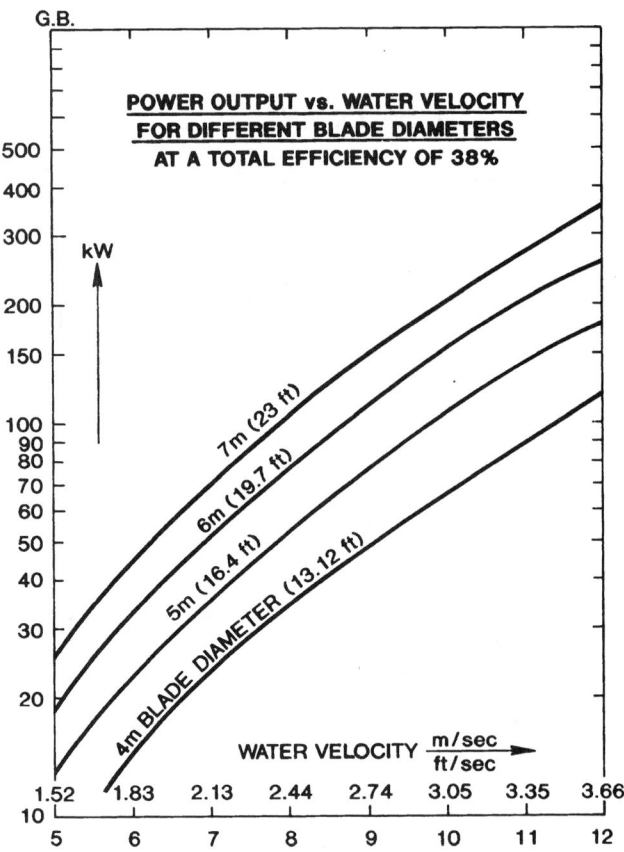

FIGURE 1. Power output vs. water velocity for different blade diameters of an underwater turbine.

projects supported by the U.S. Department of Energy were dropped. The device was disassembled and stored at NYPA.

In 1987, the London-based foundation New Emerging Sciences and Technologies (NEST) showed strong interest in the project. They obtained the KHECS on a loan basis and financed the testing of it in Pakistan. New supporting structures were designed, and part of the testing program was performed in November 1989 at the exit waters of a hydroelectric power plant in Pakistan. The final testing was to be conducted in the fall of 1992, but owing to heavy rains and flooding the testing was postponed.

FIGURE 2. How underwater generator would work.

DISCUSSION OF THE PAPER

QUESTION: If I am correct, that's a quarter of the time, or one-eighth of the time for a half cycle with the barrier in position?

GEORGE BIRMAN: We could turn 180 degrees.

QUESTIONER: There is no flow the other way.

BIRMAN: In this case, it will be one-eighth, you are right.

QUESTIONER: You would get maybe a maximum for average production half of that, maybe 8 kilowatt-hours per day per unit. Would that pay for itself?

BIRMAN: That's the big question.

Permitting the East River Tidal Barrage

JAMES W. HAGGERTY
New York District
U.S. Army Corps of Engineers
26 Federal Plaza
New York, New York 10278-0090

I wish to thank you for the opportunity to provide comments from the regulatory perspective of the Corps of Engineers with respect to the proposed East River Tidal Barrage. My comments will be very brief since my colleagues, Bob Will and Lynn Bocamazo, spelled out earlier the myriad concerns associated with this proposal and to rehash them here would be repetitive.

Although no formal determination has yet been made, it would appear that a Federal Environmental Impact Statement would be likely for this proposal. This would be to satisfy the requirements of the National Environmental Policy Act of 1969. An Environmental Impact Statement is necessary if an action that is licensed, proposed or permitted by a Federal agency is likely to cause significant impacts to the human environment.

There are several major areas of concern that would necessitate careful evaluation if a permit application for this work is submitted. It is possible that the proposed tidal barrage may meet the definition of a "dam" under the Rivers & Harbors Act of 1899. If this is considered a dam, authorization could not be issued by the Corps of Engineers. Rather, this would require Congressional authorization. The structure may also be considered a bridge, in which case authorization would be necessary from the U.S. Coast Guard. Under this scenario, the Corps of Engineers would regulate any discharge of dredged or fill material into the waterway while the Coast Guard would have jurisdiction for permitting the structure itself.

Regardless of whether this project will require authorization from Congress or the Coast Guard, the Corps of Engineers would be seriously concerned about navigational impacts associated with the proposed structure. Protection of navigational interests has long been a primary responsibility of the Corps' Regulatory Program. It was the sole focus of the program until the late 1960s after which time the program was expanded to consider a full range of public interest factors. However, since most other regulatory agencies do not consider navigation as part of their decisions to issue permits, this remains one of the major aspects of the Corps' Regulatory Program. Navigational concerns are paramount in heavily used commercial waterways such as the East River, and in fact a Department of the Army permit cannot be issued for any structure or work which would, in our judgment, cause undue interference with navigation. A formal determination in this regard would be made as part of our review of a permit application for the proposed tidal barrage.

An additional item of navigational concern which is not part of the regulatory purview is the fact that depending upon the exact location of the proposed tidal barrage, the sedimentation rate in the East River is likely to increase. At present, the Federal Navigation Channel in the East River requires little maintenance since rapid currents result in little sedimentation. Installation of the proposed tidal barrage would likely result in an increased need to perform maintenance dredging of the channel in the East River at taxpayer expense. This issue, along with many others associated with navigation, would have to be carefully evaluated as part of any permit application and/or environmental impact statement.

As part of the regulatory process, the project would be reviewed at the Federal level by the U.S. Environmental Protection Agency, the National Marine Fisheries Service of the U.S. Department of Commerce, and the Fish & Wildlife Service of the U.S. Department of the Interior. These agencies would likely be invited to serve as cooperating agencies in the preparation of an Environmental Impact Statement and their views regarding the proposal would be given serious consideration as part of the ultimate decision on the application. Their views could consist of recommendations of permit denial or conditions to be included in a Department of the Army permit aimed at mitigating adverse impacts upon the aquatic environment. The recognized expertise of these agencies makes their input extremely valuable to the regulatory process. We would also invite and welcome any comments that the U.S. Coast Guard would have to this proposal.

Pursuant to the Coastal Zone Management Act, a Department of the Army permit could not be issued until and unless the proposal is found to be consistent with the Coastal Zone Management Program of the State of New York. The state agency charged with administering this program is the New York State Department of State. Also, if the project included work regulated pursuant to Section 404 of the Clean Water Act, a permit could not be issued until and unless the New York State Department of Environmental Conservation issues a water quality certificate as provided for in Section 401 of the Clean Water Act.

In closing, I wish to emphasize that the Regulatory Program of the Corps of Engineers is neither an advocate nor an opponent of this proposal. My comments presented today constitute an assessment of some major issues that are expected to arise with respect to this project and are based upon my experience gained by working for the Regulatory Program during the past eight years. A project of this nature and scope is unprecedented within the regulatory boundaries of the New York District, Corps of Engineers, and the many issues associated with this proposal would require an extremely careful review.

DISCUSSION OF THE PAPER

VINCENT BLACK: I'm just wondering: how long do you think this would take?

JAMES W. HAGGERTY: I take the Fifth Amendment. When you are talking environmental impact statement, quite frankly, it's years. It also depends upon how you measure time. Do you measure time from the submission of the permit application which may be several years away? Or do you measure the time lapse from today? Now, if you measure it from today, obviously it is going to be a few years. With a permit application, from the time it is submitted, it is still unpredictable. We are still constrained by requirements to get permits from the New York State Department of Environmental Conservation and clearance from the New York State Department of State, but anything that requires an environmental impact statement, which we feel this probably would require, would probably take several years.

QUESTION: I'm wondering on this increased dredging, if you have any idea how East River dredging project would compare to the existing project that you have now.

HAGGERTY: Well, the existing project, as I have heard, doesn't require much in the way of maintenance. One of the speakers earlier I think alluded to potentially having a difference in the mean low water line. That could result in the need to deepen the channel, and in some areas that would involve going down to bedrock and blasting. I don't know what that would all involve though, because that's beyond my area of expertise.

QUESTION: As you said, the Corps started looking at navigational issues. A lot of the focus has been on commercial navigation. Would you ever look at changes that affect sailboaters, recreational users of the Sound? For example, what would a change in circulation patterns do to boating in Long Island Sound? Is that part of your view?

HAGGERTY: Any aspect of the project that has any kind of impact is relevant to our review. I just mentioned navigation because that is something that is near and dear to our hearts, but any kind of impact has to be evaluated. And if there is an environmental impact statement, that's all going to have to be included if it is going to be an impact to the proposal, whether it is a direct or secondary impact.

Some Initial Thoughts from a Member of The Environmental Community

TIMOTHY D. SEARCHINGER[a]

Environmental Defense Fund
257 Park Avenue South
New York, New York 10010

This paper presents the preliminary thoughts of one member of the environmental community about the proposal to construct a tidal barrage across the East River to help address water quality problems in Long Island Sound. It raises environmental concerns, legal obstacles, and alternative strategies for addressing the hypoxia problems in the Sound.

GENERAL OBSERVATIONS ABOUT LARGE-SCALE INTERFERENCE WITH NATURAL HYDROLOGY

What is the initial reaction of a member of an environmental organization? Frankly, the initial reaction is considerable skepticism. Many projects have modified nature ostensibly to make a natural ecosystem more able to tolerate the stresses of man. Often these projects have "solved" one problem only by creating many others. Natural systems in general have demonstrated time and time again how little humans fully understand them.

One example with which I am personally familiar is the Everglades.[b] Under natural conditions, the Everglades were a wetland roughly forty miles wide and a hundred miles long in which water flowed slowly south down the south Florida peninsula from Lake Okeechobee into Florida Bay. A variety of small scale drainage projects had begun to disrupt the system even by 1940. In the late 1940s, the Army Corps of Engineers did a study that planned to channelize the Everglades into a series of hundreds of miles of canals and huge pumps. Although a large purpose of that effort was to provide drainage for agriculture and water supply for both agriculture and urban areas, the Army Corps of Engineers argued at the time that the changes would be beneficial for the Everglades. According to the Corps, this managed system would prevent flooding of the system in high rainfall years, and supply water to Everglades National Park, at the bottom of the system, in low rainfall years.

[a]Currently in the Washington D.C. Office of EDF; Tel: (202) 387-3500.
[b]For scientific discussion of the Everglades problems discussed in this paper, see Davis and Ogden.[1]

In fact, the result has been catastrophic. The Everglades are now home to roughly two dozen endangered or threatened species. Breeding populations of the wading birds that once made the Everglades famous have declined by more than 90% in 50 years. Alligator and fish populations have shrunk, and the low water levels have allowed a massive invasion by non-native tree species that in turn further dry up the Everglades.

In 1970, concerned that Everglades National Park was simply not getting enough water, Congress mandated a minimum flow of water into Everglades National Park. At the time, scientists thought that would take care of many of the problems. But that amount not only turned out to be insufficient, it also turned out to disregard the importance of when the water flowed. The Everglades system is highly dependent on a seasonal pattern of water flow in which high water levels in the wet winter season gradually taper off in the dry summer. As water levels decline, fish are concentrated in shallow pools, which allows wading birds to feed during breeding without traveling long distances. The result of this minimum flow system actually turned out to be large discharges at the wrong time that further exacerbated wildlife problems.

Neither is the disturbance confined to the mainland. Water flowing south into the Everglades eventually reached Florida Bay, a semi-estuary that has historically supported abundant fisheries nestled in large seagrass beds. The alteration in the flow of water into the Bay has resulted in increased salinities over most of the Bay most of the time, supplemented by occasional bursts of freshwater flow into one inlet during flood periods. In recent years, scientists have linked those salinity changes to massive declines in the Bay including huge die-off of seagrasses, the decimation of sponge populations, and the loss of fish and shrimp populations.

A relevant issue here is that the impact of the loss of fresh water on the Bay was not at all obvious. The Bay has naturally high salt concentrations, and seagrasses can generally tolerate those concentrations. In addition, flow from the Everglades contributes only a few percent of the total freshwater to the Bay, most of which comes from rainfall. But the loss of fresh water flows has apparently led to more spikes of hypersalinity. Although sea grasses are tolerant of high salt concentrations, these spikes have crowded out many species of sea grasses and left only one, still stressed, species. A virus has now hit that species, and the virus is the proximate cause of a massive seagrass die-off. In turn that die-off has led to the release of nutrients into the water and large algae blooms over half of the Bay that have further caused declines in the sea grasses and other marine life.

Another non-obvious impact of the loss of a natural fresh water flow has been the decline of the pink shrimp. Historically Florida's largest shrimp fishery located in the Dry Tortugas has supplied tens of millions of dollars to the local economy. Scientists started noticing that years of low freshwater discharges corresponded to years of low shrimp catches. That correlation was puzzling because the pink shrimp did not seem to have a negative reaction to high salinity. It turns out that the pink shrimp navigate hundreds of miles from the Tortugas into the near coastal areas off the Everglades using the inflow of fresh water as a navigational device. Loss of that navigational aide is apparently the primary cause in the decline of these pink shrimp.

The Everglades have received a relatively large commitment of resources for ecological study. Despite these studies, a consensus has now emerged that scientists cannot determine the needed hydrology from what they know about individual species. Instead, the only way to restore the Everglades is to attempt to understand the way water naturally flowed, and then to replicate that natural flow as much as feasible.

The Everglades provides only one example of the kinds of harmful effects that have befallen aquatic ecosystems from severe changes in the natural hydrology. Science does not know very much about the dependence of different species of plants and animals on natural hydrological patterns. Science may only know that those patterns seem to be important in the evolution of the ecosystems that are out there. That suggests humility about mankind's ability to predict the impacts of large-scale hydrologic structures. In part for this reason, a report on aquatic ecosystem restoration by the National Academy of Sciences last year adopted a definition of restoration that emphasizes restoring natural hydrology.[c]

ENVIRONMENTAL CONCERNS WITH EAST RIVER TIDAL BARRAGE

How do these general observations apply to the East River Tidal Barrage? The preliminary modeling by Malcolm Bowman and Hydroqual indicates a large increase in the net quantity of water flowing into Long Island Sound from the Race, although that increase is apparently small by comparison with the total flows in the tidal cycle. The modeling also indicates a large increase in the quantity of flow from the Sound into the East River and through the Battery. If I understand it, the incoming water would be cooler, saltier and denser. Presumably the Sound would then heat up and cool off more slowly. The barrage would also cause a large decrease in the flux of sediment from the Sound into the Harbor, and potentially a large increase in the quantity of sediment settling in at least the East River. These changes raise several obvious questions.

- How would these changes impact larval forms of finfish and shellfish?
- What impacts might these changes have on the navigational tools available to migrating fish populations?

[c]National Research Council, Committee on Restoration of Aquatic Ecosystems: Science, Technology and Public Policy, National Academy of Sciences[2]: "In this report, restoration is defined as the return of an ecosystem to a close approximation of its condition prior to disturbance . . . The goal is to emulate a natural, functioning, self-regulating system that is integrated with the ecological landscape in which it occurs."

- What impacts might the increased salinity have on the full range of aquatic life?
- How would the salinity change in the tidal portions of the major tributary rivers, and what impact would those changes have on their aquatic life?
- Would the circulation changes affect the New York Bight in ways that would impact marine life?
- Even regarding the intended objective of addresses Long Island Sound hypoxia, what impacts would changed water temperatures and density have on the pynocline and its impacts on hypoxia?

A large category of concerns is whether a tidal barrage would simply move the nutrient problem elsewhere. The HydroQual modeling indicates that the barrage would decrease dissolved oxygen in some parts of the New York Harbor. Even unaffected parts of the harbor are probably unaffected because they are light-limited rather than nutrient-limited and that could change if those parts become less turbid as a result of other pollution controls.

Perhaps more importantly, the New York Bight from Apex down the New Jersey shore has also suffered bouts of hypoxia. Algae blooms apparently tend to form every year. Whether they cause hypoxic conditions in the Bight in any given year depends primarily on wind patterns and resulting hydrodynamics.

These environmental issues, which are probably only a partial category of those relevant, assures that any tidal barrage could only follow after years of scientific analysis. In addition to the environmental issues, there are obvious questions of navigation, and potentially impacts on boating recreation. A significant question is whether science could ever resolve the uncertainties sufficiently to allow a conclusion that the overall environmental impact of the barrage would be better rather than worse.

LEGAL CONSTRAINTS ON THE TIDAL BARRAGE

The large uncertainties inherent in a barrage proposal have particular significance because of the substantial legal hurdles a barrage would face. I provide only a partial list here.

Under Section 9 of the Rivers and Harbors Act of 1899, 33 U.S.C. Section 401, the tidal barrage would require approval by an act of Congress.[d] At the very least, that would undoubtedly require a substantial

[d]Section 9 reads as follows: "This it shall not be lawful to construct or commence the construction of any bridge, dam, dike, or causeway over or in any port, roadstead, haven, harbor, canal, navigable river, or other navigable water of the United States until the consent of Congress to the building of such structures shall have been obtained and until the plans for the same have been submitted to and approved by the Chief of Engineers and by the Secretary of War . . . "

consensus among the legislators of Connecticut, New York and New Jersey.

In addition, both Section 9 of the Rivers and Harbors Act and Section 404 of the Clean Water Act, 33 U.S.C. Section 1344, require a permit from the Army Corps of Engineers. That permit would require consultation with the National Marine Fisheries Service, the Environmental Protection Agency, and the U.S. Fish and Wildlife Service. The regulations of the Corps provide a fairly general public interest review for such a permit. However, the applicant would have to establish that it is not practicable to use reasonable alternative methods to accomplish the purpose of the structure, in other words, that it is not reasonable to address the water quality problems in other ways. The Environmental Protection Agency also retains the right to veto any application.

The structure would also require a variety of state approvals. The New York State Department of Environmental Conservation would have to certify that the project would not lead to violations of water quality standards. In addition, if New Jersey or Connecticut objected to the project, each would have the right to a hearing before the Army Corps of Engineers regarding whether the project would violate that state's water quality standards.

Depending on where the barrage is sited, it would probably also require a New York State tidal wetland permit (6 N.Y.C.R.R. Part 661). Flooding impacts from raised water levels might also trigger liability, and would require state review of potential impacts (New York Environmental Conservation Law Sec. 36-0111).

As a part of all these reviews, the applications would also have to satisfy requirements for general environmental review. Those include the National Environmental Policy Act, and the New York State Environmental Quality Review Act. Both impose the requirement of a comprehensive environmental impact statement. The state law also has a substantive component that requires a broadbased consideration of environmental factors in the formulation of a decision.

In addition to these requirements, approval would also have to come from New York City authorities. That would require following at least the Uniform Land Use Review process established by the New York City Charter. It sets forth a variety of procedural requirements and could potentially require a favorable vote from the New York City Council.

ALTERNATIVES TO A TIDAL BARRAGE

New York City Sewage Treatment

The variety of these legal and environmental issues suggest that the tidal barrage faces serious obstacles. That compels an examination of alternatives, in particular the alternative of reducing human sources of nitrogen. I believe a crucial premise behind the tidal barrage is not valid: namely, that the cost of removing nutrients is overwhelming.

Unlike other eutrophic estuaries, the Environmental Protection Agency estimates that point sources supply the majority of the nutrients into Long Island Sound. According to the Long Island Sound study, 50% of the human-enriched lode of nitrogen is discharged from sewage treatment plants, and another 8% results from point source discharges in the tributaries.[4] In addition, the study identifies 21% of the load in flows from the Race and below the Battery, much of which also comes from point source discharges to other coastal waters. Compared to other estuaries, the present estimates therefore point us strongly toward point sources.

Most of the direct point source inputs come from New York City's sewage treatment plants, and New York City has provided the most horrific cost estimate for reducing those discharges. It presently estimates a costs of $6 to $7 billion to retrofit only its six plants that discharge into the East River and Sound to meet concentration limits of 3 to 5 milligrams per liter.[5] Although the numbers vary from year to year, that would represent a two thirds to three quarter reduction in load. New York based these estimates on technological assumptions that meeting these levels would require a massive expansion of sewage treatment plants.

In particular, the City assumed that to reach those discharge levels, aeration tanks probably would have to provide twelve hours of detention time, final clarifying tanks would be greatly expanded, and large sand polishing filters would have to be constructed. These technical assumptions were particularly onerous for New York City because its plants now have unusually short retention times, and some are as low as three and a half hours. The City's assumptions therefore called effectively for as much as quadrupling the size of core components of the plants. The costs were particularly high because most of these plants face severe site restraints, in some cases requiring expensive construction of pilings to fit the new structures onto the plants.

Even without any new technologies, the City's assumptions represent overkill. Many sewage treatment plants have achieved high levels of nitrogen removal with far shorter detention times and without sand filters. More importantly, technologies employed in Europe have indicated a substantial possibility that New York could achieve desired levels of nutrient reduction with only limited additional structures.

Secondary treatment works by mixing sewage in a high oxygen tank with recycled sludge. Biological nutrient removal essentially requires that ammonia in the influent be converted first to nitrate by using particularly high oxygen levels and sludge concentrations, and then broken down into nitrogen gas by moving it through low oxygen areas. Low temperatures decrease the reaction rates involved in the nitrification process and make cold weather the particularly problematic period. The costs of nutrient removal under conventional efforts arise from the need to increase the detention times in the aeration tanks and the need to increase sludge concentrations (the mean cell retention times), which in turn requires larger final clarifying tanks in which the sludge settles.

Alternative technologies essentially focus on efforts to increase the concentration of microorganisms in particular ways and particular parts of the plant to achieve more rapid nitrification or denitrification, and to do so without increasing the need for final settling tanks. Another important variable involves the exact location of denitrification. Nitrification must occur before denitrification, but by recycling water through the plant, denitrifying areas can actually be placed first, and that has many potential benefits. Additionally, wastewater can be rerun through the plants several times under the theory that more nitrification/denitrification cycles at shorter times may work better than one cycle with a longer time.

In Europe, several sewage treatment plants have successively accomplished these objectives by adding synthetic plastic materials (in the form of ropes or cubes) into the aeration tanks—so called fixed film media. They allow a build-up of microorganism levels that permit a higher level of reaction. That in turn reduces the need for detention time, and, because much of the sludge remains attached to the media, reduces the need for final settling tanks. Results from West Germany indicate that with detention times as low as six hours, as much as 92% of total nitrogen can be reduced.[6]

Another promising technique involves the use of final sand filters not just to remove the final quantities of nitrogen but as an integral part of the nitrification or denitrification process. Essentially, by pumping air into the filters, they can provide a good medium for nitrification. Then, by recycling the water back through anoxic portions of the aeration tanks, the nitrate can be broken down into nitrogen gas. Alternatively, another part of the filters can act as the denitrifying medium.

In the last year, Connecticut has agreed to spend $15 million to try out these technologies. The Environmental Defense Fund is also in negotiation with New York City as part of a permit challenge to require similar pilot analyses in New York City. Our struggle has been to convince the City, frankly as much through persuasion as through threat of legal mandate, that it can greatly benefit from a program to spend a few millions to save potential billions.

Another promising "alternative" treatment option is investments in water conservation. Rather than expanding aeration tanks, New York City can provide longer hydraulic detention time simply by reducing the quantity of sewage. For treatment plants that now have 4 ½ hour detention times, a reduction of sewage by 25% would permit a detention time of 6 hours. That level of detention time might permit high levels of nutrient removal with relatively little new construction.

Is that kind of reduction realistic? I believe it is. New York City uses approximately 200 million gallons of water per person per day. That is equivalent to the use of the water-guzzling cities of the Southwest, and that use is remarkable because those cities use most of their water outside, to turn deserts into lawns. Little water in New York goes to lawns at all. That means New York probably sets the national and world record for indoor water use and leakage.

Where does the water go? Some might suspect that it is lost to water main breaks, but repeated City studies indicate only small leakage in that area. The probable answer is that it goes into highly wasteful, leaking plumbing fixtures in aged buildings that historically have not had meters. Enormous savings are available in the plumbing fixtures alone, for the City can replace 6 gallon toilets now with 1.6 gallon toilets, and showerheads that use 10 gallons per minute with shower heads that use 3 gallons per minute. The larger savings from replacing these fixtures, however, would probably come from the reduced likelihood of leaks.

Rex Management undertook a study that indicates the significance of leaks.[7] It repaired plumbing and installed low water using fixtures and meters in eight large apartment buildings. It also provided substantial financial incentives to building superintendents to keep water use down by tracking leaks. Despite these efforts, data on water use per weak over the course of a year revealed that most buildings had individual weeks in which water use was at least 50% higher than the lowest weeks and in many buildings was close to 100% higher. The difference was leaks. The overall significance of leaks in the City as a whole then becomes clear if one imagines a City filled with forty-year-old buildings that throughout that time have lacked the meters that might indicate the presence of leaks.

To its enormous credit, New York City and the Dinkins Administration are taking water conservation seriously. Two weeks ago, the Administration announced its most dramatic step, namely, that it would offer rebates of up to $260 to homeowners to retrofit older toilets with new, lower water use toilets. It expects in this way to retrofit 1.5 million toilets at a cost of $300 million. Prudently, City officials have estimated water savings modestly at roughly 90 million gallons per day. If the retrofit program proves to have large impacts on leaks, however, as some other, more modest retrofit programs have reported, the savings will be much greater.

Neither are wastewater savings the only benefits of such a program. A 25% reduction would more than close the roughly 200 million gallon per day gap in the "safe yield" of New York City's water supply system. That would save as much as $800 million dollars in the alternative construction of a new water supply tap on the Hudson River. Those savings would also save in potential filtration treatment costs. Because savings on the water supply end already exceed the cost of water conservation programs, conservation measures make an essentially free contribution to reducing the costs of nutrient removal. I am also not the only person who believes this level of reduction possible. An expert panel on water filtration appointed by the Environmental Protection

Agency also recently estimated that the City can cuts its water use almost 25% from 1377 mgd to 1100 mgd.[8]

Although New York is making some efforts to analyze alternative nutrient removal technologies, and considerable efforts to conserve water, several additional actions are warranted. Most importantly, the City needs to devote a substantial budget, on the order of $10 million per year, to examining these alternative nutrient removal strategies. In doing so, the City should utilize an advisory committee of top academic experts on nutrient removal to help direct the effort. A majority of demonstration plant construction could also be incorporated into any final technological plan.

New York should also pursue at least two additional water conservation measures. One would involve intensive water conservation demonstration zones representative of the City as a whole. In those zones, the City should complete metering, but continue to charge at the old bulk rate for at least a few months to permit an analysis of water use. The City should then implement intensive water conservation efforts and measure the extent of the savings. This program would help the City analyze, and demonstrate, the potential for conservation to address the costs of nutrient removal.

The City should also work to establish expanded maintenance programs for leak detection. In buildings with maintenance staff, that involves an effort to convince building operators and the public that regular leak detection surveys are simply good building practice. In buildings without maintenance staff capable of repairing leaks themselves, that requires the encouragement of service contracts for leak detection that would also perform these surveys. Calling a plumber to repair a leak today is too expensive because of the travel time involved and probably also because fully trained plumbers are not necessary for leak detection. Economies of scale, however, could justify regular leak detection.

Beyond New York City Sewage Treatment Plants

Obviously, other sewage treatment plants that discharge into the Sound should meet the same requirements as New York City. That means, in my view, that they should make similar contributions toward a collaborative effort to analyze alternative treatment technologies.

Beyond these treatment plants, Long Island Sound also requires addressing nutrient inputs outside of the Sound. Generally elevating nutrient concentrations are causing eutrophic conditions in principal estuaries and even open bodies of water all the way from New England to the southern Gulf Coast of Texas. Long Island Sound specifically requires addressing nutrient inputs from other discharges into New York harbor, reductions that would also benefit parts of the Harbor and New York Bight. But the time has come to require nutrient removal as a general requirement in all coastal waters. If alternative technologies demonstrate that these reductions can occur more cheaply, that requirement may become politically acceptable.

Even though nonpoint sources provide a smaller source of the pollutants to Long Island Sound than other estuaries, reductions in nonpoint sources are still necessary to alleviate hypoxia. Nothing serious has been done. EDF recommends two steps toward addressing nonpoint source pollution.

First, EPA, New York and Connecticut need to use their stormwater permitting authority to require the development of plans to address stormwater discharges into the Sound. Stormwater discharges now require permits under the Clean Water Act, and they are subject to the same obligations to meet water quality standards as sewage treatment plant discharges. Despite that fact, the costs and practical difficulties of addressing stormwater have led the agencies to be timid.

Costs are a legitimate concern, just as they are a legitimate concern for sewage treatment plants. But the agencies should utilize their permitting authority to require permittees at least to develop the information necessary to begin to address the problem. The Long Island Sound Study has adopted stormwater zones. It should set a goal of a 50% reduction in nitrogen from each of these zones, and require permittees to contribute the necessary resources for the development of plans to achieve those goals in each area. At the same time, planning teams in each of the zones should work together to explore the most cost-effective technologies. Effective stormwater controls would not only help address the nitrogen problem, but they could also help address toxics, turbidity and pathogen problems in bays and inlets that are themselves important environmental issues.

In addition to these efforts, the agencies involved in the Long Island Sound Study should identify and explore wetland and riparian area restoration programs to help address nitrogen discharges. EDF is involved with environmental organizations and government agencies from around the country in an effort to enhance the role of the water resources public works agencies in aquatic ecosystem restoration. Officials of both the Army Corps of Engineers and the Soil Conservation Service have shown considerable interest. Our region could provide an important impetus to this change in focus.

REFERENCES

1. DAVIS, S. & J. OGDEN, EDS. 1994. Everglades: The Ecosystem and its Restoration. Delray Beach, FL: St. Lucie Press. In press.
2. NATIONAL RESEARCH COUNCIL, COMMITTEE ON RESTORATION OF AQUATIC ECOSYSTEMS: Science, Technology and Public Policy, National Academy of Sciences. 1992. Restoration of Aquatic Ecosystems: Science, Technology and Public Policy. Washington, DC: National Academy Press.
4. UNITED STATES ENVIRONMENTAL PROTECTION AGENCY, EXPERT PANEL ON NEW

York City's Water Supply. 1993. Report of the Expert Panel on New York City's Water Supply. New York. Unpublished manuscript.
5. NEW YORK CITY DEPARTMENT OF ENVIRONMENTAL PROTECTION, Bureau of Wastewater Treatment Process Control Section. 1991. Long Island Sound Study: Nitrification/denitrification process design and costs estimates. Wards Island, NY.
6. RANDALL, C. W. Utilization of fixed film growth in activated sludge systems to achieve year round nitrification and total nitrogen removal. Unpublished monograph.
7. JUDD, P. H. 1991. More expensive than oil: Water metering in multifamily buildings in New York City avoiding the unintended effects. Unpublished monograph.
8. UNITED STATES ENVIRONMENTAL PROTECTION AGENCY, EXPERT PANEL ON NEW YORK CITY'S WATER SUPPLY. 1993. Report of the Expert Panel on New York City's Water Supply. New York, NY. Unpublished manuscript.

DISCUSSION OF THE PAPER

ARTHUR GLOWKA: I'm the chairman of the Long Island Sound Taskforce (LIST). I have been involved with the restoration of the Hudson River for thirty years. I've worked on PCBs, power plants, pollution suits, Westway, and striped bass tagging as well as other projects.

I like the idea of tidal gates in the East River. They would flush out the excess nutrients which are causing the hypoxic conditions in the western Sound. This hypoxic condition lasts for only a few weeks during the height of the summer heat and occurs in deep water where in fact there is very little fish life except for lobsters.

What we have here is a room full of engineers who understand very little about the fish life and biological processes which take place in the western Sound. This is the same time that we have switched the whole aquatic system from a detrital organic base to a nutrient-driven food chain. Ed Wagner has asked the question as to why, as New York City has improved its sewage treatment, the hypoxia problems have increased. We're basically going through this Long Island Sound cleanup to improve the habitat and water quality for the fish and other aquatic life. The Environmental Protection Agency and States spend about $1.5 million a year on this effort, about the same price as the average cost of a home on the Sound. They dip a lot of water to analyze and seine only in mid-Sound.

What we don't understand and have no one looking at are the basic biological structures. I presently have two LIST board member PhDs doing this work on plankton and vascular grasses. Because the academics are so specialized in their fields—and spend very little time out on the water—no one is approaching the Long Island Sound problems from the ecosystem point of view. We may not understand what we are doing when we start playing God with an aquatic system.

QUESTION: I have a question on the Clean Water Act. The modeling session this morning talked about improvements in some areas, but a decrease or downgrading in the water quality of New Jersey waters. What do you think about that in terms of the Clean Water Act?

TIMOTHY D. SEARCHINGER: Was it New Jersey or some parts of the harbor? From a legal standpoint, New Jersey would be entitled to stop this project if it could show in a hearing, which it would be entitled to have in front of the Corps, that the project would contribute to a violation of its water quality standards. So it would be a very severe legal obstacle, if nothing else.

M.L. THATCHER: You've made a very good case for not moving from where we are. And at the same time you are encouraging us to move in the direction of solving the nutrient problem, the nitrogen problem. What concerns me is the first observation, that is hard to move from where we are. There is an assumption that where we are is not as bad as where we were—which I disagree with, I think we were worse off before—but that if we try something a little bit out of line, that might be worse. In other words, the tidal barrage idea is too far out. It might be bad. I feel it's not getting a fair shake, and I feel that you are diverting our attention to: let's go back and get the nitrogen out in the first place. Now . . .

SEARCHINGER: I didn't suggest that we are not better off than we were before, certainly before sewage treatment plants.

THATCHER: . . . there's a certain conservatism in this. For those of us who are engineers, it's like viscosity. It's hard to move through all these regulations. And that's supposed to protect us from going somewhere that isn't so great. I'm wondering whether maybe we're in pretty bad shape right now. So . . .

SEARCHINGER: I think we are in bad shape right now. I'm not challenging that. I think we have severe problems.

THATCHER: Well, what about the suspended sediments, for example. A beautiful example. Suddenly, people said: the water's getting clearer, we're taking out suspended sediments with secondary treatment. Maybe we should put it back.

SEARCHINGER: No, no, no. I'm not suggesting that. What I'm suggesting is this: I was really saying that only to point out that essentially we have heavily nitrogen-enriched water, and there is a great benefit to removing the nitrogen. If your focus is simply on moving the nitrogen around with the idea of alleviating a particular problem in a particular area, there is a good chance that you will contribute to problems with that nitrogen elsewhere.Now if your chosen strategy is instead to remove the nitrogen, then you will not be contributing to that problem elsewhere and you will in fact be contributing to alleviating that problem elsewhere. If in fact it turns out that we do have severe eutrophication problems in the Bight—and I am not at all confident that that is not the case—then the tidal barrage won't help us at all and could probably hurt quite a lot. By contrast, removing nitrogen would greatly help improve any nitrogen problem we have in the Bight.

THATCHER: Aren't you saying it is that the mass of nitrogen is what's important, not the fact that the concentration would be reduced.

SEARCHINGER: Well, this is something that I would be interested in seeing. If we are taking the nitrogen that now goes out to the Sound and moving it out to the Bight, we would also apparently be diluting it somewhat with some additional fresh water, but the total mass is still going to be going out there. Now the question is: how much is that already? I mean, if your are increasing the mass—and again, you may understand this better than I do—my gut reaction would be if you are increasing the mass but diluting the concentration of what comes out of the harbor, you are nevertheless displacing other not very heavily enriched water that would otherwise be there. And therefore you have the potential to be greatly increasing the concentration once you get it out there. You may be decreasing the concentration of what you are sending out there, but increasing the total mass because you are increasing the quantity, and that's displacing nutrient-poor water that might otherwise be out there. So I think there is a real potential there.

MALCOLM BOWMAN: In all fairness, though, there is enormous potential for so much nitrogen. The whole ocean is full of nitrogen. So is the atmosphere. The atmosphere is 78 percent nitrogen. I think your concern is valid close to shore, nearest the coast, and we will have to look at that carefully. The coastal ocean . . .

SEARCHINGER: I'm not saying the whole ocean is going to get eutrophic.

BOWMAN: . . . is still a drop in the bucket.

SEARCHINGER: I'm not suggesting the whole ocean. I am suggesting near-shore waters.

BOWMAN: I think that has to looked at very carefully.

SEARCHINGER: Right. I'm not worried about algae blooms in the middle of the Atlantic or anything.

Part V
CONCLUSION

A Summary of the Symposium

DONALD F. SQUIRES[a]
Department of Marine Sciences
The University of Connecticut
Storrs, Connecticut 06268

As the Long Island Sound Study proceeded with its investigations, there were some participants who felt that the study had determined both problem and solution too quickly. The problem identified was hypoxia, or low oxygen conditions in western Long Island Sound. But, said some, was hypoxia a problem of recent (*i.e.* post-colonial) origin or, had the Sound experienced "naturally" induced hypoxic episodes? The solution identified for hypoxia was advanced sewage treatment in the Connecticut, Westchester County, New York, and New York City wastewater treatment plants discharging into water affecting Long Island Sound.

Only late in the study were efforts made to assess alternatives to advanced treatment. One such effort, an examination of alternative technologies for reducing nutrient loadings to western Long Island Sound was arranged by J.R. Schubel, Marine Sciences Research Center, State University at Stony Brook in 1991. Identified at that workshop as a technology most promising for further exploration was Professor Malcolm Bowman's concept of the establishment of tidal gates on the East River thereby rectifying the tidal flow of that strait. And so, we have today been making that first step towards assessment of an idea he first put forward 17 years ago.[1]

This symposium had its origins in the fascination of imaginative persons with Bowman's concept. That interest arises for the idea brings into play not only the engineering aspects of design and construction of such a structure, but also involves the complexity of hydrodynamics within a highly complicated coastal system, the potential for co-linking pollution abatement with river crossings for mass transit, creation of an aesthetically pleasing public space, and the potential for energy production. As of this time, there are no proponents, individual (other than those speaking in support today) or organizational. The mode of this symposium has been one of open inquiry of an interesting idea.

Several speakers today have cautioned that tidal gates should not be considered as a "silver bullet," a single expeditious solution to the water quality problems of Long Island Sound. I think that all who favorably view the concept of the tidal barrage would concur for the actuality of those problems is much more complex. In 1990 a several day symposium was held at Manhattan College to review the status of the several investigations of the coastal waters of the tri-state area. The conclusion of that symposium was that the physical interconnectedness and inter-

[a]Address for correspondence: 19 Shady Lane, Storrs Mansfield, CT 06268-1814.

dependence of the New York Bight, the New York/New Jersey Harbor Estuary (hereinafter referred to as New York Harbor) and Long Island Sound was such that they need always to be considered as a single system.[2] No solution to the vexing water quality problems of any one part of that system could be taken without consideration of the effects upon the system as a whole. One appealing aspect of the tidal barrage concept is that it seems, at this level of investigation, to have some promise of benefitting the entire system.

It seems to be generally agreed that ongoing efforts to diminish the negative effects of discharge of sewage effluents into the Bight-Sound-Harbor system must be continued. But one must ask: Are those efforts enough? Should more be done? Need more be done?

English settlers of Manhattan Island brought with them the experiences of home among which were the memories of the effectiveness with which vigorous North Sea tidal currents flush the embayments of the British Isles. The currents of the Hudson and East River, although lesser, may have seemed adequate for certainly they immediately proceeded to use these waterways for all manner of waste disposal transferring the problems of public health, odor and aesthetics from the land to the waterways. But by the end of the 19th century it had become clear to all observers that the tidal flushing of Manhattan was inadequate. As put by Anne Loop, historian of New York City's sewage treatment programs:

> The city is surrounded by water. This might be considered an advantage, but the nature of the rivers, harbor, sound and the ocean frontage create an unusual circumstance. Despite its great size and volume, the Hudson River is a relatively sluggish stream at its mouth, that is at New York City . . . This is due to the ocean tides which cause the river current to oscillate upstream and down. East River and Harlem River (really not rivers at all) are affected by the same tidal currents. The effect is to retard the conveyance of wastes away from the City and out into the open sea.[3]

The inappropriateness of the waterways as conductors of untreated or partially treated sewage had been recognized by the late 19th century (*e.g.*, refs. 4 and 5). But sanitarians found it difficult to appropriately site treatment plants both because of the expanding city and, to a lesser extent, the pattern of sewerage established by the concept of waterway flushing. And so began the long, expensive and technically difficult task of installation of sewerage and sewage treatment, a program which has reached astounding capabilities despite daunting complications. One of the most daunting was the introduction, in the early 1800s, of indoor running water which enormously increased the volume of water required to be treated (*e.g.*, ref. 6). And of course there was always the problem of population growth.

New York City faced these problems earlier than Long Island, Connecticut (that state's first sewage treatment plant was built in 1896) or New Jersey, for it was the economic and demographic engine which drove the growth of adjacent areas. Although the surrounding communities have coped, none have done so at the gigantic scale and technical skills of New York City. But for all, sewerage and sewage treatment has always been a game of catch up. "Getting ahead of the curve" has always been blocked by too few dollars, too much opposition, and a general disinterest in what I have called "yesterday's dinners."[7] In Connecticut, shallow soils and surface water supplies together recommended sewerage only in urbanized areas and large lot zoning, permitting septic systems, for less built up communities. Long Island was, until post-war population expansion, to get by entirely on septic systems.

As the sewage disposal problem periodically worsened in the Harbor's waterways, other ideas came forward. One such idea was that of Sidney Reeve who proposed, in 1922, to establish tidal gates across the East River for the avowed purpose of flushing New York Harbor with the clean waters of Long Island Sound.[8] Oh, how the times do change: today we seek also to flush those formerly clean waters of western Long Island Sound.

The oscillatory nature of the East River tidal flow had been determined by 1908 when the City of New York and the United States Coast and Geodetic Survey performed tidal studies. A float set adrift at College Point, upper East River, was followed night and day by a tug. In three days it had travelled 107.8 miles ". . . and was taken up only two miles from where it had been released."[9] Professor Bowman's concept of rectification of that tidal flow would reduce the nutrient burden of western Long Island Sound by moving those waters through New York Harbor and into the Atlantic Ocean. By his calculations, nutrient reductions in western Long Island Sound would maximally approach 70% and notably the nutrient concentration in New York Harbor would be reduced by about 50% (Bowman, this volume). Lesser reductions would be achieved in the coastal waters of New York Bight. Mr. St. John confirmed those estimates utilizing the elegant hydrodynamic and water quality models of HydroQual. But Mr. St. John also showed that there is no free lunch, for those same models showed that there would be some transference of biochemical oxygen demand (BOD) loadings, as well as slightly higher coliform levels, in the outer Harbor waters (St. John, this volume).

A colleague, Estelle Smith, observed that "what one seeks are results, what one achieves are consequences."[10] One of the consequences of a tidal barrage, identified by Bowman and St. John, would be increased occurrence of both borers and oxidation of steel pilings within the Harbor as dissolved oxygen levels within the upper Harbor areas were increased. An estimated one million unprotected wood and steel pilings were set within the Harbor during that 50 plus year period when dissolved oxygen levels were so low that borers could not survive nor would subtidal steel oxidize. There will be other, similar consequences.

Dr. Lewellyn Thatcher called our attention, with impressive graphics, to the extraordinary changes wrought to the bottom physiology of the

Upper Bay. Similarly, the East River is hardly to be considered a natural physical environment. As commerce in the Port of New York boomed, following the War of 1812, merchants agitated for the improvement of access to the Harbor not through the Sandy Hook-Rockaway transect, but rather through the tortuous passage of Hell Gate. Long Island Sound provided a protected waterway linking the two great commercial centers of the time, Boston and New York. Through the late 19th century heroic efforts were made to remove the rocks, reefs and shoals which had been responsible for as many as 1,000 shipwrecks each year (see TABLE 1). But the East River was also modified throughout its length by marginal filling which channelized the strait. Marion Klawoon, historian of the New York District Corps of Engineer, observed:

> It is estimated that if this creeping outward of piers had continued, by 1900 the East River would have been completely spanned by piers ... (p. 66)[11]

This symposium was fortunate to have the participation of Parsons Brinkerhoff and TAMS engineers. The presentations by Alex Matlin and John Szeligowski of conceptual designs for a tidal barrage gave substance to the concept and suggested opportunities which might have otherwise not been recognized. It became clear from symposium discussions that while the opportunity for creation of a new city icon, as advocated by Professor Webster, abounds, the design and construction of a barrage was a lesser task than that of achieving its required environmental impact statement and permits. Presentations by Professor Bokuniewicz on the effects of the barrage on sedimentation and Dr. Woodhead on impacts on fishes served to point out the complexities—and lack of knowledge—about the East River. As outlined by Corps of Engineers participants Ms. Bocamazo and Messrs. Will and Haggerty, the regulatory hurdles through which the project would be required to pass are formidable. So formidable were these that in the course of discussions the phrase "the billion dollar environmental impact statement" was coined.

Commissioner Lucius Riccio, at luncheon, and the afternoon presentations made a convincing point that the tidal barrage concept must rise or fall on the contribution it would make to water quality improvement. The potential values of the barrage as a river crossing enhancing transportation between boroughs, or the production of energy, or the creation of a public space are real. And while the concept of a multipurpose structure has intrinsic appeal because of the potential of getting something for nothing, such additions would have deadly consequence by merely complicating the development and permitting processes. Commissioner Riccio offered the acronym coined for the obstacles confronting city construction: BANANA (Build Absolutely Nothing Anywhere Near Anything). BANANA applies well to the approval process which would face the barrage.

Water quality throughout the Bight-Harbor-Sound system has been undeniably impaired by human activities, particularly contamination by

TABLE 1. Modifications to the East River by Rock and Reef Removal

Locality	Distance from Battery (Mi)	Least Original Depth (Ft)	Projected Depth (Ft)
Battery Reef	0.00	12.8	30.0
South Ferry Reef	0.00	17.0	30.0
Diamond Reef	0.50	15.7	40.0
Reef off Diamond Reef	0.50	19.0	40.0
Coenties Reef	0.50	14.3	40.0
Corlears Reef	2.75	—	40.0
Third Street Reef	3.00	15.9	40.0
Shell Reef	2.50–4.00	7.5	25.0
Pilgrim Reef	3.50	12.0	—
26th Street Reef	4.00	16.1	—
Charlotte Reef	4.25	14.7	30.0
Isolated Rock	—	—	30.0
Ferry Reef	4.50	14.7	30.0
Man-of-War Rock	4.75	+0.8	40.0
Rhinelander Reef	7.75	—	26.0
Middle Reef including Negro Head, Flood Rock, Hen and Chickens and Gridiron	7.50	+6.0	40.0
Heel-Tap Rock	7.75	12.1	—
Hallets Point Reef	7.50	+4.0	40.0
Frying Pan Reef	7.50	9.0	40.0
Pot Rock	8.00	8.0	40.0
Shell Drake Rock	8.00	8.0	40.0
Ways Reef	8.25	5.0	40.0
Rock off Negro Point	9.00	—	40.0
Scaly Rock	9.25	—	—
Middle Ground	10.00	11.0	40.0
Rocks off Port Morris	10.75	—	35.0
Port Morris Shoal	11.25	—	30.0
Reef off North Brother Island	10.75	—	35.0
Channel between North and South Brother Islands	11.25	19.0	40.0
North Point of North Brother Island	11.00	—	35.0
Rocks off Baretto Point	11.75	—	40.0
Baretto Reef	11.75	17.0	40.0

Data from Port of New York Annual, 1919, Vol. 1, p.56.

excessive nutrients emanating from sewage discharged into the waterways. Human sewage is a pollutant not entirely responsive to source reduction thus requiring that treatment facilities keep pace with population growth. However, technology of treatment, particularly that of nutrient removal, has not developed as quickly as population with the result that nutrient levels in coastal waters generally are higher than desirable.

During the late 1980s hypoxia, or low dissolved oxygen conditions in Western Long Island Sound worsened, causing the Long Island Sound Study to focus upon that problem. Not answered in ensuing investigations, however, was the question: had Western Long Island Sound experienced similar conditions in the past? Nitrogen budgets of inputs to the Sound suggested that the excess nitrogen in Western Long Island Sound was of human origin and that enhanced sewage treatment and best management practices undertaken by agriculturists, property owners and developers was called for. Model runs of HydroQual's LIS 2.0 water quality program suggest, however, that even if these measures are undertaken and that realistic improvements in both point and non-point nutrient reduction were achieved, the dissolved oxygen levels in Western Long Island Sound would not preclude future hypoxia events.[12]

Bill McKibben in his evocative essay "The End of Nature" noted that the effects of human society and culture are now globally apparent, omnipresent.[13] Nature, which was once present, has been replaced by a state subtly or not so subtly modified by our presence, our activities and our numbers. Nowhere is this more apparent than in the surround of major cities. Major alterations to natural systems having the effect of enhancing the environment, as it is, are therefore more acceptable. Commissioner Wagner espoused a more conservative, and traditional, view. He argued a position with which many agree, that sufficient "nature" remains in New York Harbor to make a major alteration broadly affecting that environment offensive. That argument is soundly based on our track record of fallibility in predicting all of the consequences of such an action. Despite the differences of philosophy expressed in these different views, there is general agreement that the barrage concept should be seen neither as a panacea for Long Island Sound water quality problems, nor as an alternative to enhanced wastewater treatment.

We are now at the point where it is appropriate to ask: How does the tidal barrage concept stack up against the approach of enhanced sewage treatment? We can make a stab at this by considering costs, time required for implementation, and expected effectiveness:

Cost

Messrs. Matlin and Szeligowski suggested that planning and construction costs of a tidal barrage might approximate $500 million. The necessary studies required for permitting might cost as much as $1 billion. Enhancement of sewage treatment is anticipated to cost between $6 and $8 billion.

Time for Implementation

Messrs. Matlin and Szeligowski suggested that planning and construction of a tidal barrage (post-EIS approval) would require less than a decade. The time required for studies might be equally long. Model predictions suggest that, once built, the tidal barrage would cause substantial reductions in nutrients in Sound and Harbor waters within a year. Enhancement of sewage treatment plants could take over a decade to implement. Educational programs required for effectuating non-point source reductions will also require time measured in decades. Model predictions suggest that nitrogen reduction resulting from enhanced sewage treatment and non-point nutrient reduction will occur in a time frame of a decade.

Expected Effectiveness

Model predictions suggest that the tidal barrage would result in substantial nutrient reductions in the Sound and Harbor waters, but that some adverse effects might be found in outer Harbor areas. Efficacy in reducing pathogen and toxic levels was not tested, nor was the effect upon embayment waters. Model predictions suggest that enhanced sewage treatment and non-point nutrient source reduction will reduce nutrient levels in the Sound. Most improvement will be felt in embayments where general water quality improvement (reduced levels of nutrients, pathogens, toxics, floating litter) will occur.

We must now weight the risks of unforeseen consequences, as well as predicted effects, of the novel tidal barrage concept against a more traditional approach to improving water quality. Are those risks too great to permit movement to the next step: a more extensive investigation of the tidal barrage concept? Or, are we too deeply embedded in sanctioned solutions to consider alternatives?

Our friends in the U.S. Army Corps of Engineers have catalogued a formidable agenda of studies which would be required for the furtherance of the tidal barrage concept. As an academic, I rejoice in the numbers of future students who will be usefully employed in such studies. This should be considered a positive aspect of the project and appropriately included in the cost/benefit analysis. I do hope that such studies are made, for in the process of gaining the necessary understandings, we shall learn more about the water quality problems of the system of waterways bounding this metropolitan area—and such understandings are always valued.

REFERENCES

1. Bowman, M. J. 1976. Tidal locks across the East River, New York: An engineering solution to the rehabilitation of western Long Island Sound. *In* Estuarine Processes. M. Wiley, Ed. New York: Academic Press.
2. Southerland, M. T. & K. Swetlow, Eds. 1990. Cleaning up our coastal waters: An unfinished agenda. Proceedings of a regional conference, March 12-14, 1990.

3. LOOP, A. S. 1964. History and Development of Sewage Treatment in New York City. The City of New York, Department of Health. 166 pp.
4. HUFELAND, O. 1925. Report of sewage disposal in the City of New York—A resume of thirty years investigation. *In* Manhattan (Borough) President. 1925. Report of the Business and Transactions . . . for the year ending December 31, 1924. 51-62. New York, NY.
5. LEWINSKI-CORWIN, E. H. 1918. The sewage disposal problem of New York City. A report by the public health committee of the New York Academy of Medicine. Medical Record. September 21:502-506.
6. TARR, J. E. & F. C. MCMICHAEL. 1977. Decisions about wastewater technology: 1850-1932. J. Water Resources Planning and Mgmt. Div., Proc. Am. Soc. Civil Eng. 103 (WR1) Proc. Paper 12920. May 1977:47-61.
7. SQUIRES, D. F. 1981. The Bight of the Big Apple. Albany, NY: New York Sea Grant Institute. Sea Grant Maritime Heritage Series. 84 pp.
8. REEVE, S. A. 1922. Cleansing New York Harbor. Geog. Rev. **12:**420-423.
9. SOPER, G. A. 1930. New York's Sewage Problem. Municipal Sanitation **1(3):**149.
10. SMITH, E. 1982. Fisheries management: Intended results and unintended consequences. *In* Modernization and Marine Fisheries Policy. J. Maiolo & M. Orbach, Eds. Ann Arbor, MI: Ann Arbor Science Press. 330 pp.
11. KLAWOON, M. J. 1977. Cradle of the Corps: A history of the New York District, U.S. Army Corps of Engineers, 1775–1975. New York: U.S. Army Engineer Corps, New York District. June, 1977. 310 pp.
12. UNITED STATES ENVIRONMENTAL PROTECTION AGENCY, LONG ISLAND SOUND STUDY. 1993. Draft January 1993 Comprehensive conservation and management plan. New York, NY.
13. MCKIBBEN, B. 1989. The End of Nature. New York: Random House.

Curricula Vitae

MICHAEL J. ABRAHAMS, P.E. Mike Abrahams is a vice president, senior professional associate, and manager of the structures department of the New York office of Parsons Brinckerhoff. He has directed bridge, tunnel, port, and building projects throughout the United States, and served as project manager or principal-in-charge for a number of bridge and tunnel inspection and rehabilitation programs. His bridge experience has focused on movable highway and railway bridges and includes the recent superstructure replacement and widening of the George P. Coleman Bridge in Virginia, one of the world's longest double-swing span bridges. Mike is the author of numerous articles on movable bridges and bridge inspection, and has received awards for the design of the 6,470 foot-long floating, prestressed concrete Hood Canal Bridge in Washington which has a 600-foot-long lift draw section, and for the plaza roof of the Five Points MARTA Station in Atlanta, Georgia, which was erected using segmental construction techniques.

GEORGE BIRMAN, P.E. George Birman is a consulting engineer in the field of energy, mechanical design and building maintenance (roofing, heating, waterproofing). Previously he worked on the U.S. Air Force heavy press program on the design of the largest forging and extrusion presses. Later he worked for United Nuclear Corporation on reactor and shielding design. At Columbia University he worked on the modification of the oldest syncrocyclotron. He designed, built and managed a facility to reprocess aluminum dross. He is a graduate of the Institute of Technology in Vienna, Austria, and is a licensed professional engineer in New York and New Jersey.

LYNN MARIE BOCAMAZO, P. E. Lynn Marie Bocamazo is a hydraulic engineer with the Planning Division of the U.S. Army Corps of Engineers, New York District. Her principal coastal engineering work has been on beach erosion control and inlet navigation projects on Long Island and New Jersey. Ms. Bocamazo has been the technical manager of Army Corps' New York Bight study for three years. She received a B.E. from Cooper Union (1983) and an M.S. in Civil Engineering from Polytechnic University (1988). She is a licensed professional engineer in New York State. She is currently a member of the Coastal Engineering Technical Committee of the American Society of Civil Engineers.

HENRY J. BOKUNIEWICZ, Ph.D. Henry J. Bokuniewicz is a professor in the Marine Sciences Research Center of the State University of New York at Stony Brook. He is the author or co-author of 32 refereed articles and over 56 other articles and reports, many related to sediment and dredging in New York Harbor and Long Island Sound. Some titles include: Predicted changes in tidal circulation in the Lower Bay of New York Harbor resulting from a deepening a section of Ambrose Channel; An overview and assessment of the coastal processes data base for the south shore of Long Island; Real time in-situ monitoring of dredge disposal sites; Sand mining in New York Harbor; Studies in the Lower Bay of New York Harbor associated with the burial of dredged sediment in subaqueous borrow pits; Bottom morphology of the Hudson River estuary and New York Harbor; Some management implications of sedimentation in the Hudson-Raritan estuarine system; Energetics of dredged-material dispersal; Sand transport at the floor of Long Island Sound. Professor Bokuniewicz received the degrees of Master of Philosophy and Doctor of Philosophy from Yale University and his B.A. from the University of Illinois, Champaign-Urbana Campus.

MALCOLM J. BOWMAN, Ph.D., P.E. Malcolm J. Bowman is Professor of Physical Oceanography at the Marine Sciences Research Center, State University of New York at Stony Brook. His research interests include the dynamics and modeling of coastal seas and estuaries, and the influence and control of marine ecosystems by physical processes. Over the last 20 years, he has had an abiding interest in, and published numerous papers on, the oceanography and pollution problems of New York Harbor and Long Island Sound.

Dr. Bowman has held visiting appointments at the University of British Columbia, Canada; the USSR Academy of Sciences, Moscow; Chonnam National University, Korea; and the University of Auckland, New Zealand. He is active in book publishing, holding the post of Founding and Managing Editor of the open series "Coastal and Estuarine Studies," published by the American Geophysical Union (formerly by Springer-Verlag). He was Conference Chair of the Gordon Research Conference on "Coastal Ocean Circulation" held in Plymouth, NH, in 1993. He was a Founding Committee member of the Council on Ocean Affairs, a national educational organization devoted to the promotion of ocean sciences and policy in the United States. He is a former member of the Board of Directors of the Northeast Area Remote Sensing System, Woods Hole, MA.

Dr. Bowman received his B.S. in Physics and Mathematics, and his M.S. in Physics from the University of Auckland, New Zealand. His Ph.D. is in Electrical Engineering from the University of Saskatchewan, Canada. Prior to coming to SUNY, he worked on underwater acoustics and antisubmarine warfare for the Naval Research Laboratory, Auckland, New Zealand.

HARRY EKEZIAN, P.E. Harry Ekezian is a consulting engineer with a half-century of experience in the engineering of a wide range of waterway, port, transportation, industrial and residential projects worldwide. For most of his career he was associated with TAMS Consultants, Inc., where he was in charge of the firm's Ports and Industrial Facilities Department and served subsequently as project director and senior staff consultant. On major waterway and waterfront projects for TAMS, he was technical director on studies for deepening the Lower Mississippi River, the Orinoco River in Venezuela, and the Hudson River to Albany for navigation of deep draft vessels, project manager for redevelopment of the East River waterfront in lower Manhattan, planning of the 5,000 acre Isser Port and Industrial Complex in Algeria, reclamation of the 70-square mile Site for Jubail Industrial City in Saudi Arabia, and the 5,000 acre Joppatowne Marine Oriented Community in Maryland.

He received his B.S.C.E. degree from the City College of New York. He is a licensed Professional Engineer in New York State and presently conducts a consulting practice at Mamaroneck, New York.

F. H. ("BUD") GRIFFIS, P.E. Bud Griffis is a professor of civil engineering, in charge of the construction program, and the director of the Center for Infrastructure Studies at Columbia University. He is also a Principal in the consulting firm of Robbins, Pope and Griffis, P.C. He was formerly the District Engineer of the U.S. Army Corps of Engineers, New York District. He is a consultant to the New York City Department of Transportation, Port Authority, and numerous construction companies. He has performed research in the application of three-dimensional computer models to the management of construction and their use in productivity improvement, CADD, development of integrated databases, knowledge-based systems, quality management and control, bid strategy models, preventive and corrective maintenance of bridges, pavement rehabilitation and design, queuing theory, simulation, project management and dredged material research. He is the author of numerous papers and reports. He is a registered professional engineer in the states of New York and Oklahoma.

JAMES W. HAGGERTY. James Haggerty is a supervisory oceanographer with the Regulatory Branch, New York District, U.S. Army Corps of Engineers. He has served as Chief, Eastern Permits Section, for four years with responsibility for issuance of permits for construction activities in navigable waterways and wetlands in New York City, on Long Island, and in Westchester and Rockland Counties, New York. Prior to commencing these duties, he served as a Regulatory Specialist assigned to manage some of the most complex and controversial permit applications and regulatory matters in the district. He has a bachelor of science degree in Meteorology and Oceanography from Polytechnic University, conferred in 1979.

DOUGLAS HILL, Eng.Sc.D., P.E. Douglas Hill is a consulting systems engineer concerned with energy and environmental policy, with clients in Canada, Korea, and the Netherlands as well as the U.S. At Brookhaven National Laboratory, he previously served as representative of the

United States on the Energy Technology Systems Analysis Programme of the International Energy Agency, responsible for the development and application a model of the U.S. energy system used to project technology needs. He subsequently headed this international program before leaving Brookhaven. Earlier, he was director of environmental programs at Grumman Ecosystems Corporation where he was responsible for oceanographic surveys in New York Bight and Long Island Sound and resource surveys in Alaska.

Dr. Hill has degrees as doctor of engineering science and master of science from Columbia University, and bachelor of aeronautical engineering from Rensselaer Polytechnic Institute. He is licensed as a professional engineer in New York State. He is coauthor of *Long Island Energy Plan* prepared for the Long Island Regional Planning Board (1991). Among his publications are articles in the journals *Energy* and *Science*.

LYLE H. HIXENBAUGH, P.E. Lyle H. Hixenbaugh is Corporate Vice President of TAMS Consultants, Inc., with over 30 years of experience in the management and technical direction of various major heavy civil construction projects. He is Principal in Charge of major heavy civil and major building design projects including water resources, airports, and transportation projects. These have included hydroelectric plants, dams, tunnels, highway improvements, and master planning worldwide. In his career, Mr. Hixenbaugh has supervised projects in Guatemala, Ecuador, Pakistan, Ivory Coast, Colombia, Egypt, Iran, Yugoslavia, Greece, the Phillipines, Jordan, Algeria, Venezuela, Turkey, Brazil, Morocco, and Australia, as well as the United States. Mr. Hixenbaugh began his career as an officer in the U.S. Army Corps of Engineers. He received his B.S.C.E. degree from the University of Pittsburgh. He is licensed as a professional engineer in New York, New Jersey, and seven other states.

ALEXANDER MATLIN, P.E. Alex Matlin is a professional associate at Parsons Brinckerhoff with extensive civil and marine engineering experience in the U.S., Russia, South America, and Asia. He has managed and participated in the planning, design, and studies of ports and harbors; the design of marine and waterfront structures, such as docks, piers, breakwaters, shore protection, and dry docks; the development of design manuals for port structures; and the design of a land-level ship construction facility at Newport News, Virginia, was the resident engineer during construction of a deep water container and multi-purpose marine terminal for the Port of Ningpo in China, conducted field inspections and developed repair methods for severely deteriorated piers for the Port Authority for New York and New Jersey, and has performed ship traffic analyses for a number of bridge pier protection projects.

CHRISTIAN MEYER, P.E. Christian Meyer is a professor of civil engineering at Columbia University. He spent his early years as an engineer with A.C. Martin and Associates in Los Angeles and with Stone and Webster Company in Boston. He specializes in structural analysis and design and has primary interests in concrete structures and earthquake engineering. His research activities include the development of a mathematical model to simulate the response of concrete frame elements to cyclic loads, a viscoplastic material model for concrete and mathematical modeling of complex structures for dynamic and nonlinear analysis. His most recent research is addressing the low-cycle fatigue behavior and damage mechanics of concrete and its applications to durability of concrete structures and other problems concerning infrastructure facilities. Christian Meyer is a registered professional engineer in the States of New Jersey and Massachusetts.

LUCIUS J. RICCIO, Ph.D., P.E. Lucius J. Riccio was appointed Commissioner of the New York City Department of Transportation (DOT) on February 1, 1990 by Mayor David N. Dinkins, where he leads over 8,000 employees who ensure that New York City citizens can move safely and quickly through the city transportation network of streets, highways, bridges, and waterways. Mayor Dinkins also appointed Commissioner Riccio to the Metropolitan Transportation Authority board in the summer of 1990. Before becoming Commissioner, he was DOT's Deputy Commissioner for the Bureau of Highways, responsible for maintaining New York City's 6,200 miles of city streets and 225 miles of arterial highways. Earlier, he was Assistant Commissioner of Operations Planning, Evaluation and Control at DOT. He also served on the staff of the Mayor's Criminal Justice Coordinating Council of New York City and on the staff of the Law Enforcement Task Force of the National Commission on Productivity. He was Assistant Director for Research of the Police Foundation under Patrick Murphy in Washington, D.C., and Director of Management Services for the Division of School Buildings of New York City's Board of Education. In addition, he has been an Assistant Professor of Industrial Engineering at Lehigh University, an Adjunct Professor of Operations Research in the Graduate School of Engineering at George Washington University, and an Adjunct Professor of Operations Management at New York University's Graduate School of Public Administration. He is currently at Manuel Elkin in New York City. He also serves on the United State Golf Association's Handicap Research Team. Commissioner Riccio is a licensed professional engineer. He received his Ph.D. in Industrial Engineering from Lehigh University in 1973.

JOHN P. ST. JOHN, P.E. John P. St. John is Principal Engineer and Senior Vice President of HydroQual, Inc., consultants in water pollution control. He has spent his entire professional career performing mathematical water quality modeling studies to determine the interrelationships between wastewater discharges and receiving water impacts for conventional, nonconventional and toxic pollutants. Mr. St. John has supervised projects on rivers, lakes, estuaries and the coastal ocean to determine the principal factors affecting water quality and to assess the effectiveness of various pollution control measures. He has managed water quality projects in New York Harbor, Long Island Sound, New York Bight, Boston Harbor, Delaware River Estuary, Chesapeake Bay, James River, Savannah River, San Juan Bay and San Francisco Bay. He was formerly a Principal Engineer and Vice President of Hydroscience, Inc., the technical predecessor of his present firm. He received his civil/environmental engineering education at Manhattan College in New York City. He is a registered professional engineer in New York and New Jersey and other states.

TIMOTHY D. SEARCHINGER, Esq. Timothy D. Searchinger is an attorney with the Environmental Defense Fund, specializing in water and wildlife issues. He was previously Deputy General Counsel to Governor Robert P. Casey of Pennsylvania, with oversight of education and environment legal departments, engaged with litigation at all federal and state levels, and serving as general counsel to the Pennsylvania Board of Education. Earlier he had served as a law clerk to the Honorable Edward R. Becker, U.S. Court of Appeals for the 3rd Circuit.

Mr. Searchinger received the degree of Doctor of Jurisprudence from Yale Law School where he was senior editor of the Yale Law Journal. As a Thomas J. Watson Foundation Fellow, he had earlier made a traveling study of worker participation in management in England, German, Italy, Hungary and Spain. He received his B.A. from Amherst College, graduating summa cum laude and Phi Beta Kappa. As an undergraduate, he spent a semester at the University of Zimbabwe.

Mr. Searchinger received the 1993 National Wetlands Protection Award. His work has been published in the Yale Law Journal, and for the Environmental Defense Fund and the World Wildlife Fund he wrote *How Wet Is a Wetland?: The Impacts of the Proposed Revisions to the Federal Wetlands Delineation Manual.*

DONALD F. SQUIRES, Ph.D. Don Squires is a Professor of Marine Policy, University of Connecticut. He was director of the University of Connecticut's Marine Sciences Institute from 1985 until 1992. Prior to that he was director of the New York Sea Grant Institute of the State University of New York and Cornell University for 12 years. He came to New York State as founding director of the Marine Sciences Research Center, SUNY at Stony Brook, after a period with the federal government in Washington, D.C. Trained in geology, he has been active in marine policy research for two decades. The author of numerous technical articles, he has also written two books about New York Bight: *The Bight of the Big Apple,* and *The Ocean Dumping Quandary.* He has two books in progress: *The Shaping of the Harbor: Building the Port of New York* and *Long Island Sound: A Personal Voyage.*

R. LAWRENCE SWANSON, Ph.D. Dr. R. Lawrence Swanson is Director of the Waste Management Institute, Marine Sciences Research Center, State University of New York at Stony Brook. It has responsibility for implementing activities relative to waste management in research, assessment, education, policy analysis and public service. Dr. Swanson received his B.S. in Civil Engineering from Lehigh University; his M.S. and Ph.D. in Physical Oceanography from Oregon State University. Prior to coming to SUNY, he was in the National Oceanic and Atmospheric Administration and served in a variety of capacities including Project Manager of the Marine Ecosystems Analysis Program (MESA) for the New York Bight; the Director of the Office of Marine Pollution Assessment; and the Executive Director of the Office of Oceanic and Atmospheric Research.

JOHN J. SZELIGOWSKI. John J. Szeligowski is Assistant Vice President and Principal Environmental Engineer of TAMS Consultants, Inc. As Head of the Environmental Engineering and Regulatory Affairs Department, Mr. Szeligowski is responsible for project management, engineering and environmental analyses, and coordination of project schedules and designs with regulatory requirements. He has over twenty years of experience specializing in environmental engineering, environmental analyses, and regulatory matters. He has been project manager or technical director of hazardous waste projects at various sites in New York and New Jersey including remedial work on the Hudson River PCB problem and at Liberty State Park. He has been project manager of numerous projects involving the handling and disposal of dredged material and other solid wastes. He has conducted analyses and prepared applications for permits under the Clean Water Act, the Clean Air Act, and the Marine Protection Act. He was project manager for the preparation of environmental impact statements for the U.S. Navy Northeast Surface Action Group Homeport. Prior to joining TAMS, Mr. Szeligowski acted as director of water and land use programs and as manager of the licensing subsection of the Consolidated Edison Company of New York.

Mr. Szeligowski received the degree of Bachelor of Electrical Engineering from Manhattan College and a Master of Science from the University of Arizona. He is a member of the York Sludge Management Advisory Committee and the New Jersey Alliance for Action, Ports and Port Development Subcommittee.

M. LLEWELLYN THATCHER, Ph.D. Dr. Thatcher's twenty-five years of water resources research includes a hydrological model study for the Delaware River Basin, numerical modeling of the combined sewer overflows in Jamaica Bay, Passaic River, and East River, transient salinity intrusion modeling of the Hudson Estuary to study impacts of withdrawals, and numerical modeling of the transport of contaminated sediments in New Bedford Harbor. Delaware Estuary studies include the impacts of sea-level rise and Chesapeake-Delaware Canal exchange, as well as long-term modeling. Other studies include the application of the MIT dynamic network model (hydrodynamics and water quality) to the St. Lawrence River, and a contaminated sediment study for PCB concentrations in the Upper Hudson River, and lagoon circulation studies for Loveladies Harbor development.

EDWARD O. WAGNER, P.E. Mr. Wagner is Deputy Commissioner and Director, Bureau of Clean Water, Department of Environmental Protection, New York City. He has worked in New York City's water pollution control program since 1961. Since 1971, he has been responsible for the city's water quality planning and policy development, and the operation and maintenance of the city's wastewater treatment plants, sewage pumping stations, combined sewer regulators, and sludge management program. He is also responsible for water quality monitoring and regulation of industrial wastes and stormwater.

Mr. Wagner received his Bachelor of Civil Engineering degree from City College of New York, and his Master of Civil Engineering from New York University. He is a registered Professional Engineer and Grade I-A Certified Wastewater Treatment Plant Operator in New York State.

ANTHONY C. WEBSTER. Anthony C. Webster is Director of Building Technologies and an assistant professor at Columbia University's Graduate School of Architecture in New York, where he co-teaches the required Building Technologies curriculum, and an elective exploring the relationships between habitable spaces and the technical-utilitarian systems that create and service them.

Mr. Webster has written extensively and spoken frequently on civil engineering and infrastructure design. Mr. Webster's analysis of Santiago Calatrava's contributions to the art of bridge design appears in *Calatrava: Bridges*, published by Artemis Verlag in 1993, and in The Architectural Review (November 1992). He is co-editor of *Bridging the Gap: Re-Thinking the Relationship of Architect and Engineer*, published by Van Nostrand Reinhold in 1991, and he is currently completing a book on the Japanese construction industry, portions of which to be published in the American Society of Civil Engineers' Journal of Professional Practice. Mr. Webster's articles on tuned mass dampers have appeared in *Civil Engineering Magazine* and *The Engineering Journal*.

Mr. Webster's design projects have been published in *The Engineering Journal, Newsline*, and *On Making*. His award-winning entry to the New York State AIA's Solar Canopy Design Competition (designed with Adams-Rosenberg-Kolb Architects) was recently exhibited at Columbia's Graduate School of Architecture.

Mr. Webster received a B.S. in Applied Science in Engineering from Rutgers University where he graduated summa cum laude. In 1984, he received an M.S. in Civil Engineering from Columbia University, where he was the recipient of the university's Carleton Fellowship and the

CRSI's Cameron Fellowship. In 1987, with the help of a tuition grant from Weidlinger Associates, a consulting engineering firm in New York, he received a Professional Degree in Civil Engineering from Columbia. Between degrees, Mr. Webster worked in New York City as a structural engineer at Iffland Kavanagh Waterbury, PC, and Weidlinger Associates.

ROBERT WILL. Robert Will is a marine biologist for the Environmental Analysis Branch of the Planning Division, New York District of the U.S. Army Corps of Engineers. For the past 20 years, he has written and reviewed Environmental Impact Statements related to water resource projects, such as navigation, beach erosion and hurricane protection, flood control and a variety of regulatory projects (power plants, gas and electric pipelines, highway projects, and construction in waterways in general). He specializes in the environmental impact of dredging and dredged material disposal, the delineation, evaluation and establishment of wetlands, and oceanographic related issues. He is currently responsible for managing the Biological Review Program for the Corps' New York Bight study. He received a B.S. in biology from St. John's University and an M.S. in marine biology from Long Island University. He has also done graduate study at the Marine Sciences Research Center, State University of New York at Stony Brook. He is a member of the Society of Wetland Scientists.

PETER M. J. WOODHEAD. Peter M. J. Woodhead is a Research Professor at the Marine Sciences Research Center, State University of New York at Stony Brook. He was previously Research Director, Discovery Bay Marine Laboratory, University of West Indies and State University of New York, Jamaica, West Indies. He has been Scientific Director or Scientific Officer at fisheries laboratories and research stations in Newfoundland, Australia, and the United Kingdom. In addition to his extensive studies of waters in the New York City environs, he has worked on 19 cruises to the Arctic North Atlantic, 23 cruises to the tropical South Pacific, 5 cruises in the Caribbean, and more than 40 cruises in the temperate North Atlantic. He has written more than 100 professional articles and is credited with a number of inventions for oceanographic research. Prof. Woodhead received his B.Sc. degree from the University of Durham, United Kingdom, with first class honors in zoology.

VICTOR WOUK, Ph.D. Dr. Victor Wouk, a native New Yorker, received a B.A. in Mathematics and Physics at Columbia. At the California Institute of Technology, he received the M.S. and Ph.D. (magna cum laude) in Electrical Engineering.

He has been active in the field of environmental control and improvement for more than three decades. He was a founder and member of the Executive Board of Citizens for Clean Air in New York City. He has been instrumental in reviving interest in electric and hybrid-electric vehicles in the United States and abroad, as the Technical Advisor to the United States National Committee of the International Electrotechnical Commission, for Technical Committee 69, "Electric and Hybrid Road Vehicles."

In the 1980s he was on the Board of Governors of The New York Academy of Sciences, and Vice-President for the Engineering Sciences. He has served as Vice Chair of the Engineering Section, and has been on the Conference Committee for more than a decade. Dr. Wouk holds more than ten patents and is a Fellow of the American Association for the Advancement of Science and The New York Academy of Sciences.

Subject Index

Biological oxygen demand (BOD). *See also* Eutrophication
  and algal photosynthesis, 38–40
  reduction in, 81–82
BOD. *See* Biological oxygen demand

CCMP. *See* Comprehensive Conservation and Management Plan
Clean Water Act, 152, 159, 164
Coastal Zone Management Act, 152
Comprehensive Conservation and Management Plan (CCMP), 83–84
Corps of Engineers. *See* U.S. Army Corps of Engineers

Dissolved oxygen, tide gates and, 24, 42–43

East River
  classification of, 1–2
  geology of, 105–106
  hydrology of, 7–12
  RMS tidal transport through, 7, 9–12
  shipping channel depth in, 9
  subtidal flow in
    estuarine circulation, 11–12
    tidal residual flow, 10–12
  tidal excursion in, 9–10
  water quality in, 2
East River bridges, 93–94
  Bronx-Whitestone, 94
  East River-lower midtown location, 95
  East River-midtown location, 94–95
East River fish community
  compared with neighboring communities, 58–64
  estuarine divisions of, 64–65
  species composition of, 57–58
East River Tidal Barrage. *See also* Tide gates
  alternatives to
    New York City sewage treatment, 159–163
    other sewage treatment plants, 163–164
  analysis of impact
    findings of, 45–46
    limitations of, 46–47
    recommendations, 47
  background considerations, 171–176
  benefits expected, 122–124

  construction costs and schedule, 176
  Corps of Engineers and, 72–76, 77–79, 151–152
  description of, 1
  design issues related to, 115
    construction costs and schedule, 122
    gate and gate structure, 117–120
    location, 116–117
    navigation locks, 120–122
    significant problems, 124
  effectiveness expected, 177
  engineering solutions, 101
    proposed gate concepts, 109–112
    proposed layout, 108–109
  environmental community and
    environmental concerns, 157–158
    interference with natural hydrology, 155–157
    legal constraints, 158–159
  and estuarine environment
    Corps of Engineers comments on, 73–76
    hydrodynamics considerations, 77–79
    New York City perspective, 81–84
  Federal agencies review, 151–152
  general concepts for, 115–117
  hydrodynamic impacts of, 25–31
  implementation, 176–177
  justification for, 1
  legal constraints on, 158–159
  and marine navigation, 103–105
  and nitrogen removal, 3
  other barrages, 106
  permitting the, 151–153
  ramifications of, 3–4
  sedimentation associated with
    sediment transport characteristics, 51–53
    tidal gate impact on, 53–55
  site description, 101–103
  site selection, 106–108
    factors governing, 1
  and tidal rectification, 23
  uses for, 1
  and water quality
    in Long Island Sound, 32–38
    in New York-New Jersey harbor, 38–44
  water quality impacts of, 3, 23–25
EIS. *See* Environmental Impact Statement (EIS)

189

Electricity generation. *See* Tidal electricity generation
Environmental Impact Statement (EIS), 73–76
Environmental Protection Agency. *See* New York City Department of Environmental Protection; U.S. Environmental Protection Agency
Estuarine circulation, 11
  in New York Harbor, 12
Estuarine environment, tide gates and, 69–71, 73–79, 81–85, 87–90
Eutrophication
  analysis of, 33–34
  BOD and, 38–40

Fish community. *See* East River fish community

Harlem River, RMS tidal transport through, 10
Hudson estuary
  fish community in, 57–65
  improvements in, 81–82
  migratory fish species in, 66–67
  physical changes since 1845, 69–70
  salinity gradients in, 64
  East River Tidal Barrage and, 71
Hudson River Estuary Management Act of 1987, 57
Hydrodynamic impacts
  of East River Tidal Barrage, 25–31
  System-Wide Hydrodynamic Model, 25–31
    in tide gate operation analysis, 27–31
Hydrography
  of New York Harbor, 7–21
    East River and, 7–9
    Hudson River and, 7
    Long Island Sound and, 7
    subtidal flows, 10–12
    tidal excursion, 9–10
Hydrology, interference with
  East River Tidal Barrage concerns, 157–158
  and Everglades problems, 155–157
Hypoxia, 2
  in New York Harbor, 12–14
  nitrogen concentration and, 3
  in western Long Island Sound, 32–38
  factors contributing to, 12–14

Infrastructure
  developments in, 134–136
  multiple roles of, 130–134
  as public place, 129–130

Infrastructure-design professions, critique by, 136–144

Long Island Sound. *See also* Long Island Sound Study
  hypoxia in, 23
  nitrogenous nutrient concentration in, 18
  pollution in, 2
  RMS tidal transport in, 7
  salinity changes in, 20–21
  sewage effluent released into, 9
  tidal circulation in, 13
  water quality improvement expected, 16–19
Long Island Sound 2.0 Model, and dissolved oxygen measurements, 33–34, 37–40
Long Island Sound Quality Model, 32
Long Island Sound Study
  CCMP developed by, 83–84
  findings of, 2–3
  hypoxia findings of, 23
  major concerns identified by, 83
  water quality model LIS2.0, 25, 31–38

Narrows, the, 7–8
National Environmental Policy Act of 1969, 151
New York Bight, residual flow into, 12
New York Bight Restoration Plan, 25
New York City Department of Environmental Protection, 81–84
New York Harbor
  Hudson River tides and, 7
  hydrographic and tidal regimes, 7–12
  hypoxia in, 12–14
  residual flow into, 12
  salinity changes in, 20–21, 69
  tidal rectification effects on, 14–16
  water quality improvement expected, 19
New York Harbor 208 Water Quality Mode, 25, 38, 40–41, 46
New York-New Jersey Harbor Estuary Project, 69
Nitrogen
  cost of removal of, 3
  and hypoxia, 2–3
Nitrogen concentration
  calculated profiles of, 41–42
  factors controlling change in, 19
  tide gates and, 24, 35, 37–38

Ocean Dumping Ban Act of 1988, 3
Oxygen. *See* Biological oxygen demand; Dissolved oxygen

SUBJECT INDEX

Rivers and Harbors Act of 1899, 151, 158–159
Root mean square (RMS) tidal transport
  at the Narrows, 7
  through East River, 7, 9–12
  through Long Island Sound, 7

Salinity
  changes in
    in Long Island Sound, 20–21
    in New York Harbor, 20–21, 69
  tide gate operations and, 24
Salinity gradients
  in Long Island Sound, 20–21
  in New York Harbor, 20–21, 69
Sediment transport
  and deposition, 52–53
  in East River, 51–53
  rate of, 51
  tidal gates and, 53–55
Sewage treatment
  in New York City, 159–163
  outside New York City, 163–164
Subtidal flows
  estuarine circulation, 11
  tidal residual flow, 10–11
System-Wide Hydrodynamic Model, 25–27, 38, 46

Tidal electricity generation, prospects of, 147–149
Tidal excursion, 9–10
Tidal range, at the Battery, 7
Tidal rectification
  basic concepts of, 14–16
  and East River residual flow, 14
  model simulation of, 27–28
Tidal residual flow, 10–11
Tidal transport
  at the Narrows, 7
  through Long Island Sound, 7
Tide gates. *See also* East River Tidal Barrage
  and coliform profile, 42–43
  and dissolved oxygen levels, 24, 42–44
  effects of
    on East River fish community, 57–65
    on estuarine environment, 69–71, 73–79, 81–85, 87–90
    on fish migration, 65–67
    on sedimentation transport, 51–55

energy harnessing by, 12, 16
impact of
  analysis of, 24–47
  hydrodynamic effects, 24–31
  on Long Island Sound water quality, 32–38
  on New York-New Jersey Harbor water quality, 38–44
and nitrogen concentration, 24, 35, 37–38
and nitrogen removal, 3
and water quality, 3, 7–21

U.S. Army Corps of Engineers, and East River Tidal Barrage
  and EIS, 73–76
  hydrodynamic concerns, 77–79
  regulatory perspectives, 151–152
U.S. Environmental Protection Agency (EPA), 152

Water elevations
  model calculations of, 32–33
  tide gates and, 27–31
Water pollution control plants (WPCPs), 13
  location of, 26
Water quality
  classification of, 1–2
  of East River, 2
  East River Tidal Barrage impact on, 23–25
  in Long Island Sound, 32–38
  in New York-New Jersey harbor, 38–44
  factors influencing, 12–14
  improvements expected in
    in Long Island Sound, 16–19
    in New York Harbor, 19
  in New York City waters, 1
  rate of improvement in, 19–20
  spatial profiles of, 35, 37–39
  tide gates and, 3, 7–21
  wastewater treatment and, 1
  in western Long Island Sound, 12–14
Water velocity
  model calculations of, 34–35
  tide gates and, 27–28, 30
WPCPs. *See* Water pollution control plants

Index of Contributors[a]

Abrahams, M. J., 101–114

Birman, G., 147–149
Black, V., *153*
Bocamazo, L. M., 77–79
Bokuniewicz, H., 51–56, *88*
Bowman, M. J., 7–22, *87, 113, 114, 167*
Burley, D., *88*

Ekezian, H., 115–125

Fahn, C., *145*

Gastrich, M., *90*
Glowka, A., *165*

Haggerty, J. W., 151–153
Hill, D., ix–x, 1–4, *114*
Hixenbaugh, L. H., 115–125

Kane, J., *22*

Lieber, G., *88–89*

Marchaj, T., *89*
Matlin, A., 101–114

Riccio, L. J., 93–97
Rich, C., *56*

Searchinger, T. D., 155–167
Squires, D. F., 171–178
St. John, J. P., 23–49, *87–88, 89–90*
Swanson, R. L., *22, 87, 88, 90*
Szeligowski, J. J., 115–125

Thatcher, M. L., 69–71, *166, 167*

Wagner, E. O., 81–85, *89*
Webster, A. C., 129–146
Will, R., 73–76
Woodhead, P. M. J., 57–68, *88*
Wouk, V., xi–xii

[a]Numbers in italics indicate comments made in discussion.